Routledge Revivals

Social Change in the South Pacific

Social Change in the South Pacific (1957) summarises the results of applying historical and contemporary fieldwork methods to the analysis of the processes of social change in the two small Pacific islands of Rarotonga and Aitutaki. It looks at changes in culture, social structure, social organisation and economic advancement.

Social Change in the South Pacific

Rarotonga and Aitutaki

Ernest Beaglehole

First published in 1957
by George Allen & Unwin Ltd.

This edition first published in 2025 by Routledge
4 Park Square, Milton Park, Abingdon, Oxon, OX14 4RN

and by Routledge
605 Third Avenue, New York, NY 10017

Routledge is an imprint of the Taylor & Francis Group, an informa business

© 1957 George Allen & Unwin Ltd.

All rights reserved. No part of this book may be reprinted or reproduced or utilised in any form or by any electronic, mechanical, or other means, now known or hereafter invented, including photocopying and recording, or in any information storage or retrieval system, without permission in writing from the publishers.

Publisher's Note
The publisher has gone to great lengths to ensure the quality of this reprint but points out that some imperfections in the original copies may be apparent.

Disclaimer
The publisher has made every effort to trace copyright holders and welcomes correspondence from those they have been unable to contact.

A Library of Congress record exists under LCCN 62050428

ISBN: 978-1-032-90347-7 (hbk)
ISBN: 978-1-003-55750-0 (ebk)
ISBN: 978-1-032-90348-4 (pbk)

Book DOI 10.4324/9781003557500

SOCIAL CHANGE
IN THE
SOUTH PACIFIC
Rarotonga and Aitutaki

BY

ERNEST BEAGLEHOLE

Ruskin House
GEORGE ALLEN & UNWIN LTD
RUSKIN HOUSE   MUSEUM STREET

FIRST PUBLISHED IN 1957

This book is copyright under the Berne Convention. Apart from any fair dealing for the purposes of private study, research, criticism or review, as permitted under the Copyright Act 1956, no portion may be reproduced by any process without written permission. Enquiries should be made to the publisher.

© George Allen & Unwin Ltd., 1957

PRINTED IN GREAT BRITAIN
in 10-pt Times Roman type
AT ABERDEEN UNIVERSITY PRESS

PREFACE

THIS monograph summarizes the results of applying historical and contemporary fieldwork methods to the analysis of the processes of social change in the two small Pacific islands of Rarotonga and Aitutaki. In its earlier historical sections it relies very largely upon the surviving early Cook Island missionaries' records now lodged in the London library of the London Missionary Society. I have to thank Miss Irene M. Fletcher, librarian and archivist of the London Missionary Society, for making available these records, and the Secretaries of the Society for their generous permission to use them in any way that suited the purpose of this study. My wife spent many laborious days that might have otherwise been more enjoyably used working through the early Cook Island mission files in the L.M.S. library. She also read the proofs and prepared the index. I thank her now, as always, for her unfailing help and encouragement.

The latter part of this monograph is based on some two months' intensive fieldwork in Aitutaki in the summer of 1948-49. Although my time was very short its value was immeasurably increased by the unlimited assistance, friendliness and hospitality of John Harrington and Myra Harrington. Because she was Aitutaki by birth and upbringing, later educated in New Zealand, a trained nurse by profession, Myra Harrington was the informant that all fieldworkers dream of, full of knowledge, sensitive, objective, thoughtful, moving easily between two cultures, a sure guide through the intricacies of contemporary Aitutaki custom and social life.

The first draft of this manscript was completed in 1951. My main thesis seems as valid today as it was a few years ago. I have therefore left its statement largely unchanged. I have brought statistics up to date and added sufficient notes to record some of the more significant official policy decisions, and the reports on which policy has been based, to give a fair idea of the way in which New Zealand is trying to aid the Cook Islander to re-interpret his place and rôle in the modern world. This aid has been given freely, generously and rapidly, so much so that within the past month or two it has been officially announced that loans are now available for improving Cook Islands housing, plans and specifications are being prepared for a large new government inter-island freight and passenger vessel, the Cook

PREFACE

Islands Department of Agriculture is to be strengthened, land utilization surveys initiated, a large central cool store for the citrus industry completed in Rarotonga, ways and means explored for establishing a quick-freeze industry for frozen pineapples and other tropical fruits and finally, political, constitutional, community and social welfare developments are to be further encouraged. Consolidation of economic and social development will obviously require time, patience and much co-operation on the part of administrators, technical experts and Islanders, but the new policies are a sign that goodwill and intelligent planning have at last reached the stage where social and economic advancement has become the mainspring of official policy for the Cook Islands.

Finally, I am not unaware that a more refined analysis of some phases of Cook Island social change might have been made by using a conceptual scheme that viewed island society as a system of systems and therefore proceeded separately to annotate changes in culture, social structure, social organization and personality system. Or again, using concepts derived from contemporary rôle theory the relations between missionary, trader and administrator on the one hand and Cook Islander on the other might have been formulated in such fashion as to emphasize the importance of intercultural rôle networks. But such analyses would necessarily have to place great emphasis on social theory and could well have produced a result not immediately relevant to my present purpose which has been more that of demonstrating the kind and amount of social change in one small Pacific island culture over the past 100 or more years than that of exploring the nature and use of new conceptual tools. This latter task may well be reserved for another place and another time.

The quotation from Lord David Cecil's study of Cowper, *The Stricken Deer*, that so aptly sums up the criss-crossing purposes of the early nineteenth-century Cook Islands social scene is reproduced by permission of the publishers, Constable and Company.

ERNEST BEAGLEHOLE

Victoria University College,
Wellington, New Zealand.
July 1957

CONTENTS

PREFACE — PAGE V

INTRODUCTION

1. *The Place* — 3
2. *The Problem* — 4
3. *Note on Geography and History* — 6

PART I: THE MISSIONARY ORDER

4. *Aboriginal Culture* — 11
5. *Initial Contacts* — 12
6. *Effective Contact. Aitutaki, Phase 1* — 14
7. *Effective Contact. Rarotonga, Phase 1* — 19
8. *Opposition to New Faith, 1827–33, Rarotonga, Phase 2* — 23
9. *Opposition to New Faith, 1827–33, Aitutaki, Phase 2* — 38
10. *Social Changes in Phases 1 and 2* — 40
11. *The New Order* — 43
12. *Consolidation of the New Order* — 56
13. *Economic Development* — 67
14. *Whalers, Traders and Frenchmen* — 69
15. *Introduction of Alcohol* — 75
16. *A Trading Mission* — 77
17. *Factors Influencing Social Change* — 79

PART II: MISSIONARY AND GOVERNMENT

18. *The Period of Stabilization, 1857–1901* — 87
19. *Economic Changes* — 90
20. *Mission Work* — 94
21. *Peruvian Slavers* — 95
22. *Social Problems, 1867–77* — 96
23. *The Protectorate* — 101
24. *Social Change, 1855–1901* — 118
25. *Coda* — 125

PART III: CONTEMPORARY SOCIAL LIFE

26. *Population* — 129
27. *Mortality and Fertility* — 135
28. *Public Health* — 136
29. *Migration* — 137
30. *Population Density* — 139

CONTENTS

31	Economic Organization	PAGE 142
32	Foods	143
33	Land Tenure	146
34	Work Organization	149
35	Organization for Visitors	153
36	Work Habits	156
37	Houses	159
38	Clothing	161
39	The Village Day	162
40	Households	163
41	Adoption	164
42	Kinship	166
43	Tribal Organization	167
44	Warfare	171
45	Village Activities	172
46	Village Leadership	175
47	Marriage	176
48	Sex Relations in Marriage	178
49	Pregnancy	180
50	Infancy	183
51	Age Grades	184
52	Growing Up	186
53	The Middle Years	188
54	Sickness and Death	191
55	Religion	194

PART IV: WELFARE, PSYCHOLOGY AND SOCIAL CHANGE

56	Welfare and Development	203
57	Administration	206
58	Administrative Personnel	211
59	Economic Development	212
60	Education	217
61	Intellectual Capacity	219
62	Character Structure	224
63	Rorschach Records	232
64	Development of Character Structure	235
65	Character Structure and Social Change	235
66	Social Change	237
67	Conclusion	255
	Index	263

An historical period is not a watertight compartment, containing only what it has itself created, sharing nothing with what has gone before and what comes after. It is a tangle of movements and forces, of various origin, sometimes intertwined and sometimes running parallel, some beginning, some in their prime, some in decay; streaked by anomalies and freaks of nature; coloured by physical conditions, by national characteristics, by personalities; struck across by unexpected, inexplicable stirrings of the spirit of God or of man; yet with every strand part of what is past or what is to come; a great river ever fed by new streams, its course continuous and abrupt, chequered and unfaltering, now thundering over a sudden cataract, now partially diverted into a backwater and carrying on its mysterious surface fragments of wreckage, survivals of an earlier day, not yet dissolved into oblivion.

LORD DAVID CECIL

I do not like dissenters, they are more zealous and consequently more intolerant than the established church. Their only object is power. If we are to have a prevailing religion let us have one that is cool and indifferent.

WILLIAM LAMB, LORD MELBOURNE

One generalization of importance that emerges from the studies of culture contact and culture change is, that on the whole, the people of a community tend to respond best to stimuli which have some relation to their traditional values and forms of organization.

RAYMOND FIRTH

INTRODUCTION

1
The Place

THE South Pacific consists of huge expanses of sea and occasional specks of land. The Cook Islands are to be found within that part of the Pacific expanse which is bounded north and south by the 8th and 23rd degrees of south latitude, east and west by the 156th and 167th degrees of west longitude. The ocean thus limited has an area of about 850,000 square miles. Within it, the Lower Group of Cook Islands, eight of them, and the seven islands making up the Northern Group, together have a land area of just over 56,000 acres (about 88 square miles) and a total population in 1956 of 16,424 people, all but approximately 400 of whom are indigenous Cook Islanders.

The islands of the lower group are of volcanic origin, generally rising from lowlands close to the beach to hilly or mountainous interiors. The highest peaks of Rarotonga are about 2,000 feet high, those of Aitutaki little more than 450 feet high. The soil is generally rich and fertile. The northern islands are typical coral atolls, low-lying, with infertile coral-sand soil. The average temperature of Rarotonga is about 75 degrees, the average rainfall about 80 inches. In Aitutaki the temperature ranges between 70 and 80 degrees, the rainfall being about 100 inches or a little less. Occasional destructive hurricanes visit all the islands of both groups.

The administrative centre of the Cook Islands is Rarotonga, about 1,800 miles from Wellington and 700 miles from Tahiti. The lower group is spread out in a semicircle to the north and east of Rarotonga and within a radius of 150 miles from Rarotonga, Aitutaki being 140 miles north. The northern group is from 600 to 700 miles north and north-west of Rarotonga. Communication within the Cook Group is by trading schooner, by government motor vessel and seasonal fruit ships. Aitutaki is linked with Samoa, Tonga, Fiji and Auckland by regular air service. Aitutaki is also on the route of a French air service between New Caledonia and Tahiti.

The two islands on which this study is focused are Rarotonga (area, 16,500 acres; population, 1956, 6,417, including 354 non-indigenous persons) and Aitutaki (area 3,900 acres; population, 1956, 2,590, including 18 non-indigenous persons).

2
The Problem

Rarotonga and Aitutaki are peculiarly fitted for a case study of the processes of social change. Both islands are relatively small in area and population, isolated and with a homogeneous population. For both there are adequate and detailed records of the introduction of Christianity which, within the western historical period, was the impact from outside that initiated a whole series of social changes that continued throughout the nineteenth century. Missionary records enable these social changes to be analysed, and when the records fail towards the end of the century, the full reports of the British Resident Agent enable analysis to be continued until the new century begins. At this point it is convenient to jump a time period of almost fifty years and consider the present social life of the people against the background of what has been learned about nineteenth-century social change.

In the historical study the focus is on Rarotonga primarily, because for this island documentary materials are richest, and secondarily on Aitutaki when there are relevant comparative records. In the contemporary study the focus is almost entirely on Aitutaki because this was the island on which the major fieldwork was carried out. The change from one island to another is of little methodological consequence. Both islands, their people and their customs are so similar that what is said of one applies to the other with the exceptions that are always noted as they occur.

The purpose of this study is to take a self-sufficient non-literate community in which change has been initiated by stimulus from without and then trace the effects of this stimulus in the resulting changed cultural life of the people. The aboriginal people had learnt a certain culture that was in all respects basically Polynesian. Alien missionaries with an alien culture came to the aboriginal peoples and forced them by appropriate rewards and punishments to learn new cultural ways. Later, traders, whalers and seamen introduced yet another culture, again with inherent rewards and punishments. The native peoples reacted to both foreign cultures by learning some new ways of thinking and behaving, and by resisting other changes. Many of these modifications in, and the resistance of, native culture may

THE PROBLEM

be explained by the operation of social influences. One line of analysis that runs through this study, therefore, is the consideration of the role of specifically social variables in the results of culture contact change. Other modifications and resistances, however, appear to require a psychological explanation if basic understanding is to be achieved of the process of social change. The second line of analysis that is used is thus psychological and the attempt is made to assess the value of the concept of character structure (or basic personality type or social personality) as an explanatory hypothesis. Not, it may be said immediately, as the only significant or all-important clue to the understanding of social change but as one important and often neglected key to understanding the reasons why non-literate people often act apparently unreasonably in their choice of what to accept and what to reject from the culture that is offered to, or forced upon, them by those aliens who have secured positions of power over or among them.

The first part of this study then is an analysis based upon the use of historical documents, the second part upon contemporary documents and field work. The concluding section studies the nature of social change as it has been variously viewed by social scientists and evaluates the role of the character structure of this Polynesian island group in explaining the social change documented in the preceding sections. Just as the clinical psychologist, by making a case study of one person, hopes both to understand the complicated pattern of development in this unique person and the way in which the individual is similar to, or differs from, other persons—in this, throwing light upon more general uniformities of behaviour and its development—so the social psychologist can study the case history of social change in a particular community and hope thereby to increase knowledge of the general processes of social change, more specially and initially, in the several societies of one psychological culture area.

Polynesia is well suited for such comparative studies. Many island groups have developed variations on a basic Polynesian theme. The history of these groups subsequent to first European culture contact has been varied and continuous. Some groups have been able to change in comparative isolation. Others have been forced to change in relation to constant pressures from surrounding European cultures. Some, again, of the groups have had small native populations reacting to minority alien populations, others have had to face social change with a minority native population almost overwhelmed by a large European or a large mixed European and Asiatic majority. Each of these Polynesian groups has arrived at some unique solution to the problems posed by the unique culture contact situation to which each has been forced to respond. Comparative study of the Polynesian Pacific therefore can work with a half a dozen social groups in which the basic culture is known, the history of social change documented and the resultant cultural adaptation open to modern study. It is as a contribution to what is undoubtedly an important human problem—the capacity of the Polynesian people to adjust to new challenges and pressures in their sea and island environment—and at the same time an important theoretical problem—how to understand social change and social conservatism —that the materials and hypotheses of this monograph have been assembled, analysed and elaborated.

3

Note on Geography and History

Aitutaki is the most northern of the Lower Cook Group. The wharf at Arutanga, seat of administration, is located on the Admiralty chart as Lat. 18 degrees 52 minutes 32 seconds South and Long. 159 degrees 46 minutes 30 seconds West. The island is volcanic, with a circumference of about twelve miles. It is surrounded by a barrier reef, which on the south-east side is up to six miles distant from the island. A number of islets on and within this fringing reef are of atoll formation. The island is pear-shaped, some four miles long and two miles wide. There is a passage through the reef on the western side which can admit whaleboats or a small schooner, and other inferior passages on the eastern side. Five of the seven villages are on the west coast—Amuri, Ureia, Arutanga, Reureu and Nikaupara—the remaining two, Vaipae and Tautu, 'secessionist' villages, are on the eastern side. Formerly all the villages stood inland on the ridge of hills that mounts to a point 450 feet above sea level, but under the influence of the missionaries the village sites were moved to the lagoon side. Four of the villages have each between 300 and 400 inhabitants, the remaining three having from 200 to 250 each.

Rarotonga is a high volcanic island with a circumference of about twenty miles. It is surrounded by a protecting coral reef. There is a

NOTE ON GEOGRAPHY AND HISTORY

small harbour at Avarua suitable for trading schooners except in strong northerly weather. On the east side of the island at Ngatangiia there is another small harbour formerly used as a schooner anchorage. The thirty-one villages of the island are dotted round the coastal plain.

Only eleven of these villages have between 200 to 600 inhabitants, the remainder each having considerably less. The average temperature in Rarotonga over a span of almost forty years is 74·67 degrees, the average rainfall 82·3 inches.

Discovery by Europeans of the islands of the Lower Cook Group took place towards the end of the eighteenth and the beginning of the nineteenth centuries.[1] Cook discovered the small coral atoll of Manuae in 1773, named it Hervey Island, a name afterwards applied by some to all the southern islands which now, however, are officially known as the Cook Islands. In 1777 Cook discovered Mangaia and Atiu. Bligh discovered Aitutaki in 1789. Rarotonga was probably visited by the *Bounty* mutineers in 1789, unofficially discovered by Goodenough in 1814 and later 'officially' rediscovered by John Williams in 1823. Mauke was also visited by Williams at about the same time.

Of the northern inhabited islands, Manihiki and Rakahanga (650 and 674 miles from Rarotonga) were discovered in 1822 and 1820; Tongareva (737 miles from Rarotonga) was sighted in 1788 (this island has the distinction of lying on latitude 9 degrees south, so that formerly sailing vessels could check their latitude as they passed by); Pukapuka was discovered in 1765 by Byron, who named the island Dangerous but did not land. The Cook Islands became a British Protectorate in 1888 and were annexed to New Zealand in 1901.

[1] Te Rangi Hiroa (Peter H. Buck) in his *Introduction to Polynesian Anthropology*, B.P. Bishop Museum, Bulletin 187 (Honolulu, 1945), pp. 92-96, provides the simplest guide to the historical discoveries and anthropological literature on both the lower and northern Cook Groups.

PART I
THE MISSIONARY ORDER

4
Aboriginal Culture

AT the time of the coming of the white man to the Cook Islands, we may assume from scattered references in missionary and other contemporary literature, the people of Rarotonga and Aitutaki were typical Polynesians living a life that conformed in all essential respects to a general Polynesian culture. Just as the people in their physical makeup appear to be connected more closely with the people of the Society Islands than with any other Polynesian group,[1] so Cook Island cultural emphases follow the central Polynesian pattern. No full record has survived of the culture of Rarotonga and Aitutaki before white contact. Bligh and Williams have left a few references to the dress and appearance of the people. Gill, Williams and Buzacott have written at odd points about some aspects of the social life of the people. Brief accounts of traditional history have been recorded in the *Journals of the Polynesian Society* and Moss has written, again briefly, on social organization. Buck has given a full record of the technology and arts and crafts.[2] The total picture, however, is only sufficient to indicate the main outlines of aboriginal culture and does not allow any understanding of detail. No attempt is made in this context to piece together the surviving bits of the jigsaw-like puzzle that constitutes our knowledge of aboriginal Rarotongan culture. It may be quite simply taken as a Polynesian culture and its outlines read off easily enough in the studies made of other islands in the Cook Group,[3] or with more attention to detail in the additional references already mentioned.

[1] See H. L. Shapiro and P. H. Buck, *Physical Characters of the Cook Islanders*, Memoirs, B.P. Bishop Museum, Vol. 22, No. 1, 1936.

[2] Ida Lee, *Captain Bligh's Second Voyage to the South Sea* (London, 1920); John Williams, *A Narrative of Missionary Enterprises* (London, 1838); William Gill, *Gems from the Coral Islands* (London, 1856); J. P. Sunderland and A. Buzacott, *Mission Life in the Islands of the Pacific* (London, 1866); J. Pakoti, ' First Inhabitants of Aitutaki, *Journal, Polynesian Society* (1895), 4: 59-70; D. Low, 'Traditions of Aitutaki', *ibid.* (1934), 43: 17-24, 73-84, 171-186, 258-266; *ibid.* (1935), 44: 26-31; F. J. Moss, 'Maori Polity of the Island of Rarotonga', *ibid.* (1894), 3: 20-26; Te Rangi Hiroa (P. H. Buck), *Material Culture of the Cook Islands (Aitutaki)* (New Plymouth, 1927); P. H. Buck, *Arts and Crafts of the Cook Islands*, B.P. Bishop Museum, Bulletin 179 (1944); P. H. Buck, *Introduction to Polynesian Anthropology*, B.P. Bishop Museum, Bulletin 187 (1945), pp. 92-96.

[3] See P. H. Buck (Te Rangi Hiroa), *Ethnology of Tongareva; Ethnology of Manihiki and Rakahanga, Mangaian Society*; E. and P. Beaglehole, *Ethnology of*

At the beginning of the nineteenth century both Rarotonga and Aitutaki were visited by traders and very soon after missionaries came to settle in the islands. Aboriginal culture was rather roughly disturbed, its equilibrium upset. People learned new ways of doing things and new ways of believing and thinking about things. The process of social change was initiated which in one aspect or another of the culture has been going on ever since. With the documentation that is available the problem is to analyse this process of social change; to find out who learned what, when and how; and to show how the present social situation has inevitably grown out of the process of social change initiated more than a century ago.

5

Initial Contacts

Credit for the European discovery of Rarotonga is usually given in official reports to the missionary John Williams who, in 1823, successfully located the island from information collected in Aitutaki. Gosset, however, has made a careful study of the surviving records and is able to show that at least three European vessels visited Rarotonga some years before Williams 're-discovered' the island.[1] The first ship was probably the *Bounty*. No European records attest the fact but Gosset believes the native report which is circumstantially clear about the fact that a ship resembling the *Bounty* called at Rarotonga presumably early in May 1789, and obviously after the mutiny had occurred. Since Bligh had discovered Aitutaki, 140 miles to the north about two weeks before the mutiny, it is not improbable that the mutineers, roughly retracing their old course back to Tahiti, did sight Rarotonga and traded with the people. Native tradition mentions the fact that two canoes visited the ship and bartered for

---

Pukapuka, B.P. Bishop Museum, Bulletins 92, 99, 122, 150 (1932-1934). With superb over-simplification and fantastic imagination, hard to equal even in the literature on Polynesia, Christian thus wrongly describes aboriginal Rarotongan culture: 'John Williams found the Rarotongans a race of fierce warriors, sunk in dark and cruel superstitions—a mixture of Indian Siva-worship, apparently, with some Arab and Persian cultus of the Jinns and Peris—and addicted to civil wars and cannibal abominations.' One comment might very well be: not apparently! See F. W. Christian *Eastern Pacific Islands* (London, 1910), p. 193.

[1] R. W. G. Gosset, 'Notes on the Discovery of Rarotonga', *Australian Geographer* (1940), 3: 4-15.

INITIAL CONTACTS

fowls, coconuts and bananas; from the orange seeds stolen from the *Bounty* at this time the orange trees grew that were in later years to provide the material for potent orange beer.[1]

The next recorded contact with Rarotonga is through the vessel *Seringapatam*, taken as a prize by the United States Navy into Nukuhiva in 1814, later recaptured by her crew and sailed to Sydney by way of Rarotonga which was sighted on 23 May of that year. Several Rarotongans visited the vessel but no record survives of what happened off the island.

The final known contact before the missionary visits was that of the vessel *Cumberland* under Captain Goodenough. Sometime before August 1814 this schooner entered Ngatangiia harbour and the crew began to cut down and collect the trees called *nono* (Morinda citrifolia) which may have been mistaken for sandalwood because of the dark yellow colour of *nono* timber. The trees were paid for with axes and tomahawks. However, the collecting did not proceed peacefully. Native women were molested by the sailors and *marae* or sacred enclosures were desecrated. On August 12 a melee occurred in which sailors and Rarotongans were killed, including a white woman from the schooner.[2] The trouble was temporarily patched up and Goodenough later left Rarotonga taking with him several Rarotongans, including the high chieftainess Tapairu, a close relative of Makea, then high chief of Rarotonga. The Rarotongans were left on Aitutaki before Goodenough returned to Sydney.

Although the *Cumberland* is the last vessel of which record has been kept, there may very well have been other occasional visits to Rarotonga by trading schooners between the years 1801 to 1823. Gosset notes that during these years there was a vigorous trade, principally in pork, from Tahiti to Sydney, but the schooners were always on the look-out for such additional cargo as sandalwood, pearl shell, beche-de-mer, arrowroot and *tamanu* logs. Although the logs might be obtained in Rarotonga or Aitutaki, brief visits to explore possibilities could have occurred without records being left behind.

---

[1] See also Williams, *op. cit.* pp. 201-202, for an account of the *Bounty*'s visit.
[2] Gill in his *Gems*, pp. 6-8, gives an account of the visit of the *Cumberland*, but without naming the vessel and placing the date of the visit in 1820 'or thereabouts'. According to Gill the whole history of the stay of the crew of this vessel at Rarotonga 'was a continued series of rapine, cruelty, vice and bloodshed. So disgraceful was their conduct that the captain did not, either for his own credit or safety sake, publish the latitude and longitude of this lovely island.' Gill also states that the woman killed was a New Zealand woman, that is, Maori.

From the known visits, however, it is probable that the native peoples learned very little. They were introduced to iron, steel tools and fishhooks; their intellectual horizons may have been stretched a little by knowledge of the existence of other people in the world with different skin colour, a superior technology and different ideas. But the social change initiated by these brief contacts was very slight, if indeed the contact had any effect at all beyond the temporary, ephemeral and superficial. For change to occur in any permanent way, contacts of a more long continued nature are necessary; it was left to the missionaries therefore to be the agents of social change, and it was their culture that left the most marked effects upon aboriginal native life.

6

Effective Contact. Aitutaki, Phase 1

Captain Bligh in the *Bounty* sighted Aitutaki on April 11, 1789, seventeen days before the mutiny. He returned to the island on July 25, 1792, when engaged for the second time in taking breadfruit to the West Indies. Between these two visits Captain Edwards, in the *Pandora*, had visited Aitutaki about the middle of May 1791 in search of the missing mutineers. From these three contacts little was learned by the people of the island. Thus Bligh records in his log for July 25, 1792, information about the island as he saw it from the deck of his vessel; he notes that three canoes came alongside and he made to the natives 'presents of beads and ironwork for which they gave us a few worthless spears and breastplates . . . they were confident of our good intentions towards them, and instead of any look of surprise and astonishment it was rather of complacency and admiration'.[1] Bligh's two vessels drifted off shore on July 25 and 26, finally sailing westward in hard squalls of rain on July 26. Apart, therefore, from very minor bartering which gave the people some iron and which had the effect of confirming in the people the friendly intentions of the technologically superior white man, no social change could have resulted from these brief visits.

Effective contact was therefore reserved until almost another thirty years had passed. On October 26, 1821, John Williams arrived at

[1] Ida Lee, *Captain Bligh's Second Voyage* (London, 1920), p. 132.

Aitutaki. The chief Tamatoa was invited on to the missionary vessel and informed of missionary enterprises in Tahiti and the Society Islands. He was also told that the principal gods of Tahiti had been burnt. Finally he agreed to allow ashore under his protection the two Tahitian missionaries that Williams had brought with him. Williams also learnt at this time of the existence of populous islands not far distant, including Rarotonga and this information, says Williams, 'much increased in my estimation the interest of the Aitutaki mission'.[1]

In July 1823 Williams returned to Aitutaki to enquire after the success of his native teachers. He found many signs of success: *maraes* had been burned, gods not burned were in the possession of the teachers; 'the profession of Christianity was general, so much so, that not a single idolater remained'; a large chapel 200 feet long and 30 feet wide had been erected; the Sabbath was regarded as a sacred day; all the people attended Divine Service and 'family prayer was very general throughout the island'. Subsequent events were to show that this account of triumphal success was more rose-coloured than correct—as indeed, might be expected when it is remembered that only twenty months had elapsed between Williams's two visits and twenty months are rather a short time in which to change an island of 2,000 people from one culture to another.

From conversations with Papeiha, one of the two native missionaries left on his first visit, Williams was able to record the actual steps in the process of persuading the people nominally to accept a new religion. These steps may be classified in the following way:

1. Initial acceptance, support and protection of the missionary by a person of high status in the native culture.

2. Testing of the powers of the native gods: on landing the native missionaries 'were led to the maraes, and given up formally to the gods'; a failure of the native gods to kill the missionaries or to stop their work.

3. Protests by dissatisfied groups, generally minority groups, who temperamentally fear the new or vaguely suspect that their status or occupation may be adversely affected by the teaching of the new religion. War broke out three times 'and all their property had been stolen from them'.

[1] J. Williams, *Missionary Enterprises* (London, 1838), p. 53. Information on this and succeeding pages about the initial stages in the acceptance by the people of Aitutaki of Christianity is taken from Williams's book, pp. 51-83.

4. Popular appeal to the people. The missionaries toured the island explaining the new faith to the people and engaging in arguments with native priests, trying to convict the latter of inconsistency and contradictory statements.

5. Substantial gifts made to people of status. About three months after the native missionaries commenced their work a missionary vessel arrived from Rai'atea. The captain gave to the chiefs presents of axes, pigs and goats. 'A powerful impression was thus very generally produced in favour of Christianity.' Many had ridiculed the missionaries when they had announced that a vessel would come to enquire about their welfare but now the people said, 'Behold, we called these men drift-wood, and they have rich friends, who have sent an English ship to enquire after them, and bring them property, such as we never saw before! We ridiculed and called them liars, and behold they are men of truth.' A combination of self-interest, perhaps cupidity, and a feeling of shame at being proved wrong may thus have influenced chiefs and people to learn more about the new religion.

6. Further testing of native gods and their second failure. The grandfather of Tamatoa, 'king' of Aitutaki, was still adamant in his opposition to the missionaries. But a beloved daughter was taken dangerously ill. 'The priests were immediately on the alert, presenting numerous offerings, and invoking the gods from morning to evening, day after day, in order to induce them to restore the child to health. The disease, however, increased and the girl died. *The chief was so much affected at the death of his daughter, that he determined at once to abandon the gods who were so ungrateful as to requite his zeal with such manifest unkindness*, and therefore sent his son early next morning to set fire to his marae. Two other maraes near it caught fire and were also consumed. The son, *enraged with the gods for destroying his sister*, went to a large marae, before which the people were presenting their offerings, and attempted to set it on fire; but was prevented by the worshippers, who seized and dragged him away' (italics added to Williams's text). Thus, Williams philosophises, 'by such circumstances does God, in numberless instances, work upon the minds of men'.

7. Mass movement to join the new faith. Band-wagon psychology explains Aitutaki behaviour as well as that of man in a mass age. 'On the Sabbath day after the death of the chief's daughter,' con-

tinues Williams, 'the people of several districts came, cast their idols at the feet of the teachers and professed themselves worshippers of Jehovah'—though the people can have had only the simplest or the vaguest notion of what it meant to be a worshipper of Jehovah— 'during the week the rest followed; so that by the next Sabbath, not a professed idolater remained in the whole island.'

8. *A sense of purpose fostered by enthusiastic action.* Having got so far Papeiha shrewdly channelled the new interest and enthusiasm into active and positive works. On the Sabbath on which he had 'the delightful satisfaction of seeing the whole of the inhabitants convened to worship the one living and true God', he announced an important meeting to be held on the next day. At this meeting he made two propositions: 'That all the maraes in the island should be burned, and that all the remaining idols should be brought to him . . . the second proposition was, "That they should commence immediately building a house in which to worship Jehovah". To both of these proposals, the assembled multitude yielded their cordial assent.' As soon as the meeting broke up crowds set off to burn up the maraes. District after district came in procession, chief and priest leading (and we may well imagine, in high spirits, with dancing, laughter and fun), to place their rejected idols at the teacher's feet, receiving in return a few copies of the gospels and elementary books. The people also immediately set to work on the chapel, burning coral for lime under the teacher's direction (whitewashing their hats and native garments and strutting about the settlement, ' admiring each other exceedingly'), wattling walls and plastering them with the limestone wash and finally thatching the huge roof in a diligent two days' work.

9. *The use of badges to symbolize in-group membership.* Williams remarks that on coming up to Aitutaki on his second visit his vessel was surrounded by canoes the people in which waved their hats to convince Williams of the fact that they were all Christians now on Aitutaki, Williams not reposing entire confidence in their verbal assertions. In a footnote Williams adds: 'The European shaped hat was worn only by the Christian party, the idolaters retaining their heathen head-dresses, war-caps, etc'. Thus badges of membership were important outward signs of conformity to a new order.

The nine steps that have been mentioned cover the sequence of events over a period of eighteen months during which attempts were made to teach the people of Aitutaki what was involved in the new religion. The statement that at the end of this period there was not a professed idolater on the island need not be taken too seriously. Many were at the time implicit idolaters and remained so for many years thereafter. For most, at this period, Christianity was a matter of profession: something new, exciting, interesting, strange and profitable. It is not improbable that success in introducing the people to the new faith lay largely in the fact that the agents of social change, the native missionaries, were themselves Polynesians, people of the same race, culture, manners and almost the same speech as the people of Aitutaki. After all, if Moslems from India set out to proselytize in New Zealand they would doubtless have more success using white New Zealand missionaries than with Indian missionaries. The native missionaries, being but recently converted themselves, must have had a good idea of how best to present the new faith, how to circumvent difficulties in acceptance that might occur to the Polynesian way of thinking, and not to a European mind. It is also probable that the native missionary had in his make-up the right proportion of fanaticism and easy-goingness that made it possible for him to know when the iron was hot and when pressure should be decreased. Finally it is likely that the Christian dogma, as filtered through the native missionary mind, may have been in some respects Polynesianized, rather than Simon-pure, and in this case it would win a wider acceptance than dogma which in its purity would be at first preaching rather unintelligible. The agents of social change in this case, therefore, were people without visible distinguishing marks, except clothing, which might mark them off as belonging to a different race; they were people who possessed the new and exciting technical skills of reading and writing, thus suggesting that other Polynesians too could acquire the new arts; they were courageous men and thus appealed to the Polynesian; they were self-assured and convinced of their own rightness; they were protected by secular authorities and inferentially by supernatural authority since native gods were ineffectual against them; they were a minority, but they were an aggressive and determined minority. Under all these circumstances it seems natural that the people of Aitutaki should stop, listen, query the old ways, incline towards the new.

7
Effective Contact. Rarotonga, Phase 1

On July 25, 1823, after several days of anxious searching, John Williams came up to Rarotonga and lay off the island. On board his vessel he had two native missionaries and four Rarotongan women, including the chieftainess Tapairu, who had been removed to Aitutaki by Goodenough many years previously and who had been converted to Christianity by the missionaries on Aitutaki. Again, the steps involved in the introduction of the new faith may be analysed according to the operation of the following factors:[1]

1. Preliminary favourable knowledge. Before Williams's arrival, the people of Rarotonga had had limited intercourse with white people and were favourably inclined towards friendly relations. This favourable attitude had been strengthened by the marvels related by a native woman who had come to Rarotonga after a stay in Tahiti where she had absorbed simple knowledge about the technology of the white man, such as: the use of nails instead of human bones, the use of scissors instead of sharks' teeth, glass mirrors instead of water pools; and simple knowledge about the ways of the 'Cookees' and the servants of Jehovah, the white man's god. So impressed had Makea, high chief of Rarotonga, become with this information that he named one of his children Jehovah and another Jesus Christ. An uncle of the king went a step further and built a *marae* for Jehovah and Christ to which sick and diseased persons were brought for healing; 'and so great was the reputation which this marae obtained, that the power of Jehovah and Jesus Christ became great in the estimation of the people'.

2. Protection by a chief. When the object of Williams's visit was explained to an 'immense assemblage of natives', and particularly the fact that many other islands had already accepted Christianity and that only Rarotonga was out of step the people were delighted with the prospect of having native teachers of their own. Makea therefore conducted ashore the teachers, their wives and the returning Rarotongans, including his cousin Tapairu. Makea's idea of protection apparently extended only to the teachers and not their wives. On

[1] Unless reference is made to other authorities, the basic material for the text analysis is from Williams's *Missionary Enterprises*, pp. 99-126.

the following morning the teachers came off to Williams's vessel and explained that various high chiefs had, during the night, tried to abduct the wives and only Tapairu, 'a person of influence, and a woman of great intrepidity' had been able to save them by weeping, arguing and even fighting for their preservation.

3. Determination of native teacher. Williams was greatly discouraged by this reception and was about to abandon 'this inviting field of labour' when the redoubtable, untiring and fanatical Papeiha volunteered to remain alone on Rarotonga, provided a helper could be sent soon. Williams 'rejoiced in the proposition' and allowed Papeiha to go ashore carrying only his clothes, his Testament and a few elementary books. In addition, the two Rarotongan men and four Rarotongan women, already converted in Aitutaki, remained on the island, promising 'steadfastly to maintain their profession among their heathen countrymen'. Williams did not go ashore at Rarotonga on this first visit. As in Aitutaki, all the initial labour of explaining the Gospel and persuading the inhabitants to renounce idolatry was carried out by Papeiha, joined four months later by a native colleague, Tiberio.

4. Convicting native priests of inconsistency. A favourite method of throwing doubt on the beliefs of the natives was to engage priests in discussion and then turn the disputation in such a manner that it became immediately evident that only the Gospel had all the answers to the apparent contradictions. Thus in discussions with converted Rarotongans, priests and chiefs learned that native gods and *maraes* in other islands had been destroyed without the people being strangled by the gods in anger. They also discussed the origin of the first man and the first woman in the world; having no answer themselves as to where the first woman came from they were intensely interested to learn how Christian doctrine solved the puzzle.

5. Support from the disaffected. The Rarotongans who initially showed the greatest interest in the new teachings were those who were helpless and fearful of their lives. Thus Buzacott writes: 'When the native teachers arrived, the tribes at Arorangi had been so worsted in war, that they feared and expected extermination. Tinomana, the chief of that settlement, was the first to cast away his idols, and embrace Christianity, because the new faith introduced the reign of peace and goodwill—provided protection for the weak and helpless.'[1]

[1] Sunderland and Buzacott, *Mission Life*, p. 109. See also Williams, *op. cit.* pp. 170-193.

Tinomana, to put the matter bluntly, decided to ask for instruction from Papeiha because that course must have seemed to him the only possible way in which he could save his own life and those of his defeated people not killed in previous wars. Other chiefs followed Tinomana, both defeated and conquering, the former because of Tinomana's reasoning, the latter because they probably felt they could not afford to miss teaching that might open the door to the possession of the secrets of the new faith's superiority.[1]

6. The use of dramatic gestures. On Rarotonga as on Aitutaki the native teachers insisted on the destruction of *maraes* and god-figures; or else on the figures being brought to the teachers, and later, in 1827, to Williams on his second visit, when '14 immense idols the smallest of which was about five yards in length' were dropped at his feet. (Williams incidentally took a warrior's delight in these trophies of spiritual battle: after the Aitutaki conquest he sailed into Rai'atea harbour in triumph with the rejected idols of Aitutaki hung to the yard-arms and other parts of the vessel, feeling 'as other warriors feel a pride in displaying trophies of the victories they win'.) Clearly by forcing the natives to destroy the symbols of the old religious order they helped to build up in the natives an attitude of desperation: having so insulted the old gods, little could be expected of them and now it was a matter of sinking or swimming with the new order. Under these circumstances the most prudent form of social and spiritual insurance was to profess Christianity as quickly and as vehemently as possible.

Papeiha was also a master of other dramatic gestures. Thus a priest brought his god and threw it at Papeiha's feet. Instead of adding it to his store, Papeiha cut it up, lighted a fire with the pieces, roasted some bananas on the fire and ate them. No evil resulted, but the act produced a tremendous impression. According to all native reasoning the wilful conjunction of the commonness of food with the sacredness of a god-figure should have resulted in the immediate death of Papeiha. Their astonishment at his temerity and survival can be appreciated only when we think of our own astonishment if a person claiming new faith were able to eat quantities of potassium cyanide or arsenic and survive because of the protective powers of the new faith.

Finally Papeiha insisted that the new enthusiasm should be put to work at the building of a chapel to be an outward symbol of the new

[1] See Lovett, *History of the London Missionary Society*, pp. 275-276.

faith and of membership in it. A little more than twelve months after his landing when 'the whole population had renounced idolatry' he had them engaged in erecting a place of worship 600 feet in length.[1] A few years later, in 1827, on Williams's second visit when teachers and people moved to the eastern side of the island immediate steps were taken to erect another chapel, 150 feet long by 60 feet wide. This chapel was completed, without nails or ironwork, to accommodate 3,000 persons, in the short space of two months—'a large, respectable and substantial building' with six large folding doors and windows back and front. The diligence and speed of the workers must have owed much to the enthusiasm with which the new faith was accepted. Much of the credit for this enthusiasm belongs to Papeiha.

Mr. Bourne, a missionary visitor to Rarotonga about 1825, was rather patronizing about Papeiha and his colleague Tiberio. After noting the remarkable progress in Rarotonga, Bourne continues: 'And when we look at the means, it becomes more astonishing. Two native teachers, not particularly distinguished among their own countrymen for intelligence, have been the instruments of effecting this wonderful change, and that before a single missionary had set his foot upon the island.' Perhaps Mr. Bourne was unduly worried by a 'striking peculiarity' (as Williams calls it) of Papeiha's first grand chapel: 'the presence of many indelicate heathen figures carved on the centre posts', accounted for by the fact that many of the builders being still heathens 'thought that the figures with which they decorated the maraes would be equally ornamental in the main pillars of a Christian sanctuary'. Doubtless Papeiha had little time to supervise every aspect of his new chapel. Perhaps as a Polynesian he was little worried by the apparent incongruity. Possibly he knew intuitively when to exert and when to relax pressure in his missionizing, and chapel building was where the people worked off energy. At any rate although Papeiha may not have been distinguished for intelligence, he appears at this distance of time to have been a

[1] The length of this chapel is rather astounding when it is remembered that Winchester Cathedral, the longest cathedral in England, is only 550 feet in length. But the size of Papeiha's house of worship is vouched for both by Williams (*op. cit.* p. 103) and by J. Montgomery (compiler), *Journal of the Voyages and Travels by the Rev. Daniel Tyerman and George Bennet*, vol. 2 (London, 1831), p. 121. Tyerman and Bennet spent two days at Rarotonga on a London Missionary Society inspection visit, June 18 and 19, 1824, but the published account of their visit gives practically no details of social or religious conditions in Rarotonga.

shrewd, conscientious, capable, determined and courageous person. What more could have been expected from a native servant of the Lord at this time it is hard to know.

By 1827 in Rarotonga, though in Aitutaki not until many years later (1839), the first phase of systematic contact between the new culture and the old ended. The contact had involved the acquiring by the natives of tools and some new ideas. Certain local conditions and events had been exploited by the principal agents for the transmission of the new ideas, the native teachers. Persons of status had been the first to show interest and when it was clear that the new ideas had thus received a certain cachet of respectability, the masses had thought it expedient also to be interested in the novelties. Since the new ideas promised relief from the anxiety associated with infanticide, cannibalism, violent death by warfare, equally violent death for having unwittingly angered native gods, the rewards for professing the new faith must have seemed to many almost too good to be true—good enough at least to demand a trial. Hence by 1827 in Rarotonga, almost all the population were interested in one way or another or for one reason or another in the new ideas. That the people had really learned the meaning of the new ideas is too much to say. Williams, as judged by after events, was all too sanguine about success. But that was the way his energetic, enthusiastic, practical temperament worked. However, the stage was set for the coming of the white missionaries. For them, immediately following years had more trials than triumphs.

8

Opposition to New Faith, 1827-33, Rarotonga, Phase 2

From 1827 onwards the main agents of social change were the white missionaries of the London Missionary Society, an Evangelical organization which was first supported by all faiths except the Roman but which soon became the overseas mission agency of the Congregational Church. The missionaries who came to the South Seas from England were men of a particular social class, trained in a Church with a particular tradition. Not unnaturally they reacted to the culture of Polynesia in a way consonant with their own outlook with its peculiar blindnesses and strengths. Personal notes on John Williams and Aaron Buzacott with some additional material on the other nineteenth-century Cook Island missionaries will serve to suggest a picture of the typical Congregational missionary and the type of Christianity this missionary wished to foster in the Cook Islands.

John Williams was born at Tottenham High Cross, London, on July 29, 1796, the son of Christian parents. His family was probably on the lower fringes of the middle class. In 1810 Williams was apprenticed for seven years to a furnishing ironmonger in the City Road with the intention that he should become a retail salesman rather than a workshop craftsman. He had been carefully trained by his mother in Christian principles (his father hardly appears to have exercised any Christian influence) but in his youth he began to drift into irreligious habits although continuing to live a strictly upright and outwardly moral life. On Sunday, January 30, 1814, a Mrs. Tonkin, the wife of his master, met young Williams in the street waiting for some companions with whom he proposed to pass a pleasant social evening at a nearby tea-garden, 'Or more correctly', says Prout, his biographer, 'at a tavern connected with one of those scenes of Sabbath desecration and sensual indulgence'. Mrs. Tonkin persuaded Williams to accompany her to chapel instead, where the Rev. Timothy East preached on the text, 'What is a man profited if he shall gain the whole world, and lose his own soul?' On this evening he was converted: 'my blind eyes were opened and I beheld wondrous things out of God's law', as Williams himself phrased the experience twenty-four years later. In two years' time Williams was accepted as a missionary. Three years later he had joined the mission at Rai'atea, Society Islands. Of his character Lovett has this to say: 'a man of restless energy, of sunny temperament, of strong self-confidence, of bold initiative, of resolute faith'[1]—the characteristics that would have made a great empire builder had Williams been fortunate enough to have been born into the right social class and attended the right public school. As his career shaped itself he had to be content with carving out an empire for Christ and not for Victoria. But with his adventurous spirit he cannot have been uncontent with his roving life, nor as a missionary, with his final martyr's crown.

[1] Lovett, *History of the London Missionary Society*, vol. 1, p. 238. The facts about Williams's early life I have taken from E. Prout, *Memoirs of the Life of the Rev. John Williams, Missionary to Polynesia* (London, 1843).

OPPOSITION TO NEW FAITH, RAROTONGA, PHASE 2

Aaron Buzacott, 'the model missionary' as Williams was 'the restless missionary', was born in Devon on March 4, 1800. His father was in business as a whitesmith and ironmonger and Buzacott's formal education was completed in a village school by the age of 12 years. Between the age of 12 and 15 years he worked on a farm, thereafter entering his father's business. While a farm labourer 'no thunder roll brought him to God but rather the still small voice of Divine Yearning', so that at the age of 15 he gave himself to Christ and was admitted to the Congregational Church two years later. For some years he continued his theological and missionary studies, gaining practical experience in the mission field by trying to convert London slum-dwellers. At the age of 26 he was appointed to labour in Rarotonga. He left England with his mother's blessing, but his father 'would have nothing to say', and arrived at the scene of all his subsequent labours in 1828.[1] Like Williams, Buzacott was of a lower middle class home, his mother extremely pious and religious. Buzacott's temperament, however, was very different from that of Williams. Whereas Williams was a leader and a bold initiator, Buzacott was a cautious, careful, conscientious plougher of the spiritual soil, something of a scholar and a translator of unparalleled industry. Both men were good craftsmen and mechanics. They could build furniture or a schooner or a church with almost equal ease, print a bible as successfully as they could preach the Gospel, doctor the sick with confidence and plan a new state with skilful plausibility.

The following notes, taken mostly from London Missionary Society records,[2] serve still further to emphasize the lower middle-class outlook, habits and skills of the Cook Island missionaries:

CHARLES PITMAN—Born April, 1796, at Portsmouth, his parents 'moving in a humble sphere'. He attended day school regularly till between 13 and 14 years old. After leaving school he was placed in a chandler's warehouse at Portsmouth, but not liking the business, left it. His next job was in a merchant's counting house. Then he went into the counting house of a timber merchant and contract boat-builder to H.M. Dockyard, till the contract was stopped owing to the peace. Finally he went to Chichester to superintend a concern in the

---

[1] Particulars of Buzacott's early life are to be found in Sunderland and Buzacott, *Mission Life*, pp. 1-14.
[2] I am greatly indebted to Miss Irene M. Fletcher, Librarian of the London Missionary Society, for assembling these details of the social background of the Cook Island missionaries, from library records.

foreign deal and timber trade, where, he says in his application to the L.M.S., 1820, 'I still continue'. He was converted about 1816.

WILLIAM GILL—Born January 14, 1813, at Totnes, Devon, brought up at Tiverton, Devon, whence the family had moved. His grandfather and great-grandfather were wool-combers, his father a tanner and currier. He had the usual schooling of the times until he was 12 years. His first job, of one year's length, was in a lace factory. At 13 he was bound apprentice to a cabinet maker and upholsterer, but a year later, owing to the family removal to Brentwood, the agreement was cancelled. At 15 years he was manager in a retail leather cutter's business at Kingston-on-Thames—'young as I was, I was led to accept this heavy responsibility'. From 1830 on he managed a retail tanner's and currier's shop in the West End of London until the firm went out of business, when he took similar work in Poplar for a further two years—till the end of 1835. There is no record of a conversion, his upbringing kept him in the Christian way, but his decision was made when he joined the Barbican Church under A. Tidman, the future L.M.S. foreign secretary, in 1832.

GEORGE GILL—Younger brother of William Gill, born at Tiverton, January 23, 1820. There is no record of his activities, but his background was, of course, the same as his brother's.

E. R. W. KRAUSE—Born July 10, 1812, at Torau, Prussia, '... being educated first in the Gymnasium of my native town, Torau, Prussia, and afterwards for $5\frac{1}{2}$ years in the Institute of the Berlin Missionary Society, and the University of Berlin for Medicine'. He had wanted to be a missionary from 1828. He came over to England with a party of Gossner's men expecting to go to India. His idea of his calling did not square with that of Max Muller, the agent in England of the mission to which he was designated, and he was not accepted. He was just left stranded in England. He finally applied to the L.M.S. but was turned down on the ground that funds would not permit sending a foreigner just then. Somehow, via South America, he made his way to Tahiti, and was finally accepted as a missionary.

JAMES CHALMERS—Born at Ardrishaig, Argyllshire, August 4, 1841, a fishing village on Loch Fyne, where he was brought up. His father was an Aberdonian stonemason, who mostly lived and worked at Inveraray, coming home at intervals. He went to the village school and when he was between 14 and 15 years went to work in a lawyer's office in Glasgow. He was converted in November 1859, when he remembered a boyish vow to be a missionary. In 1861 he joined the Glasgow city mission where he had 'to deal with men and women hardly less degraded and even more difficult to influence for good than the heathen of New Guinea'.

WILLIAM WYATT GILL—No relation to the other Gills. Born at Bristol on December 27, 1828. In 1847, aged 19, he went to Theological College in London. After his year at Highbury College his tutor wrote, deprecating his desire to be a missionary, '. . . malformation about his organs of speech . . . young man of rather slender abilities'. Gill changed over and spent the rest of his college life at New College, where he made good.

HENRY ROYLE—Born at Manchester in 1807, '. . . placed in one of our large Manufactories when very young where continued until about 4 years ago. I was called by the urgent wishes of my brethren to fill the office I now sustain of the Missionary Agent to the Grosvenor Street Christian Instruction Society . . .'—October 11, 1837. He went to the Manchester Mechanics' Institute for several years for English grammar, mathematical and Latin classes, attended lectures in astronomy, mechanics, and electricity and a number of other scientific subjects.

Two final points need to be kept in mind to understand the culture Buzacott and his co-missionaries brought to the South Pacific. In the first place it is very probable that as lower middle-class persons they were very intolerant of the dominant values of the upper class aristocratic English society that they left behind them with its sexual freedom, its hard animalism and rapacious worldliness, its religious conformity masking absence of religious belief, its tolerant indifference to moral values, its emphasis on the refinement and cultivation of good taste.[1] Zealous and intolerant the dissenters were in England, equally zealous and intolerant they had to be in their missionary endeavours when they realized that the values and virtues of the chiefly class of Polynesians seemed to be more than a faint echo of

[1] Lord David Cecil's *The Young Melbourne* (London, 1948), gives a vivid insight into the late eighteenth-century English society, with the dying life of which the first Cook Island Missionaries would certainly have been familiar by hearsay, observation and preaching, even if not by participation. It is probably also a not insignificant fact that the first Polynesian visitor to England, Omai from Tahiti, taken to England by Cook in 1774 and residing there for two years, appears to have fitted himself perfectly to the polished and sophisticated customs, manners and etiquette of the aristocratic society of the time. See H. Luke, 'Our First Polynesian Visitor', *Geographical Magazine* (1950), 22: 497-500.

the values of the society they had left behind them. It is more than likely that some of the driving energy behind missionary assaults on the immorality of the Polynesians came from a realization that aristocracy has many values the same whether in the South Seas or in Melbourne House.

Secondly, Congregationalism had behind it as one of its most vital traditions the pattern of the local church as a community-integrating institution, rather than a merely ornamental activity to grace one day in each week. What more natural, therefore, than that L.M.S. missionaries should take steps actively to build on their South Sea islands mission-inspired theocracies that transferred to the Pacific dreams of a good life severely frustrated by State persecution or indifference in England?[1] In almost all parts of the Polynesian Pacific where Congregationalism and Methodism were the spearheads of Christian advance, spiritual values and behaviour rapidly received the sanctions and support of the secular power of the community and this power was generously, at times intolerantly, used to stamp out behaviour not overtly congruent with Christian teaching.

John Williams discusses specifically the attitude of the missionary towards the adoption of a code of laws. After his return to Rarotonga in 1827, conditions, he says, rendered it imperative that the chiefs of Rarotonga should adopt a code of Christian laws as the basis of the administration of justice in their island. The laws enacted related to theft, trespass, stolen property, unjust possession of another's land, lost property, Sabbath-breaking, rebellion, marriage, adultery, the judges, the jury. (Only later was murder included, and the initial list reminds one of the missionary Pitman's subsequent statement, made perhaps in a moment of pessimistic clarity, that there were really only three crimes or sins on Rarotonga: fornication, adultery and thieving.) With a fine grasp of what would now be termed the functional viewpoint in the analysis of a social structure, Williams argues that those who object to the missionary interfering in the above matters forget of the natives that 'their civil and judicial polity, and all their ancient usages, were interwoven with their superstitions; and that all these partook of the sanguinary character of the

[1] The influence of the Commonwealth tradition in determining missionaries to mould the entire life of a Pacific community seems to be the point of Latourette's brief discussion in his summary of the Spread of Christianity throughout the islands of the Pacific, but his phrasing is too cryptic to admit of a ready understanding of his meaning. See K. S. Latourette, *The Expansion of Christianity*, vol. V, *The Great Century* (New York, 1943), p. 259.

system in which they were imbodied, and by which they were sanctioned; thus maintaining a perpetual warfare with the well-being of the community. The Missionary goes among them. . . . Subsequently they become acquainted with new principles . . . and soon perceive that these ancient usages are incompatible with Christian precepts and that such a superstructure cannot stand on a Christian foundation.'[1] Hence, says Williams, the missionary must give freely and fully of his knowledge. He must not assume political authority; he should interfere as little as possible in civil, legal or political affairs, and then solely by advice and influence—but he does have to realize that Christian behaviour can no more be tacked onto a heathen foundation than can a heathen superstructure rest firmly on the Christian foundation.

The persuasiveness and moderation of Williams's reasoning are both admirable. It is unfortunate that his Rarotongan code of laws came to be interpreted by native judges and police who were more fanatical in their devotion to the letter of the law than in their understanding of the Christian spirit behind the law. But Williams's own moderation can be seen in his handling of the difficult problem of polygamy. The native teachers at their first baptisms had insisted on candidates putting aside all wives but one. A number of men, however, including the king, soon took back their discarded wives, alleging that they had previously thought the separation was only temporary and had they known it was meant to be permanent they would have selected otherwise. Williams therefore thought it wise to allow the dissatisfied to make a second selection on condition that the man be publicly married to his final choice. Since the king's action would form a precedent he was prevailed upon to be the first to make his choice. Of his three wives, adds Williams, he chose his youngest 'in preference to his own sister, by whom he had three children, and his principal wife who was the mother of nine or ten'.[2] Williams admits that there may be a reasonable difference of opinion upon how to handle such a subject but he believes his solution was both 'suitable and salutary'. It is probable that he worked with a good intuitive knowledge of Polynesian psychology in this, as in other affairs, because the Rarotongan would be more likely to respond, in his new-found enthusiasm, to something difficult that would yet give him an aura of prestige by marking him off from the non-baptized, than to an easy solution of his marital difficulties.

[1] J. Williams, *Missionary Enterprises*, p. 140.   [2] J. Williams, *op. cit.* p. 135.

In any case, with the free and easy attitude of the Rarotongan to sex, the baptized person was able to bask in the public gaze as a 'different' person and at the same time indulge wayward propensities without at this time receiving public disapproval.

The laws of Rarotonga as finally drafted and revised after discussions with the chiefs, were read and carefully explained to an assembly of the people. They were then 'unanimously adopted by the chiefs and the people as the basis on which public justice was to be administered on the island of Rarotonga'.[1] But public justice, according to the missionary idea of the content of justice, could not be taught simply by the adoption of a code. Much injustice was to follow in subsequent years from a rather fanatical and tyrannical attempt to impose on the people a code of law which in some respects must have been as meaningless and as uncongenial to them as the laws of Tibet would be to the average New Zealander of today.

Pitman arrived at Rarotonga in 1827, Buzacott in 1828. Owing to chiefly rivalry it was found expedient for two mission stations to be established. Pitman therefore went to Ngatangiia to convert the people under the chief Tinomana while Buzacott remained at the first settlement of Arorangi under the high chief Makea. Both missionaries found few evidences of any understanding of Christianity. The years between 1827 and 1833 were years therefore in which much fundamental proselytizing work had to be done. They also witnessed the formation of an opposition party, irregular but persistent violence between the opposition and supporters of Christianity, severe sickness, a major hurricane and finally the formation of a church with an initial three members. These steps in the learning process and the influence upon learning of death and famine can now be discussed in more detail.

After Pitman's arrival in 1827 he was soon forced to conclude that much of what had passed for missionizing in the years between 1823 and 1827 was in fact valueless. Although the chapels were full on Sundays and Sunday school was popular with the children, none the less most of the people, noted Pitman on November 6, 1827, 'manifest a total indifference to divine truth' (L.M.S., B.6, F. 4, J.B.).[2]

[1] J. Williams, *op. cit.* p. 139. A letter from Pitman, by now a resident missionary on Rarotonga, places the date as about November 6, 1827.

[2] All references to missionary journals, letters and reports in the Library of the London Missionary Society, Livingstone House, London, are given in conformity with the following code: B., Box; F., Folder; J., Jacket; J.A., Jacket A.; J.B., Jacket B., etc. Month and year refer to the date at which the report was written from the Cook Islands.

OPPOSITION TO NEW FAITH, RAROTONGA, PHASE 2

Again, on December 16 of the same year, he writes, with the faintest touch of irony: 'It is a pleasing thing to see and hear of nations "casting away their gods"—but we wish to see and hear something more than this.' (B.7, F.4, J.B.) At about the same time Mrs. Pitman adds her burden: 'I am far from considering the generality of them *true Christians*, as many who make a profession want the *essentials*, which are, a sorrow for sin when committed and a hatred for it afterwards.' (December 12, 1827, B.6, F.4, J.B.—italics in original); and six months later Pitman takes up the same theme: 'Pray for us . . . that God would pour out His Spirit upon this New Mission and *convince* the people of sin—I am sorry to say that *deep heartfelt* sorrow for sin seems to be but little understood among the South Sea Islanders.' (July 10, 1828, B.6, F.8, J.B.)

Trying to diagnose the trouble, Pitman is forced to conclude that the failure of the mission has been due to the failure, in two respects, of the native teachers. First, Williams's account was far too rosy because he relied solely on the native teachers' statements. The teachers baptized indiscriminately and, as Buzacott informs us in June 1833, even used the *akara* or native policemen, to round up people and force them to attend on Bourne during his 1825 visit, so that the latter might have extra hordes for baptism, even though not one of the hundreds so baptized 'had anything like a scriptural knowledge of that solemn rite' (L.M.S., B.9, F.3, J.B.). In other words the attitude of the native teachers was: if the white missionaries want people to baptize then we will find them even if we have to use native police to find the people. Secondly, the natives soon learned to distrust the native teachers because of their assumption of secular power. 'In many things they have erred,' writes Pitman on November 6, 1827, 'and in none perhaps so much as in exercising undue authority over the people, as even the chiefs of the island are afraid of them. They have given them a great deal of labour. . . . When a thing is proposed to be done, the chiefs will very readily consent; but the poorer orders ought to be consulted also, as the laborious part devolves on them.' (B.6, F.4, J.B.) So imprudent and power-drunk were some native teachers that Pitman has to confess a month later: 'One of the Chiefs in private conversation said to me, and I could scarcely refrain from weeping, that they were more happy in their heathenish state, than since the Word of God came to them, alluding to the manner in which they had been treated by the Native Teachers.' (December 19, 1827, B.6, F.4, J.B.) Perhaps some of this chief's testimony may be discounted on the grounds that it was his power that was being whittled away; on the other hand, it is plausible to infer that the native teachers, with their small schooling in Christianity, knew its letter and not its practice, and easily became despotic in a status society when the opportunity arose because by origin they belonged to the commoner stratum of this society.

And as if these failings were not enough, Pitman continually recurs to the fact that the native teachers needed thorough visits and a double portion of divine grace to prevent them falling into the sin of adultery, 'the besetting sin of the South Sea Islanders' (September 3, 1833, B.6, Journal 99). Tiberio was the first to be expelled for 'illicit connexion with women. At first he strongly denied it, but as three women confessed, he afterwards acknowledged his guilt.' (December 19, 1827, B.6, F.4, J.B.). Tiberio was not above strongarm methods. According to Williams, 'He oppressed the people much, made the girls submit to his wishes by the terrors of his musket, besides oppressing the people much over other ways' (February 1828, B.6, F.8, J.B.). Three native teachers from other islands, including Aitutaki, had to be removed for the same reasons and 'such is the native character', says Pitman, 'that "in office" they soon become elated with pride and it requires great grace . . . to resist the temptations thrown in their way' (October 10, 1832, B.6, Journal 99).

The missionaries owed much to the combination of aggressiveness and shrewdness with which the native teachers introduced Christianity to the Cook Islands. It is not improbable, however, that rapidly as this introduction took place, the consolidation of the ground thus easily won was hindered by the all too human feelings of the native teachers, quickly propelled into positions of power which they were unprepared to occupy and displaying therefore all the intemperate characteristics of persons having power and tasting its delights for the first time. As teaching models many of the native missionaries were thus useless. Because their teaching and their example upset the already existing status system of native society, it was natural that many of those who felt their positions endangered should join together to form an opposition party. The process has been described in its outlines by Buzacott and Pitman and it may now be analysed.

To many minor chiefs Christianity meant great changes for the worse in their relative status, resources and influence. This more lowly status was symbolized by the code of law with its trial before a judge and jury (perhaps composed entirely of commoners) for actions now called crimes but which were previously part of accepted customary behaviour. The lower the initial place in the status ladder the more the annoyance and anxiety at the disturbance to this ladder. Former warriors whose status depended upon a continuance of warfare and former priests (Buzacott puts their numbers at seventy) now no longer in a respectable occupation which formerly gave power and prestige, also found themselves among the dispossessed. These persons therefore formed a party determined to crush the new religion. Supporting the new religion were the principal chiefs whose status and powers were confirmed by the new religion, since at the beginning no judge or jury or policeman would be bold enough to lay charges against, condemn or convict such powerful persons.

Antagonism between the rival parties was muted for a time. According to Buzacott's account the spark to open conflict was struck by a native Tahitian missionary's seduction of the daughter of a chief. 'The poor father maddened by the wrong', writes Buzacott with complete ignorance of Rarotongan psychology, 'at once joined the malcontents and the antagonism to religion at once became open and violent.'[1] No Rarotongan father would really become maddened by such a happening though he might well simulate anger if for any reason he was seeking an excuse to lower the prestige of the new religion. Pitman's emphasis is more probably correct: The Rarotongans, he avers, like most heathen nations are a very revengeful race and until this passion is fully satiated they cannot rest. 'The Chiefs of the different stations agreed to put down evil in the land and appointed judges to inflict punishment on offenders. The consequence was that the revengeful feelings of the people soon began to appear by setting fire to the houses of the inferior judges or those who were most active in their detection.' (December 16, 1829, B.7, F.4, J.B.) It is one thing to agree to the promulgation of a code of laws. It is quite another to rest content when the code is enforced with intolerance and in this statement of Pitman's there is the first hint of the operation of a system of almost unchecked power which some years later turned into a police-state which in many respects must have rivalled the severities of Geneva under Calvin or Massachusetts under the Puritans. Keeping a middle position

[1] Sunderland and Buzacott, *op. cit.* p. 41.

between Buzacott who believes the violence of this period to be due to 'heathen influences' and Moss who later wrote that the revolt of the people was 'only caused by the brutality with which the new laws were enforced',[1] it can be assumed that fanatical implementation of new laws by the recently converted together with a threatened loss of status and security by many whose position was tolerable in aboriginal society would together be good reasons for anti-Christian violence.

The opposition group first tried the technique of stirring up intertribal and inter-district jealousies so as to provoke an outbreak of warfare. Two or three districts did fight for a few days but nothing of consequence occurred and the dispute was soon settled amiably by a return of the lands occasioning the conflict. (Letter from Pitman, December 16, 1829, B.7, F.4, J.B.) Buzacott was sure that God had intervened but to be on the safe side he threatened his own chiefly protector that he would lose his protection unless the chief became more friendly and pacific. The threat was successful. (January, 1830, B.7, F.8, J.B.)

Failing to force a war the opposition party turned to incendiarism and the destruction of property. They chopped down coconut trees. They set fire to native houses and burnt them to the ground. They put flames to chapel and schoolhouse. The house of the chief judge was a special target for the incendiaries and 'for several weeks nothing heard but of houses set on fire' (Pitman, *ibid.*). Friendly chiefs set guards, however, and when an offender was caught in the act of setting fire to a building the chiefs decided to kill him off-hand. Only Buzacott's pleading saved his life. Several hundred pro-Christians guarded the persons of the missionaries against violence. Plans for the murder of the friendly chiefs by the opposition chiefs were continually revised and finally dropped owing to altercations and quarrelling among the opposition as each tried to force the other to choose as his special victim the semi-sacred person of Makea, the high chief of the island.

The violence might have become endemic had not an epidemic of dysentery (Buzacott's diagnosis) or 'inflamatory fever which in many cases turns into the typhus' (Pitman's description) suddenly broke out brought, according to Williams, by a visiting vessel.[2] Between 800 and 900 people died in the months from April to August 1830, at least one-seventh of the population. In two districts,

[1] Moss, *op. cit.* p. 22.   [2] Williams, *op. cit.* p. 280.

OPPOSITION TO NEW FAITH, RAROTONGA, PHASE 2

Pitman notes, which 'had ever manifested much opposition to the advancement of Godliness' nearly all the people died (July 2, 1830, B.7, F.4, J.B.). Buzacott was able to improve the occasion by noting the hand of God in this chastisement of the people, particularly as both missionaries, the only persons who could administer any relief to the sick natives, were themselves prostrated. But since the sickness swept away all the leaders of the opposition and completely crushed the numerous party who had set themselves against the establishment of Christianity and of law, Buzacott inquires, 'Are we wrong in coming to the conclusion which all the natives have come to, "This visitation is from God?" . . . For many years afterwards', Buzacott continues, 'this judgment was used as a text, from which class leaders exhorted their inattentive scholars; parents were wont to warn their refractory sons and daughters by reference to it; and occasionally the voice of the missionary pleaded tenderly with ungodly youth, and entreated them to believe lest they too should fall into the hands of the living God!'[1] One is not informed by Buzacott why falling into the hands of the living God should be such a terrifying experience.

Although the epidemic was thus considered by Buzacott to be evidences for Divine wrath against those who planned war against Jehovah and even jestingly and wantonly broke the Sabbath by cooking food on this day,[2] and although it may have broken the spirit of the opposition, the epidemic's immediate effects upon the spread of Christianity were not at once apparent—an illustration perhaps of the fact that punishments are less reliable than rewards in furthering the learning process. Pitman notes in several letters that the epidemic made little impression on the sanctity or Christian devotion of the natives. 'It was heartrending', Buzacott also writes, 'to witness the awful ignorance and blindness of such numbers about to enter eternity. In some were visible all the horrors of an awakened conscience—in most others a pharasaical self-complacency fancying all was well because they had observed a regular attendance on the Sabbath—in others an almost brute-like insensibility either to the joys of heaven or the miseries of the lost.' (August 17, 1830, B.7, F.8, J.B.)

Indifference to the new faith continued throughout the following year, but at the end of 1831 a second visitation was heaped upon

---
[1] Sunderland and Buzacott, *op. cit.* p. 49.
[2] Sunderland and Buzacott, *op. cit.* pp. 46-47.

the people in the form of a devastating hurricane and heavy seas. All provisions were destroyed and a terrible famine resulted. Many scoffed, according to Pitman, when they saw that the Lord did equal damage to the lands of the good and bad people alike (December 3, 1831, B.6, Journal 99), but the lesson being so hammered that rebellion, epidemic, hurricane and famine 'were the means employed by God to produce a new state of things'[1] and that even worse might be in store if the islanders did not soon enter into the Kingdom of God, some few thought it wise to learn the new ways. In May 1833 Buzacott was able to form a Church of five members, Pitman admitting three members to his Church at about the same time, seven more on August 31, 1833. Of Buzacott's members, one was a confessed cannibal, a second an old warrior 'under deep conviction of sin', and a third a sorcerer with a high professional reputation for his one-time skill in burning the 'spirits of living men upon a red-hot oven'. These three and a further convert became the first deacons of the new Church. Immediately after their conversion they began a routine of house to house visits to chiefs and commoners alike and preached their favourite sermon on the text, 'The axe is laid unto the root of the tree; therefore every tree which bringeth not forth good fruit, is hewn down, and cast into the fire'. Numbers professed to be greatly moved by this sermon and the domiciliary discourses. From this time forward, according to Buzacott, 'the days of darkness and anxious toil were now past and, as by the law of secret yet mighty growth, the whole island became as a garden of the Lord'.[2]

Yet, rather curiously, a minor epidemic of suicides occurred at this time. On February 15, 1833, a man hanged himself, 'apparently a thief who feared detection'. On May 1, Pitman records that a woman recently hanged herself, and in addition a boy of 9 or 10 years, a good pupil and assistant teacher, followed suit. On July 8 another woman hanged herself after quarrelling with her daughter-in-law over a jug; three weeks later a little boy attempted to hang himself after being punished by his mother. (Pitman, B.6, Journal 99.) Even after making due allowance for suicidal contagion it would appear as if some were being unduly weighted with a Christian conviction of worthlessness. This conclusion is strengthened by a report of Buzacott in which he enumerates examples of satisfactory confessions and conversions. In addition to a 'vile thief' now reforming,

[1] Sunderland and Buzacott, *op. cit.* p. 51.
[2] Sunderland and Buzacott, *op. cit.* p. 60.

OPPOSITION TO NEW FAITH, RAROTONGA, PHASE 2

two confessed cannibals, a chief unable to sleep after a sermon, another ill with remorse, Buzacott gives details of a 'pleasing conversation' with two women, both of whom were so 'deeply impressed as to have produced considerable effects on their bodily frame'. One woman told Buzacott that 'in consequence of the extreme anxiety of her mind she thought her body was being cut into two pieces, and the chief's wife said that on thinking over her sinful state her fear was so great as to throw her frame into a state of violent agitation' (November 18, 1833, Box 9, F.C.).

The work of schooling and teaching, however, took on new life during this year 1833. By November the two missionaries, in their schedule of returns are able to report the following statistics: in school 1,720 children, 640 adults; baptized, 88; church members 16; marriages 26; candidates for baptism 16, and candidates for communion 17. School attendance for many must have been irregular however, for Pitman notes that at one school festival enlivened by food, hymns, prayers and bible readings, 700 attended, but another 200 were deprived of this pleasure as a punishment for non-attendance or irregular attendance (May 21, 1833, B.9, F.3, J.B.)—and of this 700 there were only four lads who could be called really devout. (October 17, 1833, B.6, Journal 99.) Many of the non-attenders among the boys and girls were apparently in prison—too many of their parents Pitman complains do not look upon pre-marital experiment 'as a serious evil, not one in 10 or 20' and so the young people were sent to prison to make up for their parents' failure even though this non-attendance seriously impeded the work of the school. Pitman also looks darkly at this time on the common practice of women and girls using scent or scented flowers, for 'when they do, it is almost always found to be for the worst of purposes' (February 4, February 6, July 8, 1833, B.6, Journal 99).

Thus the year 1833 ended. The people had learned something, but not very much. Before analysing the factors at work in the process of social change in Rarotonga, it will be well briefly to outline the steps in the somewhat similar process of social change that occurred later in Aitutaki, but which follow the phase already described for Rarotonga.

9

Opposition to New Faith, 1827-33, Aitutaki, Phase 2

Towards the end of 1838 there was a persistent, unpleasant rumour current about Aitutaki in Rarotonga and an equally unpleasant, but well-known fact. The rumour was that the Catholics planned or proposed to send popish missionaries to the island; the fact that could no longer be brushed aside was that only one of the several native teachers working on the island was free from sin. Henry Royle, a recently arrived missionary reinforcement, was therefore sent off to Aitutaki, where he arrived on May 23, 1839, with a double commission: to forestall the Romans and to set Aitutaki's Christian house in order. (B.12, F.5, J.B.)

Royle arrived on the island at the beginning of June. He was met by large crowds of people all professing attachment to Christian principles, but when, says Royle, 'we detected and affectionately reproved their sins, their clamorous professions disappeared like a cloud before the sun . . . and in return for our faithful admonitions we became the objects of their displeasure' (December 25, 1840, B.13, F.4, J.D.). The prison house—for there was already a prison house to confine the sinners so judged under a code of laws similar to the Rarotongan code—was burnt down in June. In July there were eight cases of attempted murder, three cases directed against the persons of William Makea and two other chiefs, all supporters of the church, and five cases against judges (two of whom were also deacons of the church). As in Rarotonga, an insurrection was planned for October, but not succeeding, incendiarism took its place. Chapels were razed, rebuilt, razed again. Houses of pro-Christian chiefs and commoners were burnt to the ground. Some conspirators and incendiarists were caught and severely punished, the conspirators by banishment from the island. (December 25, 1840, *ibid.*)

The main source of trouble appears to have been the rigid application of the code of laws, and the resentment against this code of some few white runaway sailors living on the island. Royle believed that 'the foreign scoundrels' living on the island were responsible for introducing venereal disease and for aiding the anti-Christian party in their particular opposition to that part of the code of laws relating to sex offences and former marriage customs. In order partially to meet a long-continued opposition, the native teachers had regularized a very easy divorce, so that it had become customary for married couples to separate on the slightest cause and there were very 'few who had not been married several times'. Some of the stricter members of the church wished Royle to pass a law nullifying all the frequent marriages and divorces and thus making every person return to his first and original spouse. Royle opposed this step and urged a reform from now onwards. While he was ill, however, the strict group held a meeting and pushed through the new law. Tremendous confusion was caused and it was some time before excitement died away, aggression was muted and the Christian party was allowed to proceed with its house-to-house visiting, its preaching and school work.

Missionary progress was assisted in Aitutaki, as in Rarotonga by hurricanes, famine and deaths through introduced diseases. Royle reports the hurricane of February 1841 as a 'merciful chastisement of the people' (June 16, 1842, B.15, F.4, J.B.). A hurricane on December 17, 1842, followed by gigantic waves desolated the whole island, levelling all but three houses, and destroying much property. (May 9, 1843, B.16, F.5, J.A.) With the assistance of these chastisements and stricter control of the native teachers, Royle was able to report substantial progress. By May 9, 1843, there were 84 church members, 730 children and 500 adults attending twelve schools (*ibid.*). Testaments were being sold for 18 to 20 pounds of arrowroot for each copy. The chapel five times destroyed (twice by fire, three times by wind and sea), was to be rebuilt in a grander manner. Contributions of arrowroot to support the London Missionary Society rose from a value of about £15 for the first three years to a value of £40 in 1844. (The 4,000 pounds of arrowroot valued at £40 requires a good deal of preparation. Its real value today is probably seven or eight times the value mentioned.) By June 18, 1845, missionary visits from the two Gill brothers to Aitutaki resulted in an urgent appeal for an additional missionary appointment to Aitutaki to beat off another rumoured popish effort at settlement on the island. (B.18, F.5, J.A., J.B., J.C.) No appointment was made. None was really needed. In some four years and working with a population of about one-third that of Rarotonga, Royle had succeeded in bringing Aitutaki to the stage in the process of cultural change that Rarotonga had reached about ten years earlier.

10
Social Changes in Phases 1 and 2

By 1833 in Rarotonga and by 1845 in Aitutaki, the results of social change were clearly apparent. The people were responding to new rewards and punishments by learning slowly new ways of behaving. The rewards and the learning responses were at least partially determined by the sociological factors that were operating in the islands as the result of the cultural contact situation.[1] A brief summary of the effect of these sociological influences will therefore be appropriate.

1. *Time sequences*. The general framework of change is given by the time sequences, because time sequences are the thread upon which social change is itself strung. In both islands, the initial contact was one of acceptance. A few technological improvements were adopted and a knowledge was acquired of the fact that there were other interesting people in the world of different skin colour, customs, beliefs and with superior technological resources. The phase of missionary teacher contact was also one of acceptance, which lead mostly to a loss or destruction of customs and objects associated with anxiety or thought to block the acceptance of more important and powerful new ideas. Warfare disappeared. Maraes and gods were destroyed. Habitations were moved from distant plantation lands to sites near the missionary station. Positively the change at this stage might almost be summed up by the conditions that John Williams laid down before he was prepared to teach the word of God in Aitutaki. 'This was our word, that they must cut their hair everyone of them—wash themselves clean, lay aside their heathenish ornaments, clothe themselves decently.' (B.5, Journal 67, July and August 1823). The phase of white missionary enterprise is dialectical in its development. First there is outward acceptance of some novelties as, for instance, a code of laws, changes in marriage customs, the alphabet and reading skills; second, there is opposition and violence from those with a vested status interest in the past, rightly fearful that the new ways would rob them of their status and power. Thirdly, the opposition is broken by disease, death and famine. The people are now prepared to push aside some of the rewards of the

[1] The variables used in the following analysis are adapted from Keesing, Felix M.: 'Some Notes on Acculturation Study', *Proceedings, Sixth Pacific Science Congress* (1940), 4: 60-63.

SOCIAL CHANGES IN PHASES 1 AND 2

old social system, particularly those rewards of which the white missionaries disapprove, and to learn the responses which will bring forth the rewards promised them under a new social order.

2. *Locality influences.* The islands were small, difficult of access, and in the first two phases of contact had few economic goods to offer to the outside world. There was little pressure on available economic resources, and what pressure there was, was soon reduced by serious population decrease. Social change therefore was positively determined by the fact that the island locality attracted, in the early period, practically no European settlers and thus there were no contradictory European reward systems to confuse the learning responses of the people.

3. *Migration influences.* The islanders continued to live in their natural habitat. The missionary teachers from Tahiti and the white missionaries from England were the newcomers; the former of the same basic physical and cultural stock as the islanders, but aggressive and power-driven, having absorbed very incompletely the new faith and the new order they were charged to disseminate; the latter bringing with them lower middle-class Evangelical English puritanism and determined to reform the South Seas garden so as to bring it into a shape corresponding to their dream-world of a Christian society. The direction of social change in the early period is determined very largely by the goals the white missionaries themselves had firmly fixed in their minds and by the shaping, therefore, that they gave where and when they could to the social life of the people around them.

4. *Numerical influences.* In the first two phases the newcomers were only a tiny minority. Up to 1833 in Rarotonga, the new people probably numbered no more than twenty; in Aitutaki no more than six or seven. The native population almost immediately began to show changes from a fantastically accelerated death rate, but in 1833 probably numbered between five and six thousand in Rarotonga and perhaps two thousand in Aitutaki. Thus, social change was the result of a numerically insignificant number of people working determinedly for social change among a population three hundred times as large.

5. *Momentum.* That social change occurred at all was due largely to the aggressiveness, the energy, and the determination with which the minority exerted pressure on the majority. The majority was not

a passive majority—initially it wanted change of some kinds, later it was split into two groups, one wanting some change, the other wanting a return to the native pattern of social organization, finally most of the population were prepared to accept the new order at least passively, and a few, gaining power under the new order, actively and enthusiastically.

6. *Degree of effective contact*. During the period under review social change was influenced by only three types of people among the newcomers: in the initial period a few sailors and sailor-traders and later the native missionary-teachers and then the white missionaries. Intermingling by the first comers was probably free, though limited by outbursts of violence; the native teachers intermingled freely and the number of them that had to be dismissed or reprimanded for 'the sin' indicates that the mingling was often on a very intimate and informal level. The white missionaries brought their wives with them and tried to raise families (though the infant and child mortality in missionary families was extremely high). Hence social contact, for the missionaries, was always on the level of formal teaching or informal friendship and never the level of intermarriage. It was a sex-segregated relationship, probably free and easy in all friendship relationships, but highly formal and awe-provoking when the missionary or his wife felt the frequent duty to thunder or to chide against sin.

7. *'Race' influences*. Most culture contact situations are affected by the degree to which the groups in contact differ in visible distinguishing physical marks. It is probable, however, that these physical 'race' factors had only inconsequential influences on the islanders during the early period of contact. The native teachers were of the same race as the islanders, so race influences were of no account. There are no surviving records to show that either the earlier European sailor contacts or the later European missionary contacts were influenced by oppositions or prejudices based on the physical characteristics of Polynesian or Europeans. It is probable, however, that visible physical marks may have influenced positively the acceptance by both groups of each other. The European in general has never found the Polynesian unpleasing; in fact he has always lived easily and happily with them. Conversely, the Polynesian, at first sight, may find the skin colour of the European strange enough to be worth touching, but he has never disliked it. For many Polynesian

peoples skin bleaching was rigorously enforced among the young women of chiefly families in order to produce a more pleasing appearance. And today the Polynesian will shelter himself from the sun, if opportunity offers, in order to prevent the darkening of his skin—and will marvel at the European who may seek the sun to secure a desirable and 'healthy' sun-tan.

So much for the more important sociological influences on the course of social change. In addition to these influences, psychological factors undoubtedly helped in defining the nature of the new rewards. Thus an interest in novelty and in the superior utility of the technological devices that the white man had to offer helped the islander to accept new ways of doing things. Reduction in inner anxieties by the disappearance of warfare, infanticide, cannibalism and sorcery also helped the acceptance of the new. A sense of helplessness induced by continual missionary emphasis that death stalking the land and hunger and destruction of property by hurricane were all due to Divine wrath and punishment must have been a powerful drive towards acceptance of the new faith. If God would at least relax his punishments, as the missionaries assured the islanders He would when their behaviour conformed to missionary standards, then new ways of behaving were at least worthy of a trial. The prestige with which the islander regarded the native ideological interpretation of physical and spiritual welfare was probably at this time at a very low ebb. In turning from this ideology he naturally welcomed a new ideology which was quite exciting in its promises, all-embracing in its interpretations, and associated in obscure fashion with the technological superiority of the white man. Finally psychological influences associated with the adaptability of the islander's personality to new ways, and with certain compatabilities between the value-systems of the islander and those of the European and his culture, also helped in the acceptance of the new. An appreciation of the role of group personality influences in social change may, however, be left for later discussion.

11

The New Order

Having secured from the islanders an initial acceptance of new ways of behaviour, the missionary's task was now fairly clear. However he phrased it to himself or to his colleagues in the islands and in England, he had now in effect a double task: one aspect of his task was to enhance the rewards associated with the new order so that the new theology, new forms of social relations and new types of economic productivity would all be better learned; the other aspect was to limit the opportunities for the learning about rewards associated with ways of behaving and thinking not congruent with the Christian ethic. Hence the missionary was fearful about the results of the introduction of alcohol from Tahiti, just as he strove to limit the frequency and intensity of personal associations between the islander and visiting European whaling sailors, traders, beachcombers and other would-be European settlers. His task, in other words, was to limit as far as possible the number and types of models through the imitation of which the islander could and would learn, to those models conforming to the Christian pattern. To enforce this construction of the learning process and thus to insulate the reward-system from contradictory rewards and experiences, the missionary was able to use the code of laws previously adopted by the people. Through his personal influence on, and his advice to, the judges, juries and police supporting this code (all of them, of course, staunch and fanatical members of his Church), the missionary was able for some years to limit and canalize the process of learning so that social change took place in one way only. Pressure from traders wishing economically to exploit the islanders by providing goods that they desired, finally broke the missionary new order, but this breaking would not have occurred from outside pressure alone had not tensions within the new order produced by the attempt to build up an over-severe group super-ego made the people welcome any change that would reduce their own inner anxieties. With this general summary in mind, the operation of the new order may now be described.

The changes that took place between 1833 and 1858, when Buzacott retired from the Rarotongan Mission (having been preceded by Pitman four years earlier), were social changes in a population that was itself being ravaged by disease and death. As indicated by Table I, more than 4,000 people died in the eighteen years from 1827 to 1845, and in the next nine years a further 1,300 people were killed off by disease. The sex ratio for the population was seriously disturbed and this biological influence must have been important in making it difficult for the people to overcome 'the sin', no matter how much they were punished for adultery and extra-marital relations.

TABLE 1

POPULATION CHANGES—RAROTONGA
1827-63

	Population	Deaths	Births
1827	7,000		
1838		909	199
1840		746	
1842		273	67
1843		442	100
1844		220	73
1845	3,000	166	95
1846		280	131
1847*		168	66
1848		119	93
1849		159	95
1850		171	152
1851		119	70
1852		81	67
1853		91	92
1854	2,300		
1858		68	60
1863	2,400		

* Sex ratio in this year was 258 nubile young men and boys to each 100 nubile young women and girls. (Gill, Minutes, December 26, 1847, B.20, F.4, J.E.) According to Gill in his *Gems*, the sex ratio for the whole population in 1846 was 150 men to each 100 women.

Source: Gill, *Gems*, p. 120; with corrections and additions from Rarotongan Mission Minutes and Annual Schedule of Returns.

The high death rate was largely due to introduced diseases, for which the people had no natural immunity, and for which several generations had to pass before some sort of immunity could be built up. The passage of the years in missionary reports brings mention of one epidemic succeeding another—in 1838, 1840, 1843 (dysentery), 1848 ('hooping-cough'), 1850 (mumps), 1851 (influenza, mumps, jaundice), 1854 (measles), 1857 (measles and dysentery). And the reports are full of repeated phrases such as: 'Epidemic of deaths still raging. Lost six young teachers.' (December 30, 1840.) Three years later Pitman reports, 'Fatal dysentery cases have carried off 30 children in five weeks'—three months later this epidemic had turned into a 'divine scourge' brought to Rarotonga from Tahiti by the captain of a whaling ship. Naturally the missionaries always seized the opportunity to 'improve the occasion' by pointing out to sinners the imminent danger to salvation caused by their way of life in such hazardous times. Thus of the epidemic of 1846 Pitman writes: 'The solemn dispensation has been greatly sanctified to all at this station. The church has been aroused to enquiry and prayer. There is a manifest anxiety to improve the awful event.' (July 1, 1846, B.19, F.4, J.D.) Twelve new members joined the Church in three months and two were restored to membership as the result of this epidemic. Again Pitman writes of the 1851 sickness, that a woman who had once been a pupil but who had left school to have her fill of sin was warned by her pious mother of the wrath of God. Soon after the woman nearly died of measles. She became so terrified of her sins that she soon came to God, along with thirty other young people. (July 23, 1851, B.24, F.4, J.A.)

One unexpected result of the epidemics was the large number of orphans left destitute by the death of their parents. In 1838 Buzacott estimated the number at 200, and by 1841 at between 800 and 900. Food was no problem, but clothing was, since without clothing the children could not attend Sunday school or church. Hence Buzacott was forced to found an Orphan Clothing Society and with contributions of clothing from the London Missionary Society and help from whaling ship captains, the orphans were kept suitably clad and all proprieties satisfied.

Another result of the hammer blows of these epidemics was an apparent loss of hope when disease did strike. In 1840 Gill writes, 'The general want of energy among the sick is one of the most painful and depressing circumstances to us; when a person is slightly disposed (*sic*) he generally casts himself down on the floor of his house, spreads his native cloth over him, and in many cases is so unnerved as to refrain from seeking any relief;—but a few weeks ago I called on a young man, a teacher in the school who had been absent but a short time; his illness at first was but slight, then, however, through want of attention and energy, had quite reduced him. I succeeded in advising him to bathe every day and either come himself or send to me for medicine. This he did for a short time, but soon relapsed and is now I fear near death.' (June 24, 1840, B.13, F.4, J.C.) Fifteen years later, George Gill remarked on the same fatalism, 'an extreme apathy and indifference . . . so that it is next to impossible to get them to adopt any means which promptly and judiciously acted upon would probably prolong life'. (August 18, 1855, B.26, F.2, J.B.) In the same passage Gill suggests that fatalism may be one among many causes 'which might be assigned for the decrease of the population throughout Polynesia', thus anticipating by almost seventy years a psychological theory of depopulation advanced by Rivers in 1922.[1]

[1] W. H. R. Rivers (ed.), 'The Psychological Factor', *Essays on the Depopulation of Melanesia* (Cambridge, 1922), pp. 84-113.

THE NEW ORDER

Psychological theories of depopulation are out of fashion at the moment. But it may be noted that although epidemics are generally deadly for primitive peoples just because they have developed no immunity, and become progressively less deadly as immunity is developed in a population, none the less, sickness infects a living person, not a disembodied organ, with all his hopes and fears, worries and anxieties. If such anxieties become acute, as they surely must have been in Rarotonga during these deadly years, then modern psychosomatic medicine would suggest that the worries and anxieties themselves can very well upset the physiological balance of the person so that resistance is lowered and an interest in remaining alive changed to indifference. Measles or mumps were therefore the specific causes of island depopulation. The co-operating contributory cause, that which lowered resistance, may well have been psychological in general and emotional in particular. All the more so that there were no physicians in Rarotonga during these years and precious few drugs. Thus it would require an extreme act of faith on the part of the natives to assume that any suggestions made to them might possibly prolong life; a great act of faith, too, since the missionaries themselves, as has been noted, were not backward in implying that the sickness was God's punishment, and the natives therefore quickly learnt the lesson that none could struggle successfully against the wrath of an all-powerful and all-punishing God.

Despite setbacks caused by sin, the missionaries made slow and steady progress in their spiritual efforts. An 'awakening' is reported during 1834. Many chiefs began to attend classes and following the band-wagon many of their dependents, 'some from purity of motive and real desire but others . . . merely following their chiefs' steps'. For each class—there are eighteen of them, ten for men and eight for women—an 'overseer' was appointed, and with the overseers Pitman met once each month to question them on the conduct of class members. Those who were reported as acting in an 'inconsistent and unbecoming manner, if judged necessary, are excluded, but not without suitable exhortations to repentance' (June 5, 1834, B.9, F.7, J.C.). This 'overseeing' is the first hint of the existence of a system of prying into the private lives of the people that was soon to give almost unlimited power to church members in the control of peoples' thought and behaviour. Buzacott also notes in this year 1834 the presence of a 'spirit of religious excitement . . . and numbers manifest such a spirit of anxiety in their enquiries respecting the concerns of their souls as lead us to indulge in a hope that the good work is begun within them' (July 1, 1834, B.9, F.7, J.C.). In 1838 and 1839, pleased optimism is still characteristic of the reports of Pitman and Buzacott. Finally another great awakening is noted in 1846. Accounts are given of individual conversions. For instance the son of Iro, a native teacher, 'was deeply convinced of sin under a sermon preached by his father. In relating his own experience he said, that as his father was proceeding in his discourse, all of a sudden his attention was aroused and the Word rushed into his soul like a hurricane tearing up everything by the roots. At the close of the discourse he hastened to his room (*sic*) and there groaned aloud with fear and dismay.' (December 22, 1846, B.19, F.4, J.E.) This account of an individual conversion could have come directly from the pages of James' *Varieties of Religious Experience.* It fits well into the evangelical pattern of private conversion and indicates the extent to which the traditional evangelical patterns of Christianity had taken form in the native mind. In 1851 and 1852 a reawakening in the young coincided with the arrival in Rarotonga of the first complete edition of the sacred Scriptures in the Rarotongan translation prepared by Pitman and Buzacott. There was great rejoicing and great excitement as people paid for their copies in money, fishing net or arrowroot. Even some unrepentants prudently purchased copies, saying they might some day repent—'such sentiments as these', writes George Gill, 'may appear rather peculiar, but they faithfully represent native thought and native feeling' (April 30, 1852, B.24, F.8, J.A.).

On the debit side of these awakenings there remain the perpetual struggles against inconsistency. Pitman notes on December 20, 1841, 'After all that has been said, Rarotonga is a land of thieves, fornicators and adulterers' (B.14, F.4, J.E.). Again on November 21, 1842, two women had to be cut off from the Church after four years' membership for the 'crying sin of the islands', and their sins were aggravated by their attending services before and after the 'act'— one of the women being superintendent of the girls' school. (B.15, F.4, J.C.) Of another woman who regularly sought baptism, but was refused because of the deacons' reports on her private life, it is noted that she quarrelled with her husband and then hanged herself. 'The awful end of this woman I attempted to improve the following Sabbath', says Pitman, 'from 2 Samuel xvii. 23.' (B.15, F.4, J.C.) Finally, after other accounts of young widows who have had to be cut off from the Church soon after their husbands' deaths, Pitman recurs to his perennial complaint of the natives' lack of understanding of the evil of sin. 'If they can but conceal their sin from their teacher or deacons of the church, it seems but little concern to them the knowledge God has of all their transactions.' (December 20, 1847, B.20, F.4, J.E.) And thus Pitman and his deacons redoubled their efforts to track down evidences of sin and used the full secular power of the state to punish those detected by observation, hearsay or any other evidence.

It was the adolescent population that gave the missionaries most trouble. Samoan practice was to exclude from church membership all except married persons. This custom was not followed in Rarotonga so that Pitman has to admit that 'few can be continued in our schools when they arrive at the age of puberty' (December 30, 1840, B.13, F.4, J.D.). William Gill, nine years later confesses, 'Our most anxious solicitude is directed towards the youthful population between the ages of fourteen and twenty-three'. These young people may have knowledge, but they are often without grace. (July 7, 1849, B.22, F.2, J.A.) And it was at this time that a group of twenty to thirty unsteady youths, suffering from the frustrations of the missionary state, and led by an 'apostate years ago excommunicated for adultery' caused much trouble by trying to stir up people against the Church, even with a view to forming a new village away from the existing church-dominated villages. The matter at dispute was, however, settled peacefully when the chiefs of the Christian party made a show of force. (Pitman, July 3, 1849, B.22, F.2, J.A.)

Two further notes made may be added to indicate the progress of missionary activity during these years. The first records the building of an establishment for a missionary college or institute in which Buzacott proposed to train native married persons in a four-year course for the Pacific mission field. The building was large and impressive. It was built early in 1844 by the chiefs and people, who were recompensed for their services by food gifts, feasts and other gifts. Buzacott has left a record of the presents given to the people; it is interesting as an indication of the things that the people most valued at this time:

Piece goods and cloth from mission stocks, value £11 8 9
24 dozen knives (the gift of a friend)
4 bundles of childrens' dresses (gift of English friends)
Piece goods and cloth supplied by Buzacott, value £25 2 3

3 Large bullocks, value 30 dollars each, value £18 0 0
5 boxes of American glass, value £10 0 0
50 hogs
Presents of bolts, hasps, white lead.

Buzacott believes the people were well pleased with their presents. Buzacott was certainly well pleased with his building, particularly as this was a time of financial stringency in the affairs of the London Missionary Society and great pressure was exerted on the field missionaries to save money by curtailing their activities. It was in order to meet a shortage of funds that the people were encouraged at this time to increase their contributions of arrowroot to the local missions. The arrowroot, sold at 2½d. a pound to visiting whalers and traders, thus became financial support for the London Missionary Society. The following figures, from mission records, indicate the growth of the mission in the increase of money contributions.

1838   £4 0 0
1839   36 0 0 (including £19 for printing)
1840   12 5 0
1841   19 2 2
1842   34 7 3 (in addition £85 paid for copies of Bible)
1843   20 7 0
1845   38 0 0 (in addition £34 for printing and £30 for British and Foreign Bible Society)
1847   83 0 0 (in addition £7 7s. 6d. for the above Society and £10 16s. for the printing press)
1857   206 0 0 (708 dollars)

It is probable that the cost of the Mission on Rarotonga in these years was about £300 each year. Thus native contributions were rarely more than token contributions towards meeting this cost. But since the only form of wealth at this time was that obtained from selling arrowroot, sweet potatoes and tropical fruits to visiting vessels, it is again not improbable that the natives and particularly church members were contributing a fairly significant proportion of their incomes to the Mission.

In October 1839, Makea, paramount chief of Rarotonga, died. Buzacott took the opportunity of composing for the Rev. William Ellis of the London Missionary Society, an obituary on the life and death of this chief. This obituary is of interest not only because it is a good example of missionary writing and of the manner in which almost any incident was seized upon to improve the occasion, but also because information in it suggests vividly the changes in the social life of the people as the missionaries themselves appreciated these changes. Buzacott's account is reproduced as he wrote it in November 1839. The spelling and syntax are his. The only omissions are a long account of the incendiarism at the mission station of Avarua which has already been discussed, and some material about Makea's family.

'The Power of Divine Grace as exemplified in the Life and beautiful death of Makea a Chief of Rarotonga, through the blessing of God on Missionary exertion:

'Makea, the subject of this memoir was one of the principal chiefs of the island. He was descended from a noble and ancient family of Ariki's (chiefs of the highest order) and could trace his ancestry back to the people of the island. He descended from Karika a chief from Manuka, one of the Samoan islands, who tradition says, was the first person that landed here. Makea was a chief considerably above the common size, his height 6 ft. 4 inches, of very commanding aspect, and his legs and arms beautifully tatooed. He was naturally of a proud and haughty disposition, which had been fostered by the unlimited power possessed by the chiefs of this island, life and death literally depending on their nod. He was one of the last chiefs of importance who embraced Christianity, and it was many years after that period ere he appeared to receive the truth in the love of it.

'When we arrived at Rarotonga early in 1828 Makea and his people had nominally embraced Christianity, but on becoming acquainted with their private characters it appeared that although they regularly attended to all the external duties of religion, yet, that few of their evil practices, and those of a licentious kind, especially, had been abandoned. Makea had professed to give up all his wives except one, but in reality keeping secretly as many if not more, than while in his heathen state. . . .

'In May 1833 a church was formed at this station [Avarua]. Only six including the native Teacher Papeiha were to be found, who gave sufficiently decided evidence of piety to be received as communicants, and in consequence of the then low state of true religion, the necessity of visiting their neighbours and countrymen from house to house was suggested to them, that they might in their own peculiar and familiar phraseology urge upon them the necessity of an immediate attention to the state of their souls. The good effects of this were soon apparent. Many became concerned and a spirit of anxious inquiry was manifested. Referring to my journal I find that on August 24th of the same year [1833], Makea took the visitors into a private room and desired them to tell, "What the true source of salvation was?" and "How was it to be obtained?" requesting them to talk freely to him as it was his wish that his heart should feel for his sins etc.

'The next notice of him in my journal is as follows. Sept. 7th. "Our chief has largely manifested some concern respecting his state as a sinner in the sight of God and many things of a pleasing nature have been reported of him by our visitors—but the report today is not so favourable; he seems to be halting between two opinions, and is afraid he shall not be able to resist the power of temptation."

'Oct. 12th. "Have had some pleasing conversation with Makea. He appeared to be earnestly enquiring after the best things. Oh that these impressions may not be like the early dew which soon passeth away."

'About this time the person who held the office of chief Judge died, and Makea took the office upon himself and seemed determined to put the laws in execution. A circumstance soon occurred which put his principles to a severe test. Two of the chief women, whose husbands had not long since died, with whom he had been living in sin since the death of their husbands, became deeply convinced of the error of their ways, and the power of their convictions was so great that they could not rest satisfied until they had confessed their guilt. This, as there are not many among them who can keep a secret, soon spread and became generally known. He was now placed in a very awkward situation. He felt that he could not sit in judgment upon others unless he himself submitted to the penalty of the law. I was frequently consulted as to what he should do and as frequently declined having anything further to say than that "he ought to do that which in his conscience he considered right". He at length came to the determination of humbling himself and exalting the laws. A day was fixed and the chief judges of the other stations sent for, when Makea and his guilty paramours were fined.

'We were grieved however to learn that such vindictive feeling had been shown by the much severer punishment which had been awarded to the females who had confessed the crime.

'From this time to 1835 he became a diligent enquirer after truth. His conviction of sin was very deep and from being a haughty proud individual, he became as meek and quiet as a lamb. Almost as soon as he became acquainted with his state as a sinner, and his need of an interest in Christ he proposed himself as a member for church fellowship. He was not however admitted till more than 12 months after. Knowing as we did his former character we were desirous of obtaining more decisive evidence of the sincerity of his profession by his continuance in welldoing. In May 1835 he with 6 others were admitted to church fellowship and continued to adorn the doctrine of God his Saviour until he was called to join the church above. The account which he gave of his conversion and religious experience when admitted, was of the most pleasing kind. . . .

'On Monday especially and also on other evenings our house is generally crowded with persons who come to talk over the subjects of the preceding Sabbaths and other portions of the word of God and often at the conclusion of the subject, when they were about to leave, have I been much affected to hear him with much concern address the people and apply the solemn truths which had been the subject of inquiry to his own and their individual cases, saying "Don't let us think that other people are intended, these truths deeply concern ourselves. What do we personally know of them?" Eternity with its realities awakened in him the most solemn thoughts, and at times the most fearful apprehensions which nothing could calm but the exhibition of divine mercy in the gift of the Lord Jesus Christ. This appeared to be his only hope, his only trust.

'What a monument of divine mercy was here. A Chief born in heathenism, brought up in all the superstitions and cruelties of heathen idolatry, a Despot who had frequently imbrued his hands in the blood of his subjects for trifling offences, or perhaps no offence at all, who had been accustomed during his heathen state to exercise his savage brutality in hewing to pieces the wretched victims of his caprice and having the mangled portions of their bodies hung up in various parts of his premises. When reflecting on this part of his conduct in connection with the solemnities of an approaching judgment, he would at times be filled with consternation and horror at the thought of meeting those whom he had formerly sacrificed to his cruelty. But then he would say "I did it ignorantly". Why did you english people delay so long the sending the gospel to us? This unanswerable question has frequently been put to me. While others have said, Oh if you had come before such an individual, such a chief, such a father, and such a brother would not have been killed.

'Makea was very desirous of imitating european customs, and in 1837 after my return from the Navigator islands [Samoa], he had a new house built far superior to any he ever had before. An American carpenter was lodging with him at the time who planned and in building it. The house measures 60 feet by 30. It has two stories, 1 hall and 4 rooms on the ground floor and 6 rooms on the second, besides two garrets. It also has a verandah and Balcony in front. It was completed in a very short time and painted throughout. He then got 4 sofas made and a large dining table, 6 common chairs and 3 two armed chairs, and a good hanging press, nearly all the furniture is made of the Tamanu wood and made by native carpenters. He had two bedrooms furnished with a number of good boxes and a bed in each furnished in english stile. The large dining table stands in the hall, two sofas and most of his chairs, on the wall is a small pier glass and a few pictures which complete his furniture.

'He had a numerous family. The eldest son, our present chief, and eldest daughter are both members of the church, but he was much tried in some of the younger branches of the family. One of his sons died while he was on a visit to the Navigators with Mr. Williams, and another who was a very wild young man died in a very awful manner. The day before his death he told his friends who were sitting around him not to think he was going to heaven but to hell! and the next morning he ceased to breathe and his friends thought he was quite dead, but sometime after he opened his eyes and spoke and said that terror had driven him back, and again told him that he was lost, and wept aloud, then closed his eyes in death!

'His disease was Florid consumption, and this awful providence was improved from Proverbs 5, 11 to 14 verse "And thou mourn at the last", etc. We have reason to believe the subject was blessed to not a few, though his own brothers were little affected by it. . . .

'He generally manifested the utmost diligence, in his character as judge, for the prevention of evil, and towards obstinate offenders he would be very severe in awarding punishments and would sometimes, according to our ideas, exceed the bounds of humanity; but we have reason to believe that his over severity arose from his great desire to prevent the commission of evil. . . .

'In May 1839 Makea was taken ill, he took some medicine and partially recovered. In June I accompanied Mr. Royle to Aitutaki. I was absent about 6 or 7 weeks and on my return found him very ill. His complaint was now ascertained to be the dropsy in the stomach and bowels. I commenced by giving him some powerful cathartics which gave temporary relief, and at one time we had hopes of his ultimate recovery, but unfavourable symptoms soon returned and every means used proved ineffectual.

'The state of his mind during his illness was very pleasing: then as when in health, he always seemed prepared to talk on religious subjects, and whenever I called he generally had to enquire into the meaning of one or more passages of the sacred Scriptures which he had in the course of his reading marked for the purpose.

'Seeing that his illness was increasing I felt desirous to converse privately with him to ascertain the state of his mind in the near prospect of death, and also to urge upon him the necessity of settling his temporal affairs without delay. In reply to the former he said that he felt quite comfortable, that he trusted entirely on the Lord Jesus Christ for Salvation, that the principal feeling of his heart was gratitude to God for the blessing of the gospel and added, I might have died in ignorance. . . .

'His disease now increased rapidly which brought on a stupor from which he did not recover. While in this state he was continually muttering, but little however of what he said could be distinctly understood. Sometimes his friends could catch a few words such as "regard well. Prepare! prepare! Let us go to the teacher to enquire about the word of God". And when the bell was rung for divine service he would make many attempts to rise and make signs that he wished to go, and in this state he continued till Oct. 28th when he breathed his last, and was admitted we trust into the presence of his Saviour, a monument of Saving Grace! A coffin was made for him of Tamanu wood, and the next day he was carried into the Chapel by his mourning tenants followed by his most disconsolate widow and weeping children. All the principal chiefs were present and the solemn service was improved from the words "Blessed are the dead which die in the Lord" etc. After which his remains were carried back and deposited in a vault prepared for the purpose in the adjoining house which is surrounded by a low wall built of lime and stone, and the following inscription cut into the plastering of the vault.

> To Makea tua vaarua, i mate aia i te marama Okatoba i te po 28, 1839
>
> This is Makea's grave, he died in the month of October, the 28th day, 1839.'

Makea's house, as described by Buzacott, was the show-place of Rarotonga at this time. Belcher, who visited the Island in 1840, remarks of it as 'fit for any European', and considered that 'the roads, enclosures, church, schools, and private residences [of Avarua] are an age in advance of Tahiti. . . . It reminds me of what I had expected at Tahiti, if their laws had been enforced.'[1] In addition to church and school buildings Belcher noted the use of a covered building or extensive shed near the landing place and used as a market place. Here Belcher found Makea's son, now high chief, 'dressed in European costume—cotton shirt, white trousers and white frock-coat, superintending the purchases for the captains of the whalers. All this results', concludes Belcher, 'from a change from absolute barbarism and heathenism since 1825.'[2]

12

Consolidation of the New Order

Between the years 1833 and 1858 great progress was made in teaching the Christian faith. At the same time there were far-reaching social and economic changes going on, some of which remain to be described in a later section. Here it may be well to discuss the way in which the missionaries during these years tried on the one hand to enforce their teachings and on the other hand to insulate the people against experiences which the missionaries felt would be detrimental to the efficient learning of Christianity and therefore to the welfare of the people.

The aim of missionary endeavour at this time was clear. It was to make Rarotonga a replica or a mirror of lower middle-class England: the Islander was to become a brown-skinned brother of the lower middle-class dissenting Englishman of his time—both were to have the same moral standards, behave in the same way, believe in the same articles of faith. The job of realizing the missionary's goal was far more difficult than it was in England, for the principal reason that the Island character-structure was one emphasizing the value of impulse gratification, not impulse-renunciation, and the super-ego

---

[1] E. Belcher, *Narrative of a Voyage Round the World, 1836-1842* (London, 1843), vol. 2, pp. 15-22.

[2] Belcher, *op. cit.* The date mentioned by Belcher should have been 1823.

CONSOLIDATION OF THE NEW ORDER

internal control system of the Islander was weak, whereas that of the middle-class English dissenter was exceptionally strong. In addition the sex ratio of the Island population was extremely abnormal which must have given a somewhat abnormal intensity to the drive for impulse gratification. The missionaries used the code of laws as the statement of what behaviour was to be expected from the people. In order to force the natives to conform to this code of behaviour they used a variety of methods: exhortation and preaching about sin and hereafter punishment for sin; excommunication from the Church and consequent shame and disgrace; the appointment of deacons and trusted church members as policemen; severe fines and other punishments for all those charged with breaking the laws.

The principal laws in operation in Rarotonga, Aitutaki and other Cook Islands were directed against fornication, stealing, tattooing, breaking the public peace (by work on the Sabbath, for example), making orange rum.[1] Gudgeon, resident agent in Mangaia, repealed in 1899 ordinances allowing prosecutions for the following offences: consulting a sorcerer; being pregnant as an unmarried woman; card playing; placing one's arm round a woman, even though the offender have no torch in the other hand; trading with a European without permission; tattooing or being tattooed; going from one village to another on the Sabbath; taking an unmarried woman inland; crying over a dead woman even though not related to her.[2] These were all offences in Rarotonga, and the Rarotongan fines were doubtless similar to those mentioned by Buck for Mangaia: for example, crying over a dead woman, fine of fifteen dollars—one in cash and fourteen dollars in trade goods; fornication, the same fine; village conduct, fine of one dollar in cash, nine dollars in trade.[3]

To detect the offenders large forces of police were required. Buck notes that in 1891 for Mangaia, a population of 1,860 needed a police force of 155, one policeman to every twelve inhabitants.[4] Moss records that at the height of the system Buzacott's station of Avarua was divided into six sections, each section having up to fifty police, so that early in the missionary period, there was about one policeman to each nine or ten inhabitants.[5] (By comparison, in 1947 there were 1,520 police in the whole of New Zealand, about one policeman to each 1,192 of population; in 1949, one policeman to each 418

---

[1] Gill, *Gems*, p. 107.   [2] See *Rt. Hon. R. Seddon's Visit*, pp. 249-253.
[3] P. H. Buck, *Anthropology and Religion* (New Haven, 1939), pp. 87-91.
[4] Buck, *op. cit.* p. 88.   [5] Moss, *op. cit.* pp. 21-22.

persons in the islands of Rarotonga, Aitutaki and Mangaia.) The number of crimes dealt with each year was very large. In 1850 Gill remarks that with a population of approximately 3,000, Rarotongan courts dealt with 900 cases of crime involving about 250 convicted persons, many of them being imprisoned or fined two or more times in the year. (Again by comparison, the number of convictions in New Zealand Magistrates' Courts for 1947 would on this ratio be about 600,000 instead of the recorded figure of approximately 34,000.)

Each division of Rarotonga under its own chief had its own judge and deacon-policeman. Fines from delinquents were divided among these three and helped swell their private incomes. There was little attempt to weigh evidence for or against an accused person. The police did the arresting and the convicting, the judge automatically levied a fine or ordered imprisonment. The system was obviously open to the gravest abuses, particularly on those islands where only native teachers were stationed, but even on Rarotonga and Aitutaki where, by policy, the white missionaries left as much secular power as possible to the natives, to be administered in the manner their Christian consciences might dictate, abuses were at times so flagrant that the people were driven into violent resistance. Indeed Moss, relying on the evidence of Rarotongan Christian natives, the author of *Seddon's Visit*, and Lamont, a visitor to the Cook Islands in 1852–53, all agree that much of the violence attending early missionary efforts, the incendiarism, conspiracies and discontent in Rarotonga, Aitutaki and Mangaia, were due not so much to the evil influences of 'heathenism' but to a natural human reaction to what Moss calls the 'brutality with which the new laws were enforced' and the author of *Seddon's Visit* describes as 'ecclesiastical tyranny'.[1]

Revealing light is thrown on conditions in Rarotonga about 1840 and in Aitutaki a few years later, first by the record of a petition submitted to the Directors of the London Missionary Society about affairs in Rarotonga by two white residents of Rarotonga; secondly, by a statement of Royle's concerning complaints made by French members of a vessel wrecked on Aitutaki in 1847.

On March 26, 1841, James Chare and Thomas Turner, describing themselves as residents of Rarotonga for twelve months, wrote a

[1] Moss, *op. cit.* pp. 21-22; *Seddon's Visit*, pp. 249-253, 298; Lamont, *Wild Life Among the Pacific Islanders* (London, 1867), pp. 83, 86, 98.

CONSOLIDATION OF THE NEW ORDER

petition to the London Missionary Society, of which the following extracts give the main point of the complaints (spelling and syntax unaltered from the original: the composers of the letter would appear to be relatively uneducated persons, even confusing the London Missionary Society with Wesleyan mission organization). The first part of the letter reads:

'To the Gentlemen of the Wesley Mission Society, sirs, we think it is time some of the transactions on this Island was brought before you. when we first came on this Island the Mission told us we could not stop for the chiefs would not allow it but we went to the chiefs and they said we could stop after 16 years labour of Mr. Pitman and Buzacott their is not a Christian on the Island but what they could be turned from their religion for a few fathoms of cloth they send home letters how they have brought the poor heathens from darkness to light but believe me they say before the Mission arrived they verry seldom died but since that they have all nearly all died on the Island. . . .'

The petitioners then turn to discuss a Mr. Cunningham, whom Pitman describes on June 30, 1837: 'A gent. belonging to the church of Scotland, who came with us from Eimeo, to see if he could succeed in procuring land for the cultivation of sugar; now he is clearing about 10 acres and is encouraging the chiefs to follow his example.' Cunningham also helped Pitman with the erection of a stone chapel, but a few years later proved himself unworthy, left Rarotonga dishonourably and apparently became a Consul in Samoa. (Pitman, June 30, 1836, B.10, F.8, J.D.; November 21, 1842, B.15, F.4, J.C.) Of Cunningham, Chare and Thomas write:

'Cunningham that Mr. Pitman brought here from Otahaita and represented to the natives as a great man that the King of England sent out to tell the natives to plant plenty of arrowroot and sugar cane, he flogged one white man here in a shocking manner . . . he was soon after taken in adultery and Mr. Pitman tried to screen him from punishment but the Natives said he must be fined as well as themselves.'

Further complaints are made about the missionaries overcharging natives 'two pence worth of thread for half a dollar and they tell the natives these things cost the same at home'; about the missionaries' collecting from each sailor who comes ashore thirty dollars; about the missionaries' cattle ranging over the natives' farms, destroying food, while Pitman allegedly threatened to leave the island if fences were erected to protect crops. Again the petitioners suggest vividly the tension between missionaries and would-be residents and the power of the missionary in the following passage:

'The Missionaries here represent European that comes here in Whale Ships to be theives and robber that cannot get a living at home, here was a man run away from his ship and run into the mountains and the constables went after him but Mr. Buzacott told them not to go near him but to stone him with stones until he was down and here was another that was an unfortunate sailor caught in adultery and made his way to the Boat when the natives said let him go but Mr. Busacott told them to get him at any rate they then rushed on him with clubs and broke his arm.'

Finally, some indication of contemporary punishment for sin is given in this concluding quotation:

'the poor people are imposed upon in a shameful manner and it had ought to be looked into here is at this present time a young girl confined to a large log of wood by her wrist for being caught in adultery but she want to have the man and they both went to Mr. Pitman and told him they was both willing to marry but he said he would not marry them at any rate because they was taken in adultery how much longer she will be kept there we don't know, she has been there confined for three months. . . .'

(All Chare and Turner material is dated March 26, 1841, B.15, F.4, J.C.)

The basic complaints of the two residents appear to be that the missionaries are exercising undue power in the secular affairs of the Island; that Christianity is still only a superficial veneer over native behaviour; that the law is interpreted one way for white men, another for the natives; that the white missionary has been rather cruel in his interpretation of the law; and finally the white missionary has been accumulating material wealth in cattle and by trading. None of these complaints seems improbable, harsh as it may appear to say this. The trading aspects of the mission will be discussed later and the general tenor of missionary behaviour appears to be consistent with what is reported by other witnesses. Not that the white missionaries were cruel, heartless despots; they were, and felt themselves to be,

CONSOLIDATION OF THE NEW ORDER

humble, meek servants of the Lord, doing their utmost to save the people from sin. But it is most probable that they could not always keep a careful check on the way their subordinates used the great power placed in their hands; and it is also probable that sickness and continual frustration occasionally led them into actions inconsistent with the Christian ethic. Perhaps they would have been inhuman, if at times they did not err.

In March 1846 the new French whaler *Lemartine* was wrecked on the reef at Aitutaki. Until July 1847 thirty-five Frenchmen and five Englishmen in French employment lived on the island, 'all' says Royle, 'with the exception of two, the most profligate men I have ever met with'. The French captain made a number of complaints to a visiting Mr. Nutt on the treatment of his crew by the people and the missionaries. Royle states and replies to these complaints in a long letter dated September 19, 1847:

1. The French captain represented that he was ill-treated because the natives kept a watch on his house—but this watching says Royle, was only to prevent his own crew breaking into the house in search of liquor.

2. The captain said that the authorities forced people to attend church services: Royle remarks that of the seven chiefs on the island, three only are church members; the church membership totals 108 (mostly women) out of a population which numbers 1700 to 2000. Royle's reply could be an evasion of the complaint since at no time in mission history were none but church members allowed or expected to go to church, and chiefs elsewhere have been reported as sending out police to herd people into services.

3. A further complaint was that if a native woman made any small present to a Frenchman, without her husband's knowledge, she was made fast in the stocks sited on the chief's property as a punishment. Royle admits that he found stocks in use when he arrived in Aitutaki in 1839—a cultural gift by the native teachers to the people. One chief placed his own wife in the stocks as punishment for adultery. In shame, the wife committed suicide. Royle disapproved of the severity of the punishment and 'the chiefs now allow two pious women to sit all night with the offenders in the stocks'.

4. The French also charged that the missionary allowed the practice of cutting short the long hair of an adulteress. True, says Royle, but

the crime should be punished even more severely. 'I have mourned over the practise, as I have seen it blunt the moral feelings and fill the heart with pride—for the moment the fine flowing locks were cut off the head would be immediately adorned with a wreath of many colours, which seem to me to embolden the erring creatures in a tenfold degree.' Royle learned when he came to the Island that the native teachers approved of three local methods for punishing adulterers: hair cutting; 'lowering the female by ropes into a dry well about four fathoms deep, keeping her there for several days on scanty rations'—a punishment reported by all Moss's informants as being popular with judges and police in Rarotonga; flogging for the man. 'For a second offence a female was marched round the settlement and pelted with human and animal refuse.' Royle abolished these crueler methods of punishment, but kept the hair-cutting punishment without, however, feeling it was severe enough to fit the crime.

5. Finally the French complained that the missionary interfered in all the business of the island. Here again Royle admits to being frequently consulted, and a year earlier had written in justification: 'Missionaries who sedulously devote themselves to the objects of their calling acquire a very considerable amount of control over the minds of the people and in proportion as the missionary makes common interest with them in their joys and sorrows at the same time manifesting a holy indifference to secular affairs, does that influence rise in degree.[1] The South Sea Islander would "kick hard" though it be against the goods employed, to urge him in any undertaking in which he does not heartily concur—but get a hold on his affection and soon his sympathies are enlisted with your objects and the courses of conduct you wish him to pursue. . . . I am aware that this commanding influence is a fearful trust committed to the missionaries of these islands.' (July 22, 1846, B.19, F.4, J.D. The charges and replies of Royle are dated September 19, 1847. B.20,

---

[1] It is hard to understand that Royle could really have meant that the missionary should manifest 'a holy indifference to secular affairs'. Objective reading of the evidence forces the conclusion that the Cook Island missionaries, whether white or native, spent their lives entangled in the secular affairs of the natives, and this was certainly a dissenting evangelical tradition of long standing. Possibly, however, Royle is thinking only of activities like trading or storing up wealth as coming within his definition of secular; if so, he was always consistent in his judgment that this sort of secular affair must not be the concern of the missionary.

CONSOLIDATION OF THE NEW ORDER

F.4, J.C.) In a later report Royle, philosophizing about mission activities and the natives, remarks that 'it were easy to have impressed upon their Asiatic temperament a religious fanaticism, a danger we foresaw from the beginning and which we hope we have successfully encountered' (September 5, 1853, B.25, F.3, J.B.).

It is unclear what Royle had in mind when he spoke of the 'Asiatic temperament' of the people of Aitutaki. It is clear, however, that missionaries in other islands were not so careful as he to say to the natives, 'Come now and let us reason together' (September 5, 1853, *ibid*.). Both native teachers and white missionaries appear to have been more impressed with the urgency of their task than the means employed to achieve their goal. Thus the fanaticism with which the mission theocracy was established and thus the ideal deacon of the church: perfectionist, intolerant, incessant in labour, holy in zeal for good works, conniver at the sins of none, justice-lover but never mercy-lover. On June 9, 1840, Pitman wrote an obituary on the recent death of Tupe, one of the three first members and deacon of his church at Ngatangiia, for many years chief magistrate of Rarotonga. The account reveals not only the sort of man necessary to run the legal and moral side of a mission theocracy, but also the persistent delight of Pitman, at least, in long drawn-out deathbed enquiries. Pitman's obituary is addressed to the secretary of the London Missionary Society. The following extracts are given with his own spelling and syntax.

> 'Rarotonga
> Gnatangiia June 9, 1840

'Revd. and dear Sir,

'A short account of this good man's religious character, career, and death, will not I presume, be uninteresting to the Directors.

'His name was Tupe. He was one of the chief supporters of idolatry in the reign of superstition. Tupe was the name of a New Zealander, whom, our departed brother had made his friend, during the visit of the schooner Endeavour, Capt. Goodenough, a Colonial vessel, several years before the introduction of christianity to this Island. The officers of the above vessel suspecting that this New Zealander was putting the natives into a method of taking their Vessel, (snug in our little harbour) entered the house of his friend, and asked for Tupe; soon as they saw him, one instantly drew a pistol and killed him on the spot, which appears to be the first knowledge this people had of fire arms. Perceiving the dreadful effects of this weapon of destruction, the affrighted inhabitants fled to the mountains till darkness concealed them from the eyes of these strangers, when the Master of the house took up the remains of his friend and buried them, and ever after was called by his name, Tupe.

'He attached himself to us on our first arrival in this place in 1827. Ignorant was I then, how Providence had gone before in preparing such a valuable assistant in my future labours. In the erection of our first Chapel, he was one of the most laborious in the work, and when a suitable person was requested to take care of our tools, he was pointed out as a trust worthy man. Night after nights was he seen carefully collecting every thing entrusted to him, which he deposited in his own sleeping apartment lest any should be stolen. Not soon will it be erased from my memory, the joy that beamed in his countenance, when it was told him that I had intended to remain in this district as their Teacher, and that Brother Williams would reside with the other division [of Rarotonga] till a ship arrived to convey him to Raiatea. The very first night of our settlement amongst them, he came to our house to make enquiries respecting the great truths of the Bible; and till prevented by disease, scarcely a night passed, but he was present, at our friendly meetings for conversation, chiefly on religious subjects. Often till near midnight, have I sat conversing with him on the "great salvation". Nothing, I believe occupied so much of his attention, as the concerns of the soul; not anything more desired by him than the wide diffusion of divine truth. Indeed I may say, to the temporal and spiritual welfare of his countrymen, he was wholly devoted. Incessant in labour, and indefatigable in his efforts to forward the cause of God, he assisted me in every good work with unwearied diligence till death.

'He was a man of considerable influence in the land, and at the establishment of the laws, was appointed Chief Magistrate for this part of the Island, which office for twelve years, he faithfully discharged. Most earnestly and patiently did he investigate every case brought before him, and I have no hesitation in saying, after years of the closest observation, that he was one who regarded not the "person of Man". The word of God was his standard. He discharged the responsible duties of his office under this impression, God is here. In cases of difficulty, he would often ask my opinion, and say, "I thought of such and such a mode of procedure, Is it

CONSOLIDATION OF THE NEW ORDER

right? is it agreeable to the dictates of God's word? What does Moses say? How would he act in such a case" etc. etc. When he could come to a satisfactory conclusion in his own mind, he was firm as a rock, and undaunted would pass sentence accordingly, whoever the parties might be. At the first this brought upon him many enemies, but ultimately commanded almost universal respect. Well do I remember, at a time when we were involved in much perplexity, owing to disputes in land concerns and all parties were preparing for war, he purposed, in person, to go to the opposite party, if possible, amicably to adjust the points in dispute, in doing which he had to pass thro' a district of some desperate young fellows. I stated to him the danger of the attempt that it might probably cost him his life. Does, said he, the word of God justify my proceedings? I could not but reply in the affirmative. Then I go, regardless as to the consequences, God can, and will protect me. He, without a weapon of defence in his hand, passed through the district of these desperadoes, amidst the scoffings and revilings of all. The subject of contention was calmly debated, he returned home, and in a few days, all was quietly settled, and war prevented.

'The unflinching conduct of this good man, in all judgment concerns, his impartiality in the administration of justice between man and man, and his unwavering determination to unite with us in seeking the advancement of "undefiled religion", roused some of his inveterate enemies (Most of whom who were shortly after cut off by an epidemick which made such dreadful devastation in this Island in the year 1830, See Evangelical Mag. for November 1831) to acts of most cruel revenge, even the destruction of himself and family. This, they attempted by clandestinely setting fire to his house, when he and family were asleep. But he, who neither slumbers nor sleeps, mercifully preserved the life of his faithful servant and of his family. They escaped however, with what they had on, every thing else was consumed. On discovering the fire, the first thing he endeavoured to secure, was, what he considered his greatest treasure, a portion of the Sacred Scriptures viz. the Acts of the Apostles in the Tahitian dialect; but this he could not effect, and in attempting it lost his all. The consequences of this fire, did not end here, it communicated to the house of his son adjoining, which was speedily destroyed; then to our large Chapel, which also, was soon level with the ground. Large flakes of fire, passed by and over our own dwelling, but thro' the timely exertions of the natives we were mercifully preserved from danger. Soon as I saw him I said, Alas! Tupe, O Teacher, he replied, the book of God is consumed! My house, my property, never regard but oh, my book, my book!! and oh, the house of God! will not God punish us for this! The next morning I had the gratifying pleasure of presenting him with another copy of the book, which he so much prized, it was received with feelings of no small delight. . . .

'He, with his brother Iro (now native Teacher at our outstation), and Kaitara, giving evidence of a change of heart were the first formed into a christian church in this place in May 1833, and when the number of members increased, was unanimously chosen to fill the office of deacon. How faithfully he discharged the important duties thereof, we are all witnesses. Decided piety, deep humility, and holy zeal for the advancement of "pure religion", were the striking characteristicks of our valued friend. This, I believe, no one who knew him would call in question. His knowledge of divine truth was by no means inconsiderable, and he was eminently qualified for the responsible situations in which divine providence had placed him; tho' his own abilities he rated very low, and almost to the day of his death deeply lamented his own ignorance. He would often revert to the condescension of God in visiting such a sinful land as this, which always called forth expressions of the greatest astonishment. Conversing with him as I frequently did, on subjects illustrative of the mercy and compassion of God, he would sit, at times for hours, in deep thought, and was heard muttering to himself—Oh, the love of God! the amazing pity of the Saviour! the depth of the sacred scriptures! the hardness of the human heart! the exceeding sinfulness of sin! the Sabbath he reverenced. . . .

'As a magistrate he was exceedingly jealous lest the least encroachment should be made on Sabbath sanctification. Soon as he understood the mind of God on this subject, with the consent of his brother, the Chief, he had it publicly made known, that work of no kind whatever should be performed on the Sabbath day. For several years past, through the perseverance of this zealous man, such a thing as to fetch a pail or cup of water from the brook, has scarcely been known in any part of the settlement, on the day of sacred rest, nor (except in cases of necessity) an oven of food cooked. On Saturday evenings are to be seen, groups of children, and grown people with their calabashes etc. going to the different streams and springs to lay in their stock of water for the Sabbath day; whilst others are seen pouring into the settlement from their respective districts, with food sufficient for themselves and families till the day of rest be over. . . .

'He connived at the sins of none. This trait in this man's character, early began to display itself. Several years ago, even before he gave evidence of decided piety in himself, our house every night was crowded with people who came to make enquiries respecting the discourses delivered from the pulpit etc. Observing some more particular in their questions, constant in their attendance at the house of God, and very active in every thing proposed for the good of the community, I, one night as we were sitting alone, made enquiry into their characters, and said, I hope by their attaching themselves to us, and their ready acquiesence in putting down existing evils in the land, that they are desirous of becoming disciples of Jesus. He made no reply; after a few minutes of silence, he said, Teacher, be not in haste, do not think so well of us, be not deceived, we are a wicked, deceitful people; stop till you have been longer with us, and know more of our character, and way of living. . . .

'His words were verified, and many of those whom I had fondly anticipated were seeking the Lord, were clinging to their heathen practices, living in adultery and other hateful crimes. This discovery led me into a more particular investigation of the private character of those who united themselves to us. Most of them had been previously baptized by Mr. Bourne, in a short visit to this Island in the year 1825. Many others then baptised, have since told me that they were altogether ignorant of the nature of baptism and found that our dear friend had not in the least exaggerated in what he told me. In enquiring of him from that time either privately or publickly, the character of those making a profession of religion, I uniformly found him the same, and do not recollect an instance in which he connived at the sins of any. His word was to be relied upon. Among a people just emerging from heathen superstition and idolatry, such a man is to be ranked amongst a Missionary's greatest blessings.'

13

Economic Development

The spur to economic development in Rarotonga came in the first instance from missionary insistence that the people should wear 'decent' clothing. Aboriginal clothing had consisted of a waist band or *maro* for men, and a grass kilt or skirt for women. This amount of clothing was considered indecent and heathenish. Therefore the missionaries insisted on women dressing in long neck-to-ankle 'Mother Hubbard' gowns and men wearing trousers, shirt and a coat (if possible). In the beginning gifts of clothing were feasible, but as more and more people became church members and as clothing was required for all those children attending school, something had to be done to provide the people with the means of making their own clothes.

John Williams brought to Rarotonga a Mr. Elijah Armitage about October 1833, to teach the people the art of weaving the cotton that had been introduced into the island several years earlier. Armitage and the missionaries soon built spinning wheels, a warping machine and a loom. 'The chief's wife and daughter, and most of the respectable girls of the settlement were taught to spin and soon thirty spinning wheels were in motion all day long, and a large quantity of cotton . . . was prepared for the looms.'[1] By December 20, 1834, Buzacott reports that 330 yards of cloth had been woven and the chief seldom wore anything else (B.9, F.7, J.A.). The material was stronger than ship's cloth, but unfortunately the labour required to make it was immense, and the product was rough and unfinished by comparison with that made from machinery. Hence when the whalers began to call regularly they brought for barter Manchester prints, fine white calico and ready-made clothing which were more desirable in native eyes than home-spun material. 'The wearing of cotton', says Buzacott, 'was soon abandoned.' Armitage also taught the people to make bench vices and screws and gave general instruction in the use of tools. In this connection he was more successful than W. C. Cunningham, who, sponsored by Pitman (even though he was 'a gent. belonging to the church of Scotland') tried to grow, and to interest the people in growing sugar cane, but had to retire, as already noted, to Samoa for dishonourable reasons.

Sometime before 1831 Buzacott managed to persuade the people to take up the cultivation of the sweet potato. At first he thought of the tuber simply as an additional food supply, but later, after the cotton failure and the desire of the whalers to barter calico for sweet potato, Buzacott found the potato rapidly became an economic mainstay of the Island. 'A suitable district was fixed, and on a given week the whole population turned out, and spent some days in the

[1] Sunderland and Buzacott, *op. cit.* p. 92.

wood, clearing the ground for potatoes and arrowroot. Hundreds of acres were thus subdued to the use and gains of man.'[1] The sweet potato had the disadvantages of keeping only for a short time and of rotting quickly if touched by salt water. Buzacott therefore introduced arrowroot, tapioca, rice and coffee. Of these, only arrowroot became a staple trading article; in addition, yams, bananas, pumpkins, pineapples and oranges were also grown for trade, pigs and poultry reared. Thus between 1835 and 1840 economic development was such that whalers could refresh and replenish stores at both Rarotonga and Aitutaki. A great many whalers began to make one or other island regular stops in their Pacific cruise. The people, for their part, were able to barter for desirable goods and at the same time learn of new ways and new experiences, often contradicting those approved of by their teachers. Economic development brought the white man in greater numbers and in doing so made the policy of theocratic insulation difficult to maintain.

14

Whalers, Traders and Frenchmen

It is easy to form the strong impression, in reading the Cook Islands missionary records, that God provided many examples of His Divine Wrath, but the most frequent were hurricanes, tidal waves, famines and whaling masters—and unfortunately whaling masters and their crews were a longer lasting scourge than the first three. Buzacott records that, probably about 1840, 'sixty or seventy whale ships visited Rarotonga annually'. In 1843 Royle reports that 'not less than 35 Vessels called here [Aitutaki] during the last twelve months' (May 9, 1843, B.16, F.5, J.A.). Gosset has estimated that shortly before 1850 the American whaling fleet numbered 680 ships, all but forty of which were cruising in the Pacific. Of those in the Pacific over 100 called at Rarotonga each year for supplies.[2] French whalers were

[1] Sunderland and Buzacott, *op. cit.* p. 91.

[2] Gosset, *op. cit.* pp. 6-8—apparently basing his figures on those given in the article on *Whaling* in the *Encyclopædia Britannica*. Hohman in his book, *The American Whaleman* (New York, 1928), gives exact figures for the size of the American whaling fleet between the years 1845 and 1860. The average number of vessels in the fleet during the years 1845 to 1850 was 660, though no figures are available as to the number that habitually cruised in the Pacific. Wilkes, however,

also active about the same time. One of Royle's trials in 1847 was due to the fact that two whalers—one American, the other French—were both wrecked on the island. Royle not only complains of the debauchery and violence that occurred but also of the expense of keeping seventy destitute seamen supplied with food for almost a year. (January 10, 1848, B.21, F.3, J.A.)

It has been a common observation that the whalers hung their consciences on Cape Horn as they passed into the Pacific. They certainly brought to the island, where they were wrecked or called for refreshment, a way of life that in many respects contradicted the behaviour and values of mission theocracy. Thus Royle noted in 1843 that he was experiencing 'considerable disquietude of mind from the base and unprincipled conduct of some whaling masters' (May 9, 1843, B.16, F.5, J.A.), and four years later he was able to instance cases of conduct which would appear to be unprincipled on any standard of ethics. When the French whaler *Lemartine* was wrecked on Aitutaki in March 1846, the crew and the vessel's cargo were both rescued by the natives, but officers and sailors returned their good treatment with drinking, rape, hooliganism, violence and insults of every kind to laws, chiefs and people. 'Captain and Surgeon seemed to employ themselves in devising means to shock the religious feelings of the Islanders; they expressly set apart the Sabbath for shooting and fishing ... on one occasion, Captain asked a chief for a leaf of his hymn-book to light his cigar. The chief's feelings being shocked at this request, he replied that the book taught him the language of praise etc. for his God. "Show me your God and I will shoot him" said the captain. The good chief turned from the scoffer, his countenance bathed with tears.' With a steady optimism Royle was able to find consolation in the visit: 'The event (the visitation) is viewed by the people as a punishment for misimproved mercies—prayer is made daily by the church and People and I trust with suitable emotions—that God would interfere and in the midst

---

in his *Narrative of the United States Exploring Expedition, 1838-1842* (Philadelphia, 1845, 5 vols.), mentions that of the nearly 700 vessels making up the fleet about 1845 (total crew between 15,000 and 16,000 men), the majority cruised in the Pacific on the whaling grounds indicated by Wilkes in his map. Wilkes also adds that if the South Seas missionaries would spend a little time and money promoting 'morality, religion and temperance' among whaling crews, then whalers would no longer be thought of as 'worthless reprobates' and the arrival of a whaler at an island would no longer be a 'blight upon a dawning civilization', but 'would be hailed with delight in the ports it may visit'. Wilkes, *ibid.* vol. 5, pp. 485-582.

WHALERS, TRADERS AND FRENCHMEN

of deserved wrath remember mercy.' (February 27, 1847, B.20, F.4, J.B.) The French government sent a boat to remove the Frenchmen in July 1847. The complaints of the French captain and Royle's counter-statement have already been discussed.

Buzacott on Rarotonga also had his troubles with shipwrecked whalers. In March 1845 the large American whaler *Tacitus* was wrecked on Rarotonga and thirty sailors set a bad example to the people with their immoral conduct. The captain also sold a thirty-six-gallon barrel of rum to a chief—bad as this act was, it was made worse in Buzacott's eyes by the fact that the whaler was sailing under Temperance principles and pledges. (September 1845, B.18, F.5, J.D.)

In general the whalers affected the people morally in three ways: The first by shipwrecked sailors; secondly by runaway sailors and deserters, a fairly large number of whom persisted in leaving their vessels;[1] thirdly by the fact that islanders were shipped on the whalers to take the place of the deserters.

The number of islanders serving as crew varied from year to year. In 1849 Pitman estimates that about 100 youths from his district alone have now left Rarotonga on sailing vessels over the past few years. By 1853, however, he reports that sixty to seventy youths have gone away on whalers during the past year. Many were incited to go by the return of a few with thirty to eighty dollars each—'these sums according to their custom they soon divided among their friends, and some of them immediately shipped again, not liking to settle down on their own lands' (December 21, 1853, B.25, F.3, J.C.). For all, one may assume, it was a desire for adventure and novelty, the challenge of new experiences and new ways of life, the hardships of missionary repressions: all these as much as the lure of money, led the young men to fill the vacant places, three or four on each vessel, caused by death or desertion of white crew. The chiefs of some districts tried to stop the emigration by forbidding their young men to go to sea. This ruling was unsuccessful because the young men simply launched a small canoe clandestinely, made the ship and then cut the canoe adrift. Other chiefs insisted on written agreements from

---

[1] But Wilkes, *op. cit.* vol. 5, p. 498, notes that some whaling masters made it a habit to leave men ashore by trickery, particularly near the end of a voyage, in order so to reduce the number of crew that the 'lay' or pay-out to crew on return to home port would be reduced with more profits from the voyage to be divided on percentage basis between owners and whaling master.

the whaling masters that the young men be returned to the island. But the masters only honoured these agreements if it was convenient; many islanders were simply put ashore at Sydney or Honolulu, where they might have to live for a year or more before getting a job on a whaler or trader returning to Rarotonga. Gill notes that the lives of these young men in such ports as Sydney were often evil and profligate. He instances one young man who returned to his island and immediately threatened to fight a duel with the man whom he found living with his long deserted wife. 'I shall shoot him', said the Sydney sophisticate, 'because it is what white men do and I see it where I go.' Other young men came back advocating prostitution (perhaps as an expedient to overcome the sex disproportions in the population!) because prostitution was a white man's custom. (G. Gill, November 30, 1846, B.19, F.4, J.E.)

Those that came back were the lucky ones, even if they were the island trouble-makers, 'depraved and vicious to an alarming extent'. Many whaling masters had to report losing all their island crewsmen by death from Arctic cold, others returned with badly damaged health. Others still simply deserted their vessels at a Californian port to prospect in the newly opened goldfields and often never returned to the islands. (Pitman, January 1, 1852, B.24, F.8, J.A.) Again it is honest Royle who sees some more good in the whaling visits. When the first Bibles arrived in Aitutaki their price was fixed by his colleagues in Rarotonga at 8s. 2d. each. Only six islanders could purchase immediately and another twenty-five scratched around to beg or borrow enough small coins to make up the required sum. Everyone else was disappointed until the providential arrival of a whaler from California to spend between 200 and 300 dollars on fresh food supplies. These dollars were immediately used to buy up the remaining Bibles! (September 5, 1853, B.25, F.3, J.B.)

The problem of runaway seamen and Frenchmen, including possible French Catholic priests, was a different one for the missionaries to solve. As early as 1837 Pitman reports that what has been long dreaded has now happened: troublesome runaway seamen threaten to thwart the mission's designs for the welfare of the islanders (February 27, 1837, B.11, F.3, J.C.), and in the same letter he likens the scourge of sailors to the current influenza scourge attacking the island. At first some chiefs tried to prohibit their landing, then to prevent their taking up residence, but the chiefs were divided and the prohibition rather ineffectual. However, if runaway seamen could land, so could Frenchmen and French priests. Missionary anxiety over the status of foreigners was therefore considerably increased when news reached Rarotonga of the action of du Petit Thouars in forcing Queen Pomare of Tahiti to accept an ultimatum providing, among other things, that 'Frenchmen of every profession should be allowed to go and come freely, to establish themselves and to trade in all the islands'.[1] Pitman immediately drew up a letter, signed by both Pitman and Buzacott, to the Directors of the London Missionary Society, asking their attitude towards the troublesome Roman Catholic missionaries (it was Queen Pomare's refusal to allow two French Roman Catholic missionaries to land in Tahiti in January 1837 that brought about the initial French intervention). 'We do not for a moment wish', writes Pitman, 'to impinge upon the liberties of conscience. The question is, how far does the prerogative of the chiefs extend in allowing or disallowing foreigners to land with an intent to settle in their islands, whether for the purpose of Religion or Commerce?' (September 28, 1838, B.11, F.7, J.B.) Ten days later Pitman and Buzacott had persuaded the chiefs to concern themselves with the problem so that they were able to write on October 9, 1838, that they enclosed 'regulations drawn up by order of the chiefs of this Island respecting foreigners etc.—Will you state if there is anything objectionable in them, as they would readily alter any of them at our suggestion.' (B.11, F.7, J.B.) No record of these regulations is apparently available, but by May 23, 1839, the regulations were widened to cover runaway seamen, possible traders and a Catholic Mission, since the chiefs had by now been persuaded not to countenance anyone 'in league with that corrupt church' (B.12, F.5, J.B.).

The expulsion by the French of ex-consul Pritchard, Queen Pomare's English advisor, from Tahiti on March 3, 1844, again brought possible French designs on Rarotonga to the fore. On June 8, 1844, Buzacott wrote to the Directors of the London Missionary Society enclosing in his letter a petition to Queen Victoria from the four principal chiefs of Rarotonga (Makea, Tinomana, Pa and Kainuku) praying for help in case their island should be sought, as Tahiti was, by the French. A similar appeal for help was also sent to the President of the United States of America. There is no record of any reply being received. (B.17, F.5, J.B.)

[1] See K. L. P. Martin, *Missionaries and Annexation in the Pacific* (London, 1924), pp. 17-22, for a statement of the facts leading to the French annexation of Tahiti, November 1843.

Not only was French intervention feared, but also the effects on the Rarotongans of the increasingly frequent contacts between Rarotonga and Tahiti. Gill reports in 1848 that many young men have gone to Tahiti to serve as domestic servants for European residents in that island. As many as twenty youths and several women might be taken by a French vessel, the captain of which collected fares for transport from the new employers. After six or eight months the Rarotongans returned, to be replaced by a new group, but those returning had 'different habits, new vices and crimes, tempting and polluting others' (June 17, 1848, B.21, F.3, J.B.).

Finally a decision was reached to establish principles governing the relations of chiefs to would-be residents. The chiefs of Rarotonga met and resolved:

1. 'To offer no resistance to foreigners who might come as private individuals and desire to reside in the islands;

2. 'That if they wished to purchase land, it should only be disposed of at an annual rental;

3. 'That they should maintain the independency of their own government.' (Gill, June 18, 1845, B. 18, F.5, J.C.)

Having established these general principles and placed them on record for the world to read, the missionaries and the chiefs thereafter apparently felt free to act in a way that appears at times to contradict these principles. Thus Royle encouraged the chiefs of Aitutaki in their refusal to allow French traders to settle on the island, allowing them to cite as a reason that there would be a shortage of food if too many foreigners came to Aitutaki. (January 10, 1848, B.21, F.3, J.A.) And there is a minute of a resolution from Rarotonga: 'That we continue to explain to the people the imminent danger to which this group of islands is exposed at the present time, from the strong desire of petty merchants and others to obtain a residence on these islands—the cause of the trouble with Tahiti.' (Gill, Resolution minutes, December 31, 1848, B.21, F.3, J.A.) It is clear that the missionaries were trying to put into operation a rather devious policy: doing all they could publicly to persuade the chiefs, in Gill's words, of the 'impolicy of driving from their shores foreigners who come to reside among them in a private capacity' (B.18, F.5, J.C.)—this in order not to antagonize the French for fear of such French reprisals as indemnities and annexations; at the same time to encourage the chiefs in their stand against allowing foreigners to reside in the islands—or at least too many foreigners, or of the wrong occupation or of the wrong nationality. It is to the credit of this policy, if one wishes to assign credits, that the 'foreign policy' of the islands was pursued successfully for a number of years: 'white heathens', as the natives called them, came only sparingly to the islands, traders were kept under some control, the French never annexed the islands, and the Roman Catholic Picpus Fathers' mission was not established until 1894. The missionaries acted, of course, in the light of very simple stereotypes. All runaway sailors were *profligate*, all Frenchmen *licentious*, all Roman Catholics *venal and corrupt*, all traders *petty and dishonest*. The triumph of their policy offers the reflection that the human mind thinks and acts most efficiently when it can reduce reality to its most simple form, even though this simplicity is manifestly untrue and human responses therefore are governed by magically acting sounds, rather than objective appraisals of the real world.

15
Introduction of Alcohol

In the midst of all their worries about Frenchmen and Roman Catholics the missionaries had to contend with the introduction of alcohol. It is suggestive of the horror which they felt for alcohol and also, perhaps, of their intuitive understanding of the way in which the islanders would welcome the effects of alcohol, that the introduction is solemnly recorded in the minutes of a meeting of the Brethren held on June 10, 1845, at Ngatangiia.[1] 'That with the deepest concern', the minute reads, 'we record the clandestine introduction of Ardent Spirits among the people of Rarotonga. A large barrel of New England Rum having been purchased from Captain McClare of the *George*, an American Whaler off the island, April 1845. While

[1] The introduction of tobacco was opposed in a resolution three years later (Minutes of Resolution, December 31, 1848) on the grounds that tobacco smoking was detrimental to the people 'physically and socially'. Only 'moral means', however, were to be used to combat tobacco, not the sanctions and penalties of the law. Royle was shocked to learn on a visit to Rarotonga that rice, biscuit and flour sent to Rarotonga by the London Missionary Society to relieve temporary distress caused by the hurricane of March 16 and 17, 1846, had been freely given to the natives in such wasteful quantities that most had exchanged it with the shipping for tobacco! (Royle, December 15, 1849; Gill, December 31, 1848, B.21, F.3, J.B.)

we are happy to find that orders have been given by those in authority, to pour the said barrel into the sea, and that a strong public feeling has been expressed against its introduction, yet we have much reason to fear that as temptation increases among the people, and Captains are disposed to make it an article of barter, it will become a trend, of no ordinary character, to our stations and lead to results as awful as those over which we mourn among the Society Group. That, deeply impressed with these views and feelings, we continue to exhort the churches and the people against its use and steadily to maintain the existing laws which prohibit its introduction.' (B.18, F.5, J.B.)

Chances of maintaining the law would have been strengthened had the chiefs been stout in its defence. Unfortunately, Makea, chief of Avarua and principal chief of Rarotonga (son of the Makea whose death has been earlier recorded), died about this time from alcoholic excess. He had acquired a taste for rum in Tahiti and on returning to Rarotonga procured spirits secretly from calling vessels. The missionaries naturally took hardly to the fact that the introduction and use of alcohol had been connived at by at least one of the most influential men on the island, and a staunch member of the church in addition. At a meeting of the chiefs held on the day of the funeral those present decided to maintain the law. With one defection before his eyes Gill may perhaps be pardoned for doubting whether all the chiefs were sincere. (June 18, 1845, B.18, F.5, J.C.)

It might have been possible to control drinking had such a habit been dependent upon acquiring liquor from calling vessels. On April 6, 1851, however, youths returning from Tahiti introduced into Rarotonga the art of fermenting a liquor from oranges, pineapples and bananas. 'Drunkenness made its appearance in almost every part of the island simultaneously and required the strong arm of the law to quell it.' (Buzacott, July 1852, B.24, F.8, J.B.) Very strenuous sermons were delivered against intemperance followed by domiciliary visits and something of a religious revival followed. Pitman, Buzacott and Gill all write in 1852 as if the 'demon' were driven back, and the 'evil' defeated. (B.24, F.4, J.A. and J.C.) That alcohol could not be defeated so easily by spiritual revivals, even when helped by the most stringent measures of the authorities, is shown by the continual recurrence of the 'alcohol problem' throughout the subsequent history of the islands. But the matter need not be discussed in more detail here because it is considered at length in a later section.

16
A Trading Mission

The closing years of Pitman's work in Rarotonga were troubled by one quarrel and one scandal. The quarrel is unimportant in this context. It was a quarrel between Pitman and Buzacott as to whom should go to England to see through the press the first edition of the Rarotongan Bible. Buzacott was chosen and Pitman was greatly annoyed. The only significance to be attached to the trouble is the fact that both missionaries were thoroughly human. Long years of semi-isolation and increasing illnesses had worn them down, particularly Pitman. His work was no longer so effective as earlier and he was beginning to become a liability to the mission.

The scandal broke when Royle became more and more impatient with Pitman's trading activities. Pitman bred cattle and horses, which he sold or bartered. His horses were boarded out and natives had the right to ride them in return for allowing them to graze on their lands. With an all-or-none activity which is very Polynesian the horses were soon being ridden furiously about the countryside. One child was knocked over and died of its injuries. A man and a woman were even noted to be riding furiously on one horse, 'the female astride in the manner of men in the most indecent manner'.

Pitman also traded in goods which he sold for a profit to natives, would-be traders and visiting vessels. Royle notes that both Mr. and Mrs. Pitman industriously collected dollars and half-dollars for cotton goods. Mrs. Pitman was constantly employed in making up fancy shirts at a dollar each for the natives at all the stations. Again Royle notes that Pitman had sold large quantities of merchandise at a considerable profit (a copy of the trading transactions occupies five typewritten pages, and includes everything from calico, through check shirts, gilt buttons, tea kettles to a bottle of wine) to two adventurers named Lewis and Hardwick who had arrived mysteriously with plenty of dollars at Rarotonga, proceeded to build a fine schooner of 60 tons burden and were about to sail in it with all their newly purchased trade goods when a gentleman arrived from the Sandwich Islands with power of attorney to arrest Lewis and Hardwick and extradite them to Honolulu to face charges of having stolen 8,000 dollars in gold besides bills of value from Mr. Booth, a British merchant resident in Honolulu.

Pitman's defence against this charge of being a trading missionary is pathetically weak. He admits to selling goods, but adds that his fellow Rarotongan missionaries Gill and Buzacott did the same. The goods Pitman sold were really his wife's goods. Mrs. Pitman's family was in reduced financial circumstances. It was planned that her brother should become an island trader and goods were purchased for him, but he settled in Sydney and thus the Pitmans were left with goods on their hands which would rapidly have rotted in the climate or have been damaged by insects had they not been sold to the natives. Therefore the Pitmans sold them partly to another trader in Rarotonga and partly to the natives. Horses and cattle were also sold, but at little or no profit; the cattle particularly to visiting whalers in great distress for want of provisions. Goods were sold to Lewis and Hardwick to help them in their distress at the original cost price plus one half-penny or one penny a yard for freightage. In sum Pitman's defence is that he sold goods, but that he never purchased goods with a view to sell or to get gain from the transactions.

The whole story of charge, counter-charge, accusation and defence is set out in long reports of Royle (dated June 25, 1847, and December 15, 1849) and of Pitman (October 5, 1849), the whole running to some forty pages of typescript. No point is served by discussing the matter at greater length in this context. Royle's conclusion about trading, however, is well made. He points out that the quarrels between the missionaries on Rarotonga were well known to the natives and were destroying the morale of the mission by interfering with the single-minded pursuit of the ideals of mission teaching: schools on Rarotonga were, he said, deserted; the Rarotongan natives had become thoroughly mercenary and would do nothing except for payment; their character had in fact become corrupted. The Directors of the London Missionary Society were guided by Royle. They persuaded him to withdraw his own resignation. They wrote a delicate letter to Pitman giving him two years' notice to leave Rarotonga and offering him means to assist his comfortable maintenance elsewhere. Pitman accepted the offer with thanks and left Rarotonga early in 1855. Buzacott wrote rather brutally later in the same year that now that Pitman was gone, good work was commencing once more at Ngatangiia, adding, 'many who a short time since were wallowing in drunkenness and filth are now among the most anxious enquirers for salvation'. (Minutes, July 1852, B.24, F.8, J.A.; Buzacott, October 1855, B.26, F.3, J.B.)

Ill health had been one of Pitman's troubles in later years. Ill health soon affected Buzacott, forcing his retirement to Sydney in 1857. William Gill had retired in 1852 after the trading scandal died down. Thus between 1852 and 1857 the three missionaries responsible for the establishment and initial operation of the mission theocracy all left the islands. They had all been good men, according to their lights, sincerely interested in the spiritual and material welfare of the people. They had come to the islands as conscious agents of social change. They were determined to stamp out heathenism (that is, any and every pattern of behaviour which was or would be in conflict with Christian teaching), to teach the people a new religious theology, dogmas and ethic, to enforce the new way of life by religious and secular sanctions, to introduce such changes in economic life as would help realize Christian teaching (goods to barter for clothing to promote 'decency'), to insulate the people against ideas, customs and practices inconsistent with the Christian ethic: in other words, first to produce changes, second to freeze the new order so that no more major changes would occur once the ideal of a Christian society had been achieved. Being human beings besides being Christians, subject to ill-health, frustration and disappointment, the European missionaries often found the ideal hard to realize. Working upon people who were also human beings and only would-be Christians, a people, moreover, bred and born in another culture, subject as a population group to profound biological changes, the wonder is that so much change and so much insulation were possible in the short space of thirty or so years. To start social change and then to stop it: this was the problem that the missionary tried to solve. If he were unsuccessful, this partial failure is but another illustration of the fact that if people are difficult to change at least they will not necessarily stop changing because someone in authority arbitrarily decides that the time has come to stop the learning process.

17

Factors Influencing Social Change

The period of initial contacts, up to about 1833, has already been analysed in terms of concepts useful elsewhere in explaining the process of culture contact. The period under review, 1833 to about

1857, may now be briefly analysed, using the same concepts, to show how the process of culture contact was slowly changing in its nature under the influence of the various events already recorded.

1. *Time sequence*. The present period falls roughly into two sequences: the first includes the establishment of the church, the propagation of the faith, the success of the mission as judged by church membership, the beginnings of the population decline; the second includes the acceleration of population decrease, the beginnings of wider contacts with non-missionaries, the development of a simple cash or barter economy geared into the continuing subsistence economy of the islands.

2. *Locality influences*. The size, topography and climate of the islands exercised no significant influence during this period, except the negative influence of being unfavourable to large-scale settlement from invading Europeans. The accessibility of the islands to the routes of the cruising whalers made them convenient refreshing places and thus pushed them for part of this period into playing a minor role in the whaling trade. The decline of whaling in the second half of the nineteenth century allowed them to fall back into a peripheral position on commerce and trade-routes.

3. *Migration influences*. These have been dealt with as adequately as the materials allow, in the discussion of the cultural background of the missionary. Native teachers continued their independent work in some islands, but in Rarotonga and Aitutaki they were now under the direction and control of white missionaries. Thus the petty tyrannies, the misinformation and more importantly, the unconscious adaptation of Christianity to Polynesian culture that occurred as Christianity was filtered through the mind of the Tahitian or native teacher, were no longer significant in the culture contact situation. Of the culture of the runaway seamen, Frenchmen and whalers it is not possible to write with any scientific certainty, except in the negative way that this culture was probably antagonistic in many respects to that of the lower middle-class evangelical missionary.

4. *'Race' influences*. Differences of visible physical marks do not appear to have had any influence upon the culture contact situation in the Cook Islands during this period.

5. *Numerical influences*. The proportion between natives and newcomers altered during the period because of the native population

decrease on the one hand and because the white population increased to an unknown extent through the presence of the runaway sailors. No estimates are available in missionary or other records of the numbers of non-missionary whites residing on any island. At a guess one would be inclined to judge that the numbers on Rarotonga were probably never more than twenty to twenty-five; on Aitutaki, with the exception of an occasional shipwreck crew for a temporary period, never more than about five. Thus the general situation would remain the same in this as in the preceding period: a large mass of natives being influenced by a small minority of Europeans, the European minority in this period, however, being divided into a tiny group of white missionaries and a larger group of non-missionary Europeans.

6. *Momentum.* Throughout the period one may continue to think of the larger group of natives as being relatively passive (though to be sure, they were interested in learning new ways, and a minority of returned native sailors with Tahitian, whaling or even Californian experience were even more interested in new experiences), the tiny minority of European missionaries with their native supporters (deacons, native teachers, policemen, judges) as being actively aggressive, the minority of sailors and other Europeans beginning to be aggressively interested in commercial exploitation, only lukewarm in their support of mission theocracy. The pressure exerted by the mission group continued, however, to be steady and heavy. The majority responded to this pressure with slow change. The pressure was not great enough nor the change fast enough to produce any reaction in the form of a revivalistic or messianic movement. It is probable that the pressure was intuitively kept within limits which produced change without at the same time producing marked manifestations of maladjustment.

7. *Effective contact.* The mingling between the peoples was limited to that resulting from miscegenation or intermarriage between sailors, traders and natives. The mingling was free, easy and without anxiety or discrimination on either side. The missionaries continued to keep themselves apart from the natives except on a friendship, master-servant or other formal or informal basis. Although there are no Cook Island records to support the statement, it is probable that, judged on performance, the Cook Island missionaries were following the rule laid down by the first London Missionary Society

missionaries to Tahiti when it was resolved (November 20, 1797) 'that to marry a native woman was contrary to the word of God';[1] contrary, that is, for a missionary to marry a native woman, but not for other white persons. Missionaries in Tahiti who married native women left the Society for this reason. It can be assumed that no race prejudice was involved in this resolution, only perhaps the good sense that made the missionaries realize that their work, their judgment and their independent, impartial position as teachers in the native community would be invariably weakened if they allied themselves by marriage with one or other of the rival groups in native society.

8. *Factor of adaptability.* Native society continued to show its adaptability by the capacity of the members of the society to adjust to the great population changes and to the steady missionary pressure without showing any significant signs of continuing social or personal maladjustment. In some respects, of course, this adaptability was a forced adaptation. The people were not free to choose. Fines, imprisonment, excommunication from the church and other even more severe punishments were used at times to force a conformity. But the people were able to adapt in the sense of at least outwardly conforming to new rules of conduct. The society was not so rigid that it refused to have anything to do with the newcomers, nor did it respond to pressure in this period with violence or nativistic cults. It is probable, however, that for those on whom pressure was too great, passive conformity became an escape mechanism, and for others, young men particularly, escape to Tahiti or on whalers was an unconscious method of avoiding a too intense social pressure.

9. *Prestige factors.* It is hardly likely that by 1857 many natives had left any feelings of pride in their own aboriginal culture. They had been told too many times of the sinfulness of aboriginal ways and punished too often for behaving in ways characterized as heathen for them to have felt that there might be some good somewhere in aboriginal patterns. On the other hand it is also probable that they had not learned to think of themselves as inferior to the white man. They probably thought of themselves in some vague sense as equal to the missionary, and definitely superior to those seamen and other drifters whom they had learned to call 'white heathens'. The native attitude therefore was probably one of self-satisfaction. Having changed to the new way of life they were probably prepared to

[1] Quotation from records noted by Martin, *op. cit.* p. 12.

accept it fatalistically while at the same time keeping something of an open mind for other novelties if and when they appeared.

10. *Factors of compatability.* These factors are analysed in a later section. All that it is necessary to note here is the fact that the islander, partly compounded as he is of free and easy-goingness with sudden upsurges of violent emotionalism and aggressiveness found in the fervour of evangelical Christianity something quite congenial to his personality, just as he was never prepared to take terribly seriously the intense fanaticism with which new doctrines were taught. It is the capacity of the islander to bend when pressure is intense without snapping or being permanently twisted, that has been responsible both for the ease with which he has appeared to respond to social change and for the implicit resistance which he has offered to pressures which otherwise would have turned him into the South Seas' version of the lower middle-class dissenting Englishman.

PART II

MISSIONARY AND GOVERNMENT

18

The Period of Stabilization, 1857-1901

WHEN Buzacott left Rarotonga in 1857, after thirty years work on the island, he was able to look back on a number of satisfactory social changes consequent upon the Mission's having achieved fairly successfully its most important goal, the salvation of sinners. In his memoirs Buzacott lists the changes under the following headings: clothing, dwellings, food, employments, education, laws, religion— the most important headings, so far as the work of a Christian missionary was then conceived. A brief summary of the changes will serve to sum up some of the trends in the previous period and provide a sort of base line against which trends in the present period may later be evaluated.

1. *Appearance and dress.* In 1827 men wore the *maro* loin-cloth, women a short petticoat of bark cloth, children up to ten or twelve years nothing. In 1857 the men wore coats, waistcoats, shirts, trousers, hats; some, shoes and stockings. The women wore an inner garment of bark cloth, on top a long flowing robe; on their heads bonnets of finely wrought plait trimmed with gay ribbons. All children were 'decently' clothed. Although this clothing was all completely unsuitable for the climate the missionaries were thoroughly satisfied that the changed circumstances were meet and proper.[1]

2. *Dwellings.* In 1827 dwellings were of customary island style, described by Buzacott as 'mere wigwams'. By 1857, every family was said to have a good cottage for itself, those of the poor being made of wattle, those of the industrious and upper classes being made of block coral. Chairs, tables, sofas and beds were the furniture in all

[1] Gill in his *Autobiography* adds the detail that about one in twenty wore stockings and shoes and then continues, 'the general appearance of the whole population is appropriate to their climate and habits, and in this sense is civilized, decent and respectable' (Gill, *op. cit.* p. 253). It is an interesting instance of the social determination of perception that whereas Gill thought it appropriate to the climate and habits of the people that they should wear in Rarotonga the clothing of an English winter, the contemporary student or visitor is more likely to consider such clothing completely inappropriate to the climate and to believe that decency can be preserved in ways other than by the wearing of waistcoats, coats, Mother Hubbard dresses and 'finely wrought plait bonnets'.

houses. Again the missionaries were satisfied with the change, though it is known today that this housing helps materially in the spread of tuberculosis.

3. *Food.* In 1827 the diet was made up of coconuts, taro, breadfruit, bananas and fish. By 1857 Buzacott notes that in addition to cattle and poultry, some seventeen fruits and vegetables had been introduced into the island.

4. *Employments.* Under this heading Buzacott is able to give little information because quite clearly the people were still mainly subsistence farmers and only secondarily crop farmers. Sheep breeding had been tried but with very indifferent success. Cotton and indigo were occasionally cultivated. For those who wished for a small money income, however, the only opportunity was that of raising food to sell to calling vessels of which about one hundred came to Rarotonga in 1857.

5. *Education.* In 1827 none, naturally, could read. In 1857 the whole of the population could read while the majority could write and do some ciphering. Enough books had been translated and printed in Rarotongan to make in Buzacott's judgment, a 'very respectable little, library, including the complete Bible, a few commentaries on books of Scripture, and the immortal allegory of John Bunyan'.

6. *Laws.* In 1827, as Buzacott phrases the matter, 'The only law was the arbitrary will of Makea, influenced by any motive which might sway his heart, full of the violent passions which despotism and heathenism usually foster in savage natives'—a rather arbitrary and one-sided reading of the nature of Polynesian social and moral sanctions, as these have been analysed by contemporary anthropologists. Two codes of law were operating in 1857: one for the natives that has already been discussed, and a second for foreigners. Concerning this second code, Buzacott gives little information, but apparently it was mainly a set of regulations stating the conditions under which goods could be bartered and sailors might land on the island. Judges and police were to be found in each settlement and were not wanting in the quick detection and punishment of crime.

7. *Religion.* In 1827, idolatry had been abolished, but not one conversion had taken place. By 1857 nearly half the entire population of

THE PERIOD OF STABILIZATION, 1857-1901

the whole island 'furnished clear evidences that they were new creatures in Christ Jesus; and having given themselves to Christ had also become members of His Church'.[1]

Summarizing these changes in the most general way one may say that the people's clothing and housing had been changed completely, but, as is now suspected, for the worse; diet had been expanded and given new variety; half the island belonged to the Church; all of the island was kept superficially law-abiding by a combination of secular and spiritual punishments. The power that had motivated these changes came largely from the fanatical drive of the three white missionaries in Rarotonga and the one in Aitutaki: Pitman, Buzacott, Gill and Royle. By undermining the authority of the chiefs and giving power to judges and policemen whose main qualification for administering the new laws was skill at scripture elucidation and preaching, the missionaries had created a new society which was largely dependent on them for its drive and integration. It was a society, moreover, in which a premium was placed on conserving the new order, on making it ever more perfect. It was certainly not a society in which anyone was being trained for leadership, nor a society in which anyone seemed to think that any more change of any sort would or could come. The principal chiefs, in bowing to the majesty of law and the *status quo* that the law stood for, had lost initiative and independence in the society. Successive chiefs were not strong enough as persons nor experienced enough as administrators to make the new state function efficiently when later missionaries were weaker persons than the original four, and thus more and more initiative had to be placed in the hands of the natives themselves. The period from 1857 to 1901 therefore shows first a society that is coasting along on the momentum derived from earlier days; then later a society that could not throw up the type of person required to make the social changes necessary to adapt the society to new problems and new demands from inside and outside the social structure. In 1888 British protectorate and in 1901 New Zealand annexation put an end to possible independent development under native leadership. The 'coasting along' period and the 'protectorate' period may now be briefly analysed in order to complete the study of seventy-five years of social change.

---

[1] The information given in the preceding paragraphs is summarized from Sunderland and Buzacott, *op. cit.* pp. 236-246.

19

Economic Changes

In the previous period the economic prosperity of Rarotonga and Aitutaki had largely depended upon the American whaling fleets. Whereas in the early years Gill records that he was often for six or eight months without seeing any vessel from the outside world, during the autumn and spring of 1850–51 no less than seventy-five ships came to Rarotonga for the purpose of obtaining yams, bananas, coconuts, potatoes, firewood, oranges and water in exchange for cloth, cotton goods and money.[1] Up to sixty of these ships would normally be whaling ships. Trading was rigidly controlled. An appointed salesman met the landing captain and conducted him to the market house where the salesman filled the captain's order and was paid for it from the chest of American or English goods that the captain brought with him. The salesman then loaded the goods into boats which transferred them to the vessel. Royle remarks of the market in Aitutaki in 1853, 'A laudable concern for the public wealth seems to animate the young and old alike which is most conspicuously seen in the arrangements of their markets: they sell by a fixed law of rotation. He that hath much, whatever be his consequences on the Island, can sell no more than he that hath little, provided the article for sale be the same in quality. No female is allowed to enter the market: the popular feeling is against it and law forbids it. But the widow and fatherless females have their turn by law: their marketable articles are fruitfully sold and the product honestly conveyed to their houses free from any charge whatsoever all to the highest satisfaction of the shipmasters touching here.' (Royle, September 5, 1853, B.25, F.3, J.B.)

Shipmasters and captains doubtless appreciated the orderliness of trading and the fixed prices set by missionaries. Trading was also carried on at a fixed exchange rate between the United States dollar and the pound sterling. Wilkes notes that the exchange in Honolulu in 1842 was $4·30 to the pound sterling, with a 12 to 15 per cent. discount rate,[2] and this rate probably ruled in Rarotonga as well.

[1] W. Gill, *Autobiography*, p. 251.
[2] C. Wilkes, *Narrative of the United States Exploring Expedition, op. cit.* vol. 5, appendix 17, p. 538.

By 1850 the rate of exchange had risen to about $4·866 to the pound sterling, with probably a similar discount rate in most South Sea ports.

If the shipmasters liked orderliness, it is most probable that the sailors did not. Some of the problems caused by runaway sailors have already been mentioned—and that these problems were not slight is suggested by the average desertion rate for American whalers at this period—between 1843 and 1862 the average whaler lost almost two-thirds of her crew from desertions and discharges. Not all of these desertions occurred in South Sea ports, of course, and it is unfortunate that available statistics do not particularize the desertions by ports or countries,[1] but it is probable that a sizable proportion of the desertions would occur on islands such as Rarotonga if opportunity and circumstances allowed a successful escape from the rigours and anxieties of the whaleman's life.

What the escaped sailors brought to South Seas life can only be inferred from records of the social and economic groups from which the average whaleman's crew was recruited. Hohman classified these groups as follows: adventurous youths from farm and workshop; spoiled sons of indulgent parents; reckless and impatient persons temperamentally unfitted for the conventions and restraints of their own society; immoral and unprincipled wretches, including confirmed drunkards, vagrant ne'er-do-wells, unapprehended criminals, escaped convicts, dissipated and diseased human derelicts. Inexperience, vice, depravity and criminality were the characteristics of a typical whaler's crew,[2] and the characteristics therefore that missionaries were likely to have to contend with among the deserters, and the recruited islanders to face when they shipped themselves as replacements for those of the ship's crew lost on the previous part of the voyage.[3] It is perhaps not to be wondered at therefore, that the missionaries strove to enforce rules against the landing of sailors, or their becoming residents, acquiring land or even marrying native women.[4] Although not always successful in their campaigns against

---

[1] See Hohman, *The American Whaleman*, pp. 63-64 and appendix B, pp. 316-317.

[2] Hohman, *op. cit.* pp. 52-59, discusses the conglomeration of races, occupations and social strata represented in whaling crews of the period up to about 1850.

[3] According to Hohman, it is estimated that in 1844 from 500 to 600 South Sea Islanders were to be found on American whalers, *op. cit.* p. 53.

[4] Gill, *Autobiography*, p. 252.

the newcomers, the missionaries may be pardoned at this date for thinking that their own way of life was probably less harmful to the natives than the values and standards of the average deserting whaleman.

American whaling was at its peak in the years between 1830 and 1860. Thereafter the effects of the American civil war and the rapid development of coal gas and petroleum as sources of lighting were rapidly to destroy the economic base of the whaling industry. There were immediate repercussions in Rarotonga. On June 25, 1861, Krause, who had succeeded Pitman and Buzacott as resident missionary in Rarotonga, notes that whereas it was customary for Rarotonga to expect between forty to sixty whaleships for trading each season, during this season no more than seven had called. (June 25, 1861, B.28, F.3, J.B.) A year later he notes that the failure of whaling had brought poverty to the people. He persuaded some natives to try again planting cotton, which at this time was selling for high prices in England because of great shortages due to the American civil war blockade of the southern states' ports. Krause also persuaded the people to extend their coffee plantations and he introduced the culture of vanilla. A small trade in fruit, oranges and pineapple had sprung up between Rarotonga and Auckland, which served to help the natives when the cotton boom markets fell and it was no longer worth while to grow Rarotongan cotton.

Krause, however, had difficulty in making up his mind about the advantages of this infant Auckland trade. On the one hand he was concerned about the economic welfare of the islanders who so obviously needed trade or money to purchase clothing and Bibles, and to support the London Missionary Society. On the other hand he feared the effects of increased trading activity and the settlement of traders in the island. Krause wrote therefore on August 29, 1862, 'Darker days are nigh at hand. The rapidly increasing population of New Zealand[1] has caused some rich Auckland merchants to cast a speculative glance at our fair isle and a plot appears to have been formed at Auckland to get possession of it per fas et nefas; they say these islands ought to be to New Zealand what the West Indies once were to England.' The 'plot' was probably mostly of Krause's own imagining, but he was troubled at the time by the rather unscrupulous and unfair behaviour of a trader named Captain Irvine who also

[1] The European population of New Zealand had increased from 22,100 in 1850 to 97,900 in 1860, and was to increase in the next ten years to 254,900.

hated missions and missionaries. Krause was thus led to think that a projected visit to Rarotonga of Sir George Grey, Governor of the Colony of New Zealand, might have some bearing on Auckland merchant ambitions—but all he could do in his letters to the Directors of the Society was to state his apprehensions and to ask for another missionary colleague at Rarotonga to help him face the trading peril. (Krause, B.29, F.2, J.A.)

One year later Krause returns to his fears when he writes: 'the tide of events is becoming every year more critical. Foreigners try to settle in the Island, enterprising and unscrupulous merchants try to get workmen [presumably natives] from here for America and Australia and all seem to feel that it is only the missionary who hinders what is called in the Auckland papers "The opening up of Rarotonga".' (October 14, 1863, B.29, F.3, J.C.) Krause clearly felt beset by worries from within and from without. Those from without were materially increased when he read in the *Auckland Weekly News* for August 13, 1864, of a suggestion to help a whole Maori tribe from the Maungatapu and Tauranga districts of New Zealand migrate to and settle down in Rarotonga.[1] It was even rumoured that the British Colonial Office was prepared to furnish a ship for the migration and buy land for the settlers in Rarotonga in return for the cession to the New Zealand Colonial Government of the New Zealand tribal lands of these Maori groups. Between five and six hundred Maori tribesmen were said to be involved, and what was equally bad from Krause's point of view was the fact that he supposed they would all be members of the Church of England, and thus only a short step removed from the Church of Rome. Krause wrote to Sir George Grey for information and help, but it is not recorded what reply he received. (B.30, F.1, J.B.) The suggestion, if it was ever seriously made, came to nothing and thus neither Krause nor his successors had to face the economic, social and religious problems of dealing with 600 Church of England Maori settlers.

Despite changing economic circumstances between the years 1857 to 1864, sufficient coffee was grown and sold to traders to provide steady contributions to London Missionary Society Funds. The population of Rarotonga was still decreasing during this period, but contributions averaged about $430 each year.

[1] In 1863 the Waikato Maori war had commenced. There was severe fighting in the Waikato and east coast districts between 1863 and 1865, when peace was proclaimed.

20
Mission Work

Missionary work on Rarotonga between the year 1857 when Krause arrived and 1867 when he returned continued in a slow and jerky manner. Krause complained of the prevailing mercenary spirit in Rarotonga on his arrival. And there is a confirmatory note in Buzacott's memoirs where a native teacher in 1865 mourns over what he described as a strong desire to acquire wealth among the Rarotongans together with their occasional drinking to excess.[1] Royle, who probably wished himself to move to Rarotonga from Aitutaki and who was thus disappointed when Krause was appointed to Rarotonga from Tahiti, would only help Krause by saying that the latter could conquer in the end by love and by love only. Krause therefore decided on a 'revival' campaign, but this time without the usual domiciliary visits. By the end of 1860 he reports a genuine awakening among the people and as proof adds that he has already sold on credit 200 copies of the Bible, to be paid for from next year's coffee crop. This credit sale is a triumph for Krause and he is not slow to point out that his predecessors had imagined they had saturated the island Bible market since they had been able to sell no more copies even after reducing the price by one-half. (December 11, 1860, B.28, F.1, J.D.) Also Krause notes that when he arrived in 1857 two-thirds of the young men of Rarotonga were drunkards and there were no young men in the Church. Now by 1861 many of these young men wished to join the Church and cast away their 'rum buckets'. Church statistics show that of the 2,400 inhabitants of Rarotonga at this time, there had been an increase in membership of 100 or 11 per cent. between 1855 and 1860 and a further increase (due to the revival) of 6 or 7 per cent. between 1861 and 1863. At this latter date Church membership numbered 1,056, which with the exception of 150 persons in the Church candidates' class, practically included the whole of the adult population of the island. (Krause, April 10, 1863, B.29, F.3, J.C.)

By the middle of 1863 Krause was in trouble with his colleagues Royle and W. W. Gill. Royle accused Krause of the same old sin of trading. In reply, Krause refused to allow Royle on mission property

[1] Sunderland and Buzacott, *op. cit.* pp. 239-240.

in Rarotonga. Native teachers wrote to the Directors of the Society complaining that Krause neglected his mission duties and made nought of his brother missionaries' words. The Directors therefore removed Krause from his charge in April 1865, reinstated him one year later, only to have Krause resign from mission duties at the end of 1866 owing to an entire failure of health.

21

Peruvian Slavers

Probably the greatest worry of the Cook Island mission during the period up to 1867 was caused by the visits to the majority of the islands staffed by Rarotongan native teachers of Peruvian slave vessels. About 1860 agricultural developments in Europe suddenly made Peruvian guano valuable. The fertilizer was also extensively needed in the new cotton plantations of Peru, Fiji, Tahiti and Queensland. Peru experienced an agricultural boom in cotton and sugar. To work the plantations cheap labour was required. Between 1860 and 1863 Peruvian ships sailed the Central and South Pacific collecting by guile, deceit or any other means something like 10,000 Pacific islanders to work in the mines, on the plantations and among the guano deposits. All but a fraction of these islanders died in Peru. The slave trade was abandoned because the islanders proved poor workers, because many Pacific islands became almost literally depopulated and because Britain and France joined in bringing pressure on Peru so that the latter officially banned blackbirding and slave raids.[1]

The Peruvians were of course too sensible to try to raid islands such as Rarotonga, Aitutaki or Mangaia where there were resident white missionaries. They did call at Mangaia, however, when W. W. Gill was absent, but their main efforts were directed towards other islands in the Cook Group: Atiu, Pukapuka (Danger Island), Tongareva (Penrhyn), Manihiki (Humphrey's Island), on each of which there were resident London Missionary Society native teachers whose headquarters were in Rarotonga. Krause was well aware of the Peruvian danger to the relatively unsophisticated native teachers and to the completely unsophisticated natives of these mission islands.

[1] See T. Dunbabin, *Slavers in the South Seas*, pp. 250-264.

He wrote on January 23, 1863, 'The greatest trial has come from the Peruvian Government who have sent out a number of vessels (14?) to the various groups around us to entice the people to go to work for them under promise of good wages. The poor people were not aware that their destination was the Chincha Islands,[1] there to work in hopeless servitude in the worst possible kind of slavery. The French Government has captured two of these vessels. I have informed His Excellency Sir George Grey (who seems to take a great interest in our mission according to his letters to me) and I have written to each Island where I could get an opportunity, warning our dear Native Teachers of that danger.' (January 23, 1863, B.29, F.3, J.C.) Unfortunately Sir George Grey was unable to do anything to help, mainly, as he explained to Krause, because of the loss of his only warship the *Orpheus*, wrecked on Manukau Bar with the loss of 181 lives early in 1863. Having thus warned everyone, Krause felt he could do no more.

William Wyatt Gill, however, took more vigorous action. By accident he was at this time visiting the outlying mission stations on the mission vessel *John Williams*. He collected information at each island about the slave raids and wrote two damning reports about the Peruvians which he forwarded to the Foreign Secretary of the London Missionary Society with urgent suggestions that the Society should appeal to Her Majesty's Government for immediate action. It is probable that Gill's reports spurred the British Government to make successful joint representations with the French to the Peruvian Government.

22
Social Problems, 1867-77

Krause was unreasoningly optimistic when he felt that he had brought drinking under control by a religious awakening. Throughout the ten years that James Chalmers, Krause's successor, spent in Rarotonga, Chalmers considered his main problem to be a fight to win what his biographer Lovett calls the 'drunkards of Rarotonga' to the leader-

[1] The guano deposits were on the Chincha Islands off the coast of Peru, about 120 miles south-east of the port of Callao, from which all the slavers cleared. Dunbabin, *ibid.* on p. 261 on the authority of the missionary Samuel Ella, puts the number of Peruvian ships involved in the slave traffic at twenty-five.

ship of his Saviour.[1] Not that other fights were not worth winning. Chalmers notes in 1867 that the people still do not consider theft and adultery very bad. Mrs. Chalmers adds that the people know that such actions are wrong 'but when anyone has been proved to have been guilty of such offences they are put out of Church membership, and are fined by the judges; but there it stops. After the fine is paid, they are received as formerly. Real shame for such sin they do not feel, nor can it easily be impressed upon them that such deeds are truly great sins in God's sight.'[2] Another observer of Rarotongan behaviour at this time notes in effect that native attitudes to sex have been among the most resistant to change in the native culture, and persist almost unchanged beneath a veneer of Christian observance.[3] Whatever Chalmers's success with the drunkards, he was not to have much success with reforming the sex standards of the people.

It seems fairly clear that by the time Chalmers arrived in Rarotonga drinking had become almost a cult and had taken on many of the features assumed in other societies by nativistic movements, that is, ritualistic or cult movements whose function it is to act as a native defence against the anxieties produced by the pressures of social change. Chalmers was shocked to find that drinking had even invaded religious ordinances. Thus he writes: 'For many years, since the first missionaries left, as stated by the deacons—the ordinance of the Lord's Supper had been sadly abused by the Church members. They literally drank of the wine or the mixture—coconut milk and wine. At all the stations I preached on the subject, and exhorted them to better behaviour; but still the abuse continued. So eventually I did away entirely with foreign wine, and confined ourselves entirely to coconut milk.' It is ironical that with the Church so opposed to drinking alcohol, people should have been joining the Church for twenty-odd years partly for the purpose of drinking alcohol at the communion service.

The drinkers of the island, particularly the young men, formed themselves into a military organization, a 'volunteer corps' in Chalmers's term. They were drilled by a man returned from Tahiti. The majority were men who never attended church services, for whom Sabbath and week day were both alike. When not drilling, the

[1] R. Lovett, *James Chalmers* (London, 1903), p. 6.
[2] Lovett, *op. cit.* pp. 88-89. All the quotations and references to Chalmers in succeeding pages are from Lovett's chapter on Chalmers's life in Rarotonga, *op. cit.* pp. 71-121.
[3] Pembroke and Kingsley, *South Sea Bubbles* (London, 1872), pp. 153-190.

young men met large numbers of young women 'in places cleared in the bush for these meetings, and the scene then enacted had better be left in the dark . . . a drinking meeting would frequently number as many as four hundred . . . in their sacred grove at night, round orange beer barrels, and a great fire, naked and fierce'. These drinking parties were obviously designed to lift for a time the Christian repression on sex expression, and numbers equally obviously gave group-support to the young people in their rebellion against church-inspired rules. The parties also served the purpose of deflecting aggression from the missionaries on to less hostile subjects. This deflection is vividly suggested by Chalmers's description: 'I have seen the natives in the thirsty stage, the talkative stage, the singing stage, the loud talking, quarrelling stage, the native fighting stage, the dead drunk stage. I have seen them fighting among themselves. I have seen them after returning to their houses, beating, kicking, cutting their wives, and pitching their children out of doors. I have known them to set their houses on fire, or to tear up every stitch of clothing belonging to their wives and children. I have heard cursing and swearing in English (a native, when drunk, talks and swears in English more than in native) in a manner that would make the hardened English swearer blush.' The choice of objects against which drunken aggression was directed must have been psychologically symptomatic of the frustrations of the period: houses and clothing were alike symbols of the mission culture; and swearing in English, which presumably included blasphemy and obscenity—the language that of the missionary, the content that which the missionary hated—must again have provided a satisfying aggressive outlet. Obscenity is impossible in native culture, using native language, only insults are possible. And blasphemy, to produce a really significant cathartic effect, clearly had to refer to sacred objects in the language of the superior supporters of, and believers in, these sacred objects.

As a nativistic or messianic movement, this Rarotongan military-drinking organization was a failure. Partly the people were too easy-going, partly the excesses of the movement itself must have so exhausted reservoirs of hate that the people lacked the energy to propound a dogma, a stable ritual and a lasting emotion. In addition, Chalmers handled the possible threat of the purely military side of the organization with great skill. Realizing that he could not suppress the group he persuaded them to accept a commander, superior to their own drill sergeant, and this new captain was Christ! He allowed them to continue dressing in their dark-green uniforms and to drill with their wooden muskets and rusty fowling pieces.[1] But he also persuaded them to march to church on Sundays, which flattered the young men, to form themselves into a very exclusive Bible class, which also appealed to their vanity, and even allowed them, as a great privilege, to undertake special repairs to the stone wall round the church yard. Royle, old fashioned, wrote from Aitutaki that he was aghast at this 'novel method of administering religious ordinances through the medium of military evolutions'. Chalmers replied to Royle on behalf of his wife and himself: 'We are both very well, very happy, and very busy!' Of the drinking habits, however, Chalmers is only able to report two years later (1872) that now only two or three drinkers meet at a time, generally in hidden places, women not generally joining such assemblies. With each partial improvement he had to be content, since he had no practical alternative to the policy of complete (theoretical) forbidding of liquor on the island.

Towards the end of his mission on Rarotonga, Chalmers was of the opinion that the type of foreigner on the island was changing for the better. Whereas former traders were mostly from Tahiti, persons 'who would sell their own souls to make a few dollars' and certainly sold lots of alcohol, of late 'traders of a very different stamp from Auckland have taken up the trade of the island. These bring Manchester and Sheffield goods, excellent in quality and abundant in quantity, as well as provisions and whatever other things may be desired by the natives. These find it to their interest to oppose the liquor traffic.' Chalmers was thus pleased to have on the island a 'respectable class of foreigners', concerned apparently only with respectable trading and with the encouragement of trade. He must therefore have been unaware of Krause's rather gloomy forebodings as to what would happen in the islands with increasing commercial penetration, even of a respectable class of Auckland foreigners. With his intense preoccupation with the problem of island drunkards, however, it is understandable that Chalmers had little time for considering the immediate future of the islands. He did think that the Rarotongan was unnecessarily limited in his outlook on the world. He therefore began the publication in Rarotongan of a monthly four-page newspaper which contained short articles on shipping news,

[1] Pembroke and Kingsley so describe the dress and arms of the group, *op. cit.* p. 174.

news from other islands, pieces culled from newspapers and books, letters from natives, articles on history and small digressions on Scripture. The newspaper created much interest. It is doubtful whether Buzacott or Pitman would have approved of such secular adventures when Scripture was relegated to such a minor place in those monthly four pages.

On one other matter Chalmers tried to prepare the natives for participation in a wider world, this time by making them more independent at home. He noted the way theocracy tended to place power in the hands of the missionary. 'He [the missionary] was a kind of high chief', as his biographer phrases the matter, 'and although always careful not to interfere in matters merely political, in many respects the missionary wielded an influence far greater than that even of the chief himself. Only in very rare instances indeed was there ever open and aggressive opposition to his wishes.' By 1874 Chalmers had formed the opinion that in the older Polynesian mission fields the natives should be encouraged to rely more upon their own efforts, and to take a more active part in the conduct of church life and church affairs. 'So long', he adds, 'as the native churches have foreign pastors so long will they remain weak and dependent', so long will they be not allowed 'to bud forth, and to think and act for themselves.'

It is true that in his thinking Chalmers was partly trying to justify to himself his own desire to leave the Cook Islands and try his hand at missionary work in New Guinea—a desire that had been frustrated for years by lack of European missionaries to replace him in Rarotonga. It is true also that he was thinking solely of church life and church affairs, not of the wider social and political problems of a native polity. On the other hand, since it could be said with truth that the Rarotongan Church was the Rarotongan state, more initiative and independence in church affairs, had these been allowed the Rarotongans in good time, might well have budded forth in greater political independence. To the older missionaries, full with the experience not only of the good works of native pastors, but also of the way in which power had often corrupted when the teachers had been left in sole charge of churches on other Cook Islands, the very idea of giving independence to native pastors would have seemed fantastically ill-advised. It is probable that in his very lack of experience Chalmers was wiser in his reasoning than the older, more experienced missionaries. However, what little independence Chalmers was able to secure for the Rarotongan native pastors before his great moment came and he was ordered in 1867 to open up the New Guinea field was not sufficient, nor in time, to help the people face the problems of greater and closer foreign pressure with any prospect of successfully retaining political independence.

23

The Protectorate

On September 22, 1888, R. Exham, acting on instructions from Her Britannic Majesty's Principal Secretary of State for the Colonies, the instructions being conveyed to Exham by Captain Bourke of H.M.S. *Hyacinth*, declared a British Protectorate over the islands of Rarotonga, Mangaia, Aitutaki, Mauke, Mitiaro and Manuae. Exham, a trader in Rarotonga, was asked by Bourke temporarily to assume the duties of Resident Agent and Adviser to the chiefs of these islands, so that the Proclamation would be in order and the chiefs would be helped in meeting the changed circumstances caused by the Proclamation.[1]

For many years there had been increasing anxiety among the chiefs in the islands over the possibility of unwelcome foreign interference in the domestic affairs of the islands. Their memories went back to Tahiti and du Petit Thouars, to the wars between Maori and Europeans in New Zealand, to international trouble in Hawaii, Samoa and Fiji. They had hoped by laws forbidding the alienation of land to foreigners, forbidding foreigners to marry native women, and laws governing trade and trading to control the growth of foreign influence in the islands.[2] Missionary influence tended to support native opinion. The missionaries undoubtedly hoped that it would be possible to build up in Rarotonga and elsewhere in the Pacific relatively strong and independent native polities, firmly based on Christian principles

---

[1] Foreign Office Correspondence Memorandum by Hertslet, January 4, 1889. Additional details of the negotiations leading to the establishment of the Protectorate have recently been summarized from all the relevant documents by R. P. Gilson, 'Negotiations leading to British Intervention in Rarotonga (Cook Islands)', *Historical Studies Australia and New Zealand* (1955), 7: 62-80. This account should be consulted by those interested in a fuller account of the political events preceding the Protectorate.

[2] W. Gill in his *Autobiography*, pp. 157, 170, summarizes native opinion on these points.

and uncontaminated by the materialistic and often un-Christian principles and behaviour of traders and the general run of white settlers. But towards the end of the nineteenth century it appeared to the islanders that if they did not wish to accept British protection then they would be forced to accept French or German protection under the threat of warship guns—a French man-of-war, for example, had recently called at Mangaia and Rarotonga and this visit was thought by many to presage renewed French interest in island annexation. Under the circumstances therefore British protection was asked for and accepted. Captain Bourke visited in turn each island of what is now the southern or lower Cook Group. On every island he hoisted the British flag and handed to the responsible chiefs a copy of the following declaration, appropriately filled in:

'Declaration given to Chiefs on hoisting Flag:

'The English Government having been petitioned to grant the protection of the British flag to the Cook Islands, group of Islands, I, by virtue of orders received, have this day hoisted the same over the   , and I do hereby declare to the Ariki thereof, in the name of Her Majesty Queen Victoria, that   territory has become part of the British Dominions.

'All laws and customs at present recognized will remain in force, and administration over the island (or district) will not be interfered with.

'I enjoin   to exercise   authority with moderation and care, to rule the people with justice, and to remember that he now belongs to the great country which has done so much for the advancement of civilization in all parts of the world.

'I further declare that all persons, of whatever nationality, who choose to reside in the country, must conform to the laws thereof.

      Edmund Bourke, Captain,
      Her Majesty's ship "Hyacinth" '[1]

When a copy of Bourke's form of declaration was received in London it was felt by the Foreign Office that the declaration was equivalent to annexation rather than to the establishing of a protectorate and that the chiefs of the Cook Islands should be immediately informed that these islands had not become part of Her Majesty's Dominions, but had only been placed under Her protec-

[1] Foreign Office Correspondence, Bourke to Admiralty, November 13, 1888.

tion.[1] In reply to this neat point, the Colonial Secretary, Lord Knutsford, agreed that although it would be unwise to annex the islands, none the less any direct repudiation of Bourke's form of declaration would cause misapprehension in the colonies, among foreign powers and in the islands themselves, where the chiefs would not understand the subtle distinctions involved. Knutsford therefore recommended that 'it be announced to the natives of the Cook Islands that it is not the intention of Her Majesty's Government to exercise within them at the present time the full duties of Sovereignty or to establish within them a Civil Administration which would be far too costly for their present requirements and resources, and that the British authority within them take the form of a Protectorate'. Knutsford went on to state that since a valuable harbour might be made in Aitutaki, this island should be annexed outright, leaving the other islands under Exham's protectorate.[2] Also, he added, 'a very early notification should be issued through the Resident that, as in New Guinea, no white men will be allowed to acquire proprietary rights in land inside the group except through Her Majesty's Representative and that no land to be sold at present in Aitutaki, which may become an important naval station'.[3]

Thus the meaning of protection was defined. Admiralty plaintively asked to be supplied by the Foreign Office with notice 'when declaring a Protectorate or annexing', otherwise mistakes might be made!'[4]

Exham, however, was not thought in Rarotonga to be a suitable person for Her Majesty's representative. The 'Queens' of Avarua, Aorangi and Ngatangiia (the three main districts of Rarotonga) soon forwarded a petition to the Foreign Office asking for the removal of Exham: 'He is not a suitable man for consul, being a merchant on the land. Further he has been fined by the Government for striking men and women. Further he has been fined for selling drink to

[1] Foreign Office Correspondence, F.O. to Colonial Office, February 19, 1889.

[2] Annexation of Aitutaki clearly made little sense to the people of the island. When Ranfurly, Governor of New Zealand, was on an annexation cruise of the South Pacific in 1900, he called at Aitutaki. Ranfurly's despatches were unable to tell him whether the island had been annexed and the people were equally unclear. The proclamation annexing (if there were such a document) must have been buried, they said, with the body of the late chief. They offered to dig up the body to see if the proclamation could be found. Ranfurly could not agree to this unconventional way of checking an imperial decision, so a proclamation ceremony was in due course performed to make matters sure. See F. W. Christian, *op. cit.* p. 31, quoting from an account placed at his disposal by Ranfurly.

[3] Colonial Office to Foreign Office, F.O. Corres., March 20, 21, 1889.

[4] Admiralty to Foreign Office, F.O. Corres., April 3, 1889.

natives, and still sells drink.'[1] The Queens asked to be given a Resident from New Zealand. Their wish was soon granted. F. J. Moss was appointed in place of Exham and given the job of securing a federation of all the islands, except Aitutaki, and the establishing of a customs at Rarotonga as the port of entry for the group.[2] The bounds of Moss's jurisdiction were also enlarged a year later by the declaration by H.M. Ship *Curacoa* of a protectorate over Danger Island and Nassau. (June 2 and 3, 1892.)[3] Thus the political status of most of the Cook Islands was now fixed in a form that was to last for the next ten years. It was difficult to tell at this time whether the next years would see the development of a responsible and strong island government leading along the road to nominal independence (the road that Tonga took and the road incidentally that Moss, first British Resident, hoped the Cook group would take),[4] or whether events would force the metamorphosis of protectorate into annexation.

Captain Bourke wrote a fairly full report on his mission to the Cook Islands and some of his remarks are worth recording as an indication of social conditions in the islands at the end of 1888. Bourke's first problem was to settle the question of what sort of flag a protected native polity might display. Exham, basing his action on the former custom of the French in the Society Islands, had quartered the English on the native flag and given this new flag to the chiefs. Bourke insisted that only one flag could be flown in a protected

[1] Petition to the Foreign Office, signed by the three Queens, F.O. Corres., May 30, 1890.

[2] Onslow to Knutsford, F.O. Corres., April 15, 1891.

[3] Admiralty to Foreign Office, F.O. Corres., June 25, 1892 (enclosing telegram from C.-in-C. Australian Station). It had been discovered in the Foreign Office that Pukapuka had been bonded as a guano island to the Guano Company of New York under the U.S. Act of Congress, 1856, but since the island had been apparently abandoned by the Americans, Foreign Office saw no reason for not snapping it up. Though a protectorate was declared over Pukapuka, it was only later that this island became officially part of the Cook Islands. See Memo from Hertslet, F.O. Corres., February 18, 1890, and F.O. Corres., June 25, 1892.

[4] Moss wrote in one of his early reports: 'The endeavour now being made to build up in the Cook Islands a self-governing people, of the Maori race under the protectorate of Great Britain, is doubly interesting. If successful, the inhabitants of this group must acquire great influence among their kindred or neighbouring archipelagoes ... and ... the success of the present experiment might fairly be regarded as the extension of New Zealand's influence, and to her becoming the commercial and ultimately perhaps the political centre of an island federation.' F. J. Moss, 'Report on the Trade of the Federated Cook Islands', New Zealand House of Representatives, *Appendices to the Journals*, vol. 1, A-3 (1892), p. 35.

THE PROTECTORATE

territory and this flag was the Union Jack. Feeling ran so high that only a compromise could avoid trouble and Bourke therefore agreed to hoist the Protectorate colours of Exham, but underneath the Union Jack. He explained that the Jack was hereafter the 'nominal' flag of the islands, to be shown for instance to passing vessels, the other was only personal, to be exhibited by the chiefs as indicative of their unimpaired authority over the people.[1] Because the change of flag was likely to diminish the power of the missionaries, a process that would be accelerated by a Resident and Adviser to the chiefs, Bourke felt that any method of stabilizing the power of the chiefs over their own people, even by the use of personal flags, was to be encouraged.

Bourke noted that the laws were similar in all the missionary controlled islands. These laws 'are made by the Chiefs in Council acting more or less, and sometimes entirely, under the influence of the Missionaries; I cannot hear of any that are absolutely repugnant to those of Great Britain. All crimes are punished by fines alone, fornication being the most frequently brought forward. As white settlers increase, changes will have to be made. At Rarotonga their number is so large (about 40) as to render them beyond the control of the natives, and they may be said to be outside the law. I am bound to admit that, considering the circumstances, they live more peaceable than might have been expected.' Bourke has here noted one of the perennial problems of the native mission polity: the problem of how to exercise control over a white minority which finds many of the laws it is asked to obey repugnant and which in any case giving allegiance already to another country is not prepared to acknowledge the power and authority of the native chiefs in whose territory the minority chooses to reside. The chiefs cannot expel the foreigners without causing trouble (Tahiti showed that once and for all time); they can try to enforce laws against intermarriage and land alienation, the last more successfully than the first; but when the time comes the foreigners will find native control so hampering that they will try to secure power for themselves and put the natives in the dependent position. Thus despite the necessity for protection if the islands were not to become French or German, the missionaries probably realized that protection meant the end of a mission

[1] All summaries and quotations from Bourke in this and the following paragraphs are from Bourke to Admiralty, H.M.S. *Hyacinth* at Tahiti, F.O. Corres., November 13, 1888.

theocracy. Caught in a dilemma, they had no choice but to recommend protection.

In connection with trading activities Bourke remarks that missionaries had managed to keep all white people except themselves out of Mangaia and Aitutaki, allowing traders only temporarily to expose their goods in a market house and paying tolls for this privilege. 'I have warned the Chiefs it is not probable they will be able to maintain the policy of exclusion.'

The police in the islands, Bourke goes on, consist of all church members, i.e. communicants, who have as such the right to arrest offenders, the fines inflicted being shared by the informers (police) and chiefs; a sentence of excommunication deprives them of their position as police, 'and the missionaries hold, and sometimes exercise, the right of being consulted before a member of the church can be proceeded against'. There is no point in analysing again the naïvety of this system of justice and the obvious tyranny that it must have engendered. Bourke's testimony is evidence that in 1888 the system was operating strongly with full missionary support and sometimes intervention.

In regard to land tenure Bourke is fairly explicit. No land, he reports, has been alienated except for a few small patches given to the early missionaries. These patches included, of course, plots of land given for missionary houses, for schools and chapels, for the Rarotongan Bible Institute, and plots of land for missionary gardens and plantations. Land in general 'is held by the chiefs, the native occupiers paying in kind and labour. In Mangaia and Aitutaki the people possess their own family freeholds and the chiefs are consequently of far less importance than on Rarotonga; at Aitutaki they are numerous and no one appeared to have a leading position, which was unsatisfactory. I find that on some islands considerable tracts are let to settlers or companies on leases extending to thirty years.' The difference that Bourke noticed between Rarotonga on the one hand and on Mangaia and Aitutaki on the other, may be rephrased and expressed more clearly by saying that family and lineage groups were more important in the social structure of the last two islands than they were on Rarotonga, where a process of consolidation of power had probably been going on just prior to white contact which resulted in district tribal chiefs gaining power at the expense of the lineage groups. Thus the three Rarotongan tribal district chiefs were quite powerful during the years of missionary influence. In Aitutaki, tribal chiefs were not all-powerful or all-important, but the lineage descent groups headed by *mataiapo* retained the large measure of social and political power.

Bourke next summarizes the liquor position in the islands. He notes that the laws against liquor are practically inoperative—the laws that is, against the importation and sale of liquor, not the laws against native drunkenness, which were fully operative. He wisely observes that the laws were so severe that they could not be carried out where white people reside. 'I regret to say that all traders import and sell for native consumption, of this the chiefs make great complaint; it is much to be desired that some means may be found of preventing the sale to the natives, as their being able to get it is rapidly producing evils not noticeable elsewhere; it is, however, to be observed that the art of making intoxicating drinks from oranges and other fruits has been acquired.'

The liquor problem remained an insolvable problem throughout the protectorate. The natives wanted spirits. The laws of the islands said they should not have them. But traders obligingly and illegally provided wines, spirits and beer, and objected strongly when various attempts were made to stop their illegal activities. Indeed the occasional disputes between Resident Agent, traders and native chiefs during the period 1888 to 1901 can most of them be traced directly or indirectly to troubles over the enforcing or breaking of liquor laws.[1] It was not until New Zealand some time after annexation, invented the expedient of making liquor available only by medical prescription for medical or restorative purposes that the liquor problem was solved, as far as imported spirits were concerned—the making of home brew being only a minor aspect of the liquor problem and not such as to cause social unrest or much harm to the people.

Concerning the economic situation of the islands Bourke has little to say. He notes, however, that the islands have neither taxes nor custom duties; the principal currency is Chilean and other South

[1] Chalmers had been optimistic when he wrote in 1887 that bush beer parties had disappeared. A Dr. Caldwell, an American medical person who had been in practice on Rarotonga for some years, wrote to Moss, July 15, 1897, describing in his letter some of the frequent orgies in the bush around the Sunday 'beer barrel'—men, women, sometimes children, drinking until they were crazed, half-naked, singing 'lewd songs' until stupified. Frequently the beer was mixed with foreign spirits to make it more potent, and much of the drunkenness was evident on Sunday afternoons and evenings, 'due to the enforced Sunday idleness of those who do not care to spend time in church'. New Zealand House of Representatives, *Appendices to Journals* (1898), A-4, p. 11.

American silver, introduced from Tahiti,[1] whose value has been maintained, notwithstanding the depreciation which has taken place, and gold is therefore used at a loss. Trade, adds Bourke, is carried on principally by barter; it is admitted to be unsatisfactory, and an English money basis is desired by the traders, but they are not prepared to bear any share of the loss that might result in changing from South American silver to English gold.

Finally, in bringing his report to an end, Bourke notes that hitherto all marriages have been performed by the missions, including a number of marriages between whites and natives which by the laws of the islands are illegal. Because the legal status of the partners in these mixed marriages is thus doubtful, Bourke recommends as immediately desirable, retrospective legislation to clarify their position. He also encloses in his report a letter from 'Queen' Pa of Ngatangiia, dated November 6, 1888, imploring the English Government to appoint as governor of the islands 'a man fresh from the English Government, a good man, new to the country whose heart is "tender" to native and white alike. We do not want a man living on Rarotonga to be Governor over us, as we know all their ways and characters.' Knowing all their ways and characters—it is hardly a testimonial to the forty Europeans on Rarotonga at this time that not one could pass the wide-eyed scrutiny of Queen Pa, but she had to wait, even so, until the Moss appointment of 1891 before she could get the impartial, but tender-hearted, outsider she required as her ideal 'governor'.

Exham, as befitted his new dignity as acting temporary Resident and Adviser and proclamation reader at each island, also sent in a report early in 1889 to Lord Salisbury at the Foreign Office. The report adds little to Bourke's statement. It notes the population on most islands visited, gives the names of the three importing firms in Rarotonga, the import and export figures for 1888, recalls that cotton is now neglected, the coffee crop recently destroyed by a hurricane, and that fruit is being steadily exported to Auckland. Exham adds several details on the difficulties of enforcing liquor laws, which again suggest a partial breakdown of native administration. 'The Native authorities are totally incapable of carrying out

[1] The value of the Chilean dollar generally fluctuated with the value of silver. In 1891 its nominal value was 4s., but its real export value was between 2s. 10d. and 3s. 3d. Its value in 1902 was 1s. 9d. Though still used by Tahitian trading firms at that date it had been given up in Mangaia and Aitutaki in favour of Sterling, and almost given up in Rarotonga. See *N.Z. Official Year Book* (1902), p. 573.

THE PROTECTORATE

their laws where foreigners are concerned, and moreover they will take bribes, therefore all sorts of liquor are sold and in a few cases only have authorities been able to enforce fines on importers, the principal reason being that the authorities have connived at the sale of liquor by people who pay them well and consequently the others will not pay their fines. The chiefs want the sale of liquor stopped but they are either afraid or too indolent.' Thus, bribery, fear, easy-goingness, and refusal to pay fines was making the liquor law ineffective and worse, building up in governed and governors alike a knowledge that native administration was in some respects corrupt and weak.

This impression would be supported by Exham's information about police administration. 'Because communicants are all policemen, most of them unfit for duties', he says, 'most people who get drunk are either sons or relations of these so-called police; they do not care to arrest them and will only be strict on sailors or natives from other islands who are working on the plantations of foreigners [the Census of 1902 gives the number of these natives as 459]. All punishments are made by fines and if the man who is fined has nothing, his relations have to pay for him, and in the case of a native from some other island who has no friends, if he is unable to pay, he gets off free.'[1] It is interesting to note in this connection that it soon became the rule to judge the healthiness of the native polity by the promptness with which liquor fines were paid and the amounts collected. Thus in a dispatch from Onslow to Knutsford at the Colonial Office early in 1891, the information is given that £150 of fines have been collected for the offence of selling liquor without a licence and this promptness indicates that the liquor law is working well because public opinion now favours the law. In other words, the more the law is broken, the more people favour the law—a queer twist in the logic of the colonial administrator.[2]

Moss, the Resident who succeeded Exham in 1890, was by arrangement with the Colonial Office nominated and paid for by the New Zealand Government. New Zealand found it difficult to understand England in allowing the Germans to secure their foothold in Samoa and despite Chamberlain's soothing dispatch on the matter,[3] undoubtedly felt that Britain might again not be so thoughtful as she

[1] The information from Exham in this and the preceding paragraph is taken from Exham to Salisbury, F.O. Corres., February 4, 1889.
[2] Onslow to Knutsford, F.O. Corres., April 15, 1891.
[3] Seddon, Prime Minister of New Zealand, wrote a memorandum dated April 16, 1900, on the subject which was only a more forceful expression of the views

should be of all the strategic problems of the South Pacific. Partially to ensure against any sudden or bargain disposal of Rarotonga and adjacent islands by the British Government, the New Zealand Government arranged for its own paid Resident to be adviser to the chiefs of Rarotonga and therefore report his activities directly to Wellington, and not only to the Colonial Office in London. One of Moss's first official acts was to implement a Constitution Act for the Cook Group. This he did by establishing a Cook Islands Federal Parliament in 1891.

This Parliament possessed an Executive Council with Queen Makea, paramount chief of Rarotonga, as its elected president; in addition there was a house of representatives made up of three representatives from each of the Cook Islands, chosen as the people of that island might desire. The representatives met regularly on a day fixed by law, they were members of mixed ages (Moss's idea was to wear down the old prerogatives of the chiefs by attrition from the ideas of the younger generations) with an elected chairman and with majority decisions. Modest revenues were obtained through import duties. There was also a supreme court of law.

Each island also had its own governing council. That for Rarotonga, for instance, consisted of a House of the Chiefs which included all the chiefs of Rarotonga and a House of the People made up of the judges of each of the three island districts, three others appointed yearly and six others elected yearly on a universal suffrage of all those over 21 years of age, and including foreigners resident in Rarotonga for longer than twelve months. For a small island with a small population this Rarotongan type of council seems cumbersome and was probably not very efficient.[1]

It had been Moss's hope that, given time to learn the art of government, the Cook Islands Federal Parliament would be able to build up a sense of corporate life so that the government would not only

---

of his predecessors. The memorandum and Chamberlain's reply are given in the New Zealand House of Representatives, *Appendices to the Journals* (1901), A-1, pp. 5-6 and *ibid.* A-2, p. 14. Extracts from the dispatches are to be found in the *Cambridge History of the British Empire*, vol. 7, pt. 11 (Cambridge, 1933), pp. 211-212.

[1] Particulars of the Rarotongan Council, as established by Ordinance of September 22, 1893, are given in New Zealand House of Representatives, *Appendices to the Journals* (1894), vol. 1, A-3, pp. 10-11—the interesting point is that by this date the foreigners in Rarotonga were powerful enough to be entitled to a vote and to be elected as members of the Council. The long-gone missionaries must have turned in their graves at this prospect.

THE PROTECTORATE

be efficient but also would be able to exercise a beneficial influence over adjacent Pacific island groups.[1] This was not, however, to be the case. Seddon, Prime Minister of New Zealand, felt strongly that strategic considerations dictated the step of so enlarging the boundaries of New Zealand 'as to include the Cook Group, the Fiji, the Friendly and the Society islands, or such of them as might be included within the extended boundaries with advantage and without causing complications'.[2] In May of 1900 Seddon made a Pacific Island tour that included Tonga, Fiji and the Cook Islands. He was confirmed in his views about the possibility of annexing the Cook Islands at least, without complications, and strengthened in them by petitions presented to him in Rarotonga by 'forty white residents' (of whom four bore Chinese names) praying for New Zealand annexation to protect the trading community against the 'independent and irresponsible character of our Courts of Justice' which made the traders (many of them closely connected with Auckland firms) feel 'insecure and dissatisfied' with their present condition.[3] In the years between 1891 and 1900 there had developed increasing tension between Moss and the federal parliament. By 1897 Moss had decided that a supreme court presided over by a European judge was necessary to deal justly with the growing number of cases involving disputes between Europeans or between Europeans and natives. His Federal Court Bill, however, was objected to most strongly by the chiefs who saw in the bill a scheme to deprive them of their authority and power by subordinating them to a supreme European. Encouraged by unscrupulous Europeans and worried in addition over proposals for establishing complete prohibition, for compulsory, secular education, and for the teaching of English in schools, the chiefs petitioned for Moss's removal. Moss had by now become something of a scapegoat upon whom the chiefs projected

[1] Moss, *op. cit.*   [2] Seddon memorandum, April 16, 1900, *op. cit.*
[3] *Rt. Hon. R. J. Seddon's Visit, 1900*, p. 334. Of some at least of these European residents it is salutary to read Gudgeon's acid comments (Gudgeon succeeded Moss in September 12, 1898): 'a very indifferent class of settlers'—'men from whom the Maoris can learn nothing'—'dissipated and fugitives from other countries, the presence of such men is not calculated to raise the European in the eyes of the Maori'. Gudgeon, *Report on Trade and Social Condition in the Cook Islands*, New Zealand House of Representatives, *Appendices to the Journals* (1900), vol. 1, A-3, pp. 23-24. It is curious the attraction that islands variously labelled 'of Eden' or 'of Paradise' or described by such adjectives as faery, mystic, scented, enchanted, rainbow, have had, not for the good and the innocent but for the wicked and sophisticated. Can it be a fact that only the bad are at heart poets and incurably romantic?

all the hostility and aggression engendered by Moss's efforts to hurry them along the path to independence. They panicked, dug in their toes and refused to have any more political change. The Chief Justice of New Zealand, Sir James Prendergast, was sent to Rarotonga to investigate the social and political conditions. His report vindicated Moss and criticized the chiefs for their inability to subordinate their personal feelings to the rule of law and for their incapacity to handle problems involving foreigners.[1] Moss had by now outlived his usefulness in the Cook Islands. With all his vision, honesty, conscientiousness and impartiality he had failed in his own job of helping the islands to become self-dependent very largely because he could not go slow but hurried the chiefs until in the end both became impatient and resentful of each other.

Comparison between the number of laws or ordinances passed before and after the Protectorate was established, serves as a rough index of the pressure put upon the chiefs to adapt to the changing circumstances. When Moss arrived in Rarotonga he found the laws a 'mixture of ecclesiastical and secular rules and enactments'. The last compilation had been made in 1879, with only one law passed between that date and 1891, this law being only a renewal of the prohibition against the importation of liquor. Moss had to hunt hard even to find a copy of the laws, at last unearthing a bound copy, almost the only one on Rarotonga, in the library of the resident missionary. The code was a simple one with forty-six short provisions.[2] Between 1891 and 1901, however, not only were major laws passed establishing Federal and Island Parliament and Councils, together with amendments from time to time, but at least fifty additional laws were passed ranging in content all the way from laws prohibiting rape and sorcery, establishing a Federal flag, regulating divorces, prohibiting the landing of sick seamen and the use of

[1] Prendergast, as if foreseeing the future added, 'I am inclined to the opinion that it is only a question of time, and that ere long it will be found inevitable to give up the Protectorate, or modify the position of the British Agent, or to annex these islands to the British Crown. . . . Legislative powers might be left to the Federal and local Parliaments on all the subjects not dealt with by the Crown or the Crown's appointee.' Prendergast to the Governor of New Zealand, January 24, 1898, *Correspondence relating to requests for the removal of F. J. Moss, Esquire, British Agent*. New Zealand House of Representatives, *Appendices to the Journals* (1898), vol. 1, A-3, pp. 14-86. The Prendergast report prints a large number of documents on contemporary social, political and personal problems in Rarotonga.

[2] Moss, New Zealand House of Representatives, *Appendices to Journals* (1891), vol. 1, A-3, pp. 19-36, where the Code is set out in Rarotongan and English.

THE PROTECTORATE

dynamite for killing fish, to laws eradicating guavas and restricting the admittance of Chinese on the grounds that they were leprous, smoked opium and were morally objectionable.[1] No wonder if the chiefs at times speculated uneasily on what next in the way of laws Moss had for their solemn but uncomprehending debate, specially when they remembered that in the thirteen years before the protectorate no new laws had been necessary, whereas in the ten years after, at least fifty new laws were required.

Almost immediately following Seddon's visit, implementing the Premier's urgent views as to strategic, commercial and improved administrative necessities, and hastened by a petition from the chiefs of Rarotonga asking for annexation, the House of Representatives passed a Resolution, September 28, 1900, extending the boundaries of the colony to include the Cook Group. The Governor of the Colony at once proceeded to Rarotonga where the ceremony of annexation was carried out on October 8, 1900. The Cook and Other Island Government Act, 1901, established a form of government, including a Federal Council for the whole group, and regulated the laws that might in future be passed for the group.[2]

The later history of the Federal Council[3] is a melancholy commentary on Moss's high hopes of 1892. The Council continued to

[1] In addition there were statutes for each island to be revised and codified by the Federal Parliament. The Statute for Aitutaki, 1899, for instance, made it no longer lawful for police to prosecute for such acts as being pregnant as an unmarried woman, card playing, placing one's arm round a woman, going from one village to another on the Sabbath, tattooing or being tattooed, taking an unmarried woman inland; but even so the revision left fifty-three positive laws for the islanders to watch carefully on pain of fine or forced working on the roads. See New Zealand House of Representatives, *Appendices to the Journals*, (1900), vol. 1, A-3, pp. 17-20.

[2] The debate on the Resolution is reported in *New Zealand Parliamentary Debates*, vol. 114 (1900), pp. 348-353, 387-426. When Seddon was asked by members of the House of Representatives the reasons for his haste in wanting the resolution of annexation passed, he replied with this poetical outburst: 'There is the cruiser "Mildura" in our harbour buoyant and ready. Her engines are throbbing. She is tearing at the hawser. She wants to get away as the messenger of peace and expansion. What is her mission? Her mission is to help you, to help this colony, and to help the Empire . . . delays are dangerous. There are those who have for long looked with longing eyes; there are those who for years have always envied New Zealand's position respecting the Cook Island Group.' *Ibid.* p. 423, Seddon did not bother to particularize the dark enemies of New Zealand's mission in the South Pacific. The annexation petition of the chiefs of Rarotonga is reproduced in the debate and given separately in New Zealand House of Representatives, *Appendices to the Journals* (1900), vol. 1, A-J. pp. 1-2.

[3] A summary of the provisions of the Act of 1901 is given in the *New Zealand Official Year-Book* (1902), pp. 573-575.

exist in an attenuated form until some time in 1912, its last ordinance being dated May 20, 1912. Poor shipping communication, however, between Rarotonga and other islands of the group apparently prevented members of the Council from outlying islands from attending meetings in Rarotonga. As a result the functions of the Federal Council were absorbed by the Island Council of Rarotonga which virtually became an Executive Council for the whole group. Between 1912 and 1915 the Federal Council ceased to function. It was not until the Cook Islands Amendment Act of 1946 was passed that the defunct Federal Council was revived in the form of the Legislative Council of the Cook Islands—and Moss's hope of developing a sense of corporate government for the whole group given a new life and a new enthusiasm, fifty-four years after he made the first attempt.

The two positive influences that brought about the end of Cook Island independence were strategic considerations and pressure from trading interests in the islands. The two negative factors were on the one hand the failure of the native government to solve the problem of conflicts between native and trading interests induced by the pressures of a small but economically powerful foreign population and, on the other hand, the failure of the missionaries to teach the natives how to rule in a society subjected to pressures from a foreign population. Native government inspired, directed and controlled by missionary teaching and advice had been satisfactory enough throughout the period from 1823 to 1888. Society was stable. Problems of administration looked simple. But the native polity was essentially a sheltered polity, dependent upon missionary help. No native person strong in sagacity and in personality was found within the polity to build up a tradition of competence and independence in Rarotonga from which wise leadership for the whole group would most naturally stem. Instead the chiefs of Rarotonga, for much of the time between 1890 and 1901, devoted their energies to a continuation of their old jealousies and feuds. Moss observed in 1891 that each Rarotongan chief carried out or observed at his or her own pleasure the laws passed by the general council of that island. Each was jealous of interference from the other and the jealousy was put to good use, but for their own purposes, by some of the foreign residents. Jealousies between Rarotonga, Mangaia and Aitutaki were superimposed upon these internal feuds.[1]

[1] Moss in his annual report for 1891. New Zealand House of Representatives, *Appendices to the Journals* (1891), A-3, pp. 19-20.

THE PROTECTORATE

Again, in 1898, Moss recurs to the obstinacy of the Rarotongan chiefs as a supreme obstacle in building up a form of corporate, though independent political life. In a dispatch, dated April 25, 1898, he writes, 'The ariki are now imbued with the idea that Captain Bourke's Proclamation in 1888 secured to the arikis that their individual administration would not be interfered with. The presence of a British Resident with the least power is therefore regarded by the arikis as an infraction of their mana, and of their claim to control the Government, and specially the revenue that has come with it, at their pleasure.'[1] Moss not only had in mind the refusal of the chiefs to pass his Federal Court Bill, but also the boiling up of jealousies that occurred in 1895 when the five principal chiefs of Rarotonga were involved in a bitter dispute over the right of one of them personally to appoint before her death an adopted son as her successor. The remaining chiefs refused to have what they called 'a cockroach crawling on their mat'; and at one time it appeared as if blood would be shed. The trouble died down in due course, but not the rivalries, suspicions and jealousies.[2]

Indeed it may be said with great truth that the first missionaries arrived in Rarotonga too soon for the ultimate good of the people. At the time of their first landings, one tribe, the Takitumu people, had beaten, and were about to annihilate, the other tribes of the island, thus establishing virtual hegemony over the whole of Rarotonga. The missionaries put a stop to the warfare, the defeated tribes drifted back to their lands, the Avarua and Aorangi people

[1] Moss to the Governor, April 25, 1898, in New Zealand House of Representatives, *Appendices to the Journals* (1899), vol. 1, A-3, p. 3.

[2] Moss gives an amusing instance of the way in Aitutaki chiefly power was used to control debate. 'In the Aitutaki Council free speech has been effectively crippled by the practice of the Chief Judge (who is also a chief of high rank) fining heavily, and on the spot, without trial, any member who made what he considered to be "a lying statement", for the making of which, by any person, their laws have long provided such penalties. The most curious feature was that the members themselves seemed to consider the judge quite right; though they complained bitterly that what he sometimes called "lying statements" they themselves believed to be truths. This was the only ground on which they objected to the practice!' New Zealand House of Representatives, *Appendices to the Journals* (1893), vol. 1, A-6, p. 41. At about this time, the contest for various offices in Aitutaki that gave power, money (from fines) and superior status, was so strenuous that divisions, discontents and hostilities were marked features of Aitutaki social life. Between 1860 and 1884 two new villages were established on the island by seceding groups which felt themselves too bitterly aggrieved in the struggle for power to be able to co-operate with the majority. Moss, *op. cit.* (1892), vol. 1, A-3, pp. 20-21.

soon becoming wealthy in fact and in prestige because they were closest to the main port of the island. Thus Takitumu fell behind and its rivals went ahead, the Makea (chief) of Avarua even becoming recognized as the paramount chief of Rarotonga. It is understandable, therefore, that from the Polynesian point of view later events were only a perpetual insult to Takitumu people and both traditional and contemporary jealousies made co-operation difficult, at times impossible.[1]

If the missionaries could not help landing on Rarotonga in the year they did, it is at least fair to believe that they could have done much more to weaken old rivalries and dampen jealous enthusiasms than they were apparently prepared to do. Probably in their missionary efforts to play off one district against another and thus by competitive rivalry to increase church membership or Sunday school successes or arrowroot contributions to missionary funds, they were blind to the ultimate political effects of this policy. As events turned out, therefore, the period between 1888 and 1901, which witnessed the waning of missionary control and the final triumph of secular control, was too short a period within which to develop either the persons or the institutional forms of co-operation which together were needed to make possible some form of independent native polity.

Thus the fate of the Cook Islands contrasts strongly with that of Tonga. George Tubou, king of Tonga from 1845 to 1893, united the scattered islands of the Tongan group into an independent kingdom which he ruled with skill and good judgment, using missionary help to form a constitutional theocracy of which he, for most of the time, was the ruler. The years from 1880 to 1890, in which the ex-Wesleyan missionary Shirley Baker was Premier and virtual dictator of Tonga, were years in which government continued to be strong, if at times arbitrary. When financial difficulties and international rivalries forced Tonga to look for protection from a Great Power, it was still possible for Tonga to negotiate a Treaty of Friendship and Protection with Great Britain (signed May 18, 1900, supplementary Agreement, 1905), which gave the Tongan government control over its internal affairs, subject to the right of the British Consul to review estimates, veto inadvisable expenditure, and to control foreign

---

[1] Moss gives a succinct account of these jealousies in his dispatches to the Governor of November 18, 1895, and April 2, 1896. New Zealand House of Representatives, *Appendices to the Journals* (1896), vol. 1, A-3, pp. 25-27, 37.

THE PROTECTORATE

affairs.¹ Tongan independence was a limited independence, perhaps, but at least there remained many opportunities for the development of more efficient and satisfactory social institutions while relieving the government from the anxieties over foreign affairs which the weakness and the inexperience of the Tongans would inevitably occasion. If, therefore, the development of independent native polities based on Christian principles was a significant aim of Christian missionaries in the South Pacific in the nineteenth century, the conclusion must be that the missionaries succeeded in Tonga and failed in the Cook Islands. They failed in the Cook Islands because they could not, or would not, build up a native polity with a strong chief at the head, preferring to subordinate existing chiefly powers to their own missionary control in the interests of a more rapid evangelization and 'moralization' of the native people. In the closing years of the nineteenth century, therefore, the Cook Islands in general, and Rarotonga in particular, were ill-equipped with experience and political wisdom to face the challenge of foreign pressure from within and without the islands. They were annexed and thus spent the next forty-five years dependent upon a New Zealand administration paternally, kindly, and effectively enough governing them from above. It required the rumblings of new ideas seeping into the islands from the experience of the Second World War to start ticking again the hands of the social clock that had in effect been stopped in 1901.

Or, more exactly, the clock of political change. During the years of the protectorate, one has the strong impression that the life of the common people went on at a steady and relatively unchanging rate. They had no part to play in petitions for annexation ('The inferior people have not of course been asked their opinion on this question'),² nor any comprehension of the struggle over a Federal Court Bill. They were living their lives unaffected by the political struggles of their superiors, eating the same foods, dying from the same introduced diseases,³ getting drunk just as frequently, wearing the same

[1] For a summary of the development of Tonga during the nineteenth century, see A. H. Wood, *History and Geography of Tonga* (Auckland, 1938), pp. 43-62. K. L. P. Martin, *Missionaries and Annexation in the Pacific* (London, 1924), pp. 94-99, gives a brief review of the later years of Baker's career in Tonga.

[2] Gudgeon to the Governor, September 8, 1900, in forwarding the petition of the Chiefs of Rarotonga for annexation. See footnote 2, p. 113.

[3] O. W. Andrews, Surgeon R.N., of H.M.S. *Ringdove*, made a special survey of the health and disease problems of Rarotonga during a visit of that vessel in August 1893. His *Report on the Health of Rarotonga, Cook Islands*, is printed in

unfortunate clothes—living, laughing, loving, quarrelling with all their usual Polynesian zest. Their rooted objection to working more than was necessary to maintain a lowly standard of living was the frequent cause of gloomy complaints from their European administrators. Gudgeon in 1902 believed that a waning population that would not work hard would soon have to be replaced with 'men and women of British descent'.[1] He was but repeating one of Moss's prophecies of 1891 when Moss advocated the wholesale importation of Japanese—Christian-Japanese, however—to cultivate 'the abundance of very fertile land now lying waste and useless'. It was Moss's sanguine expectation that the children of such Japanese migrants by being taught English 'would become English in life and sympathy', while the 'introduction of new blood from a kindred race would be in all respects of great value'.[2] It is fortunate that Moss's suggestions did not receive consideration, because in a few years the population of Rarotonga was to show signs of great vitality and an upward trend in population became evident. Thus the principal changes during the protectorate were attempts upon the part of the native governing class to learn how to govern themselves in an increasingly complex Pacific world while the mass of the population clung to their way of life as it had become stabilized in the previous period.

24
Social Change, 1855-1901

The theoretical analysis of the process of social change during the nineteenth century may now be completed by a summary of the effect of the influences or factors already discussed in the earlier periods of social change.

1. *Time factors.* As far as the general pattern of change and stability is concerned during this period, time factors appear to be relatively

---

full in New Zealand House of Representatives, *Appendices to the Journals* (1894), vol. 1, A-3, pp. 17-24. Among the causes for the high death rate, Andrews assigns principal place to tuberculosis, the debilitating effects of syphilis, unfortunate alterations in dress and mode of life introduced by the missionaries, and too much tobacco smoking, specially excessive inhaling by women and young girls, *ibid.* p. 20.

[1] Gudgeon, New Zealand House of Representatives, *Appendices to the Journals* (1902), A-3, p. 55.   [2] Moss, *op. cit.* (1892), vol. 1, A-3, p. 35.

SOCIAL CHANGE, 1855–1901

insignificant. The pattern was one of general social stability marked by a very slow increase in foreign pressure, which resulted in the acceptance of British protection in 1888. Politically, therefore, this date marks the change from independent to semi-dependent polity with a now increased pressure from foreign interests.

2. *Locality influences.* These remain fairly constant during the period. Population was still decreasing in Rarotonga, though at a slower rate than in the preceding period. There would therefore have been room at the time for foreigners to settle, either Europeans or Maori, except for the laws against alienation of land and intermarriage which had the psychological effect of hemming in those foreigners who did get a foothold by leasing land or contracting a marriage not technically recognized by the law. The native population thus had the feeling of free space. It was the small foreign population which felt constricted, and which responded by increasing agitation and pressure against what it felt to be limitations on legitimate settlement.

3. *Migration factor.* The missionary and his cultural equipment remained a stabilizing influence during this period. The influence of the whaler and sailor with their outlook and habits waned though it continued in the first part of the period and was reinforced by actual or hearsay knowledge of the depredations of the slavers. The relatively uncultivated habits, outlook and beliefs of the trader were, for the most part, contrary to the values of the missionary, and were often of divergent and confusing national origin as well. Exham, for instance, notes that the three principal trading firms at Rarotonga in 1889 were a New Zealand firm, a branch of the German firm 'Société Commerciale de l'Oceanie' from Tahiti and an American importing house.[1] Thus the cultural pressures to which the native was subjected were a mixture of Evangelical middle-class Christianity and European or American commercialism.

4. *Race influences.* These influences still continue to be unimportant. By 1895 to 1901 seven to eleven Chinese, five Portuguese, one Jamaican and one native from New Guinea had been added to the dominant native population and the seventy-five Europeans then in Rarotonga. No reference is found anywhere, however, to race prejudice, race antagonism or heightened race consciousness. Legal restrictions on intermarriage were not motivated by race separatism but by the feared inability of the native government to handle the

[1] Exham to Salisbury, F.O. Corres., February 4, 1889.

problems likely to be created by the presence in the islands of numbers of Europeans married to, and therefore having claims upon the land of, native women.

5. *Numerical factor*. Throughout the period the population of Rarotonga and Aitutaki remained preponderatingly Polynesian. At the very end of the period, the census returns of 1895 and 1901 record that only 3·9 and 3·8 per cent., respectively, of the population of Rarotonga was European, the remainder, with the exception of the Chinese mentioned in the last paragraph, being either Cook Islanders or other Polynesian islanders. On Aitutaki the Census of 1901 records no European resident on the island. Thus at no time during the period was a numerical factor by itself important in social change except in the sense that the absence of a large European population permitted, even encouraged, social stability. The numerical factor was, however, significant in the sense that the majority of the Europeans on Rarotonga were interested in making a living, making in fact as good a living as possible, or else interested in the spiritual welfare of the people. Thus the factor of momentum was more important than the factor of numbers.

6. *Momentum*. During the present period the pressures on native society become far more complex than in the preceding periods and for the purpose of analysis may be roughly classified as spiritual, economic, strategic and idealistic. The spiritual (meaning by spiritual, religious and philanthropic) pressures of the missionary as exerted through church activities and supported by secular sanction continued to be intense. Instead of all the pressures being cut from the one cloth so to speak, economic pressures became during the period sufficiently strong to challenge some of the values of the theocracy. A simple index of the growth of economic pressure is given by trade figures. Whereas in 1850 Gill is able to report that 'in the entire group, not less than one hundred ships annually trade with the natives, and receive produce of native labour in exchange for manufactured wares, amounting to not less than three thousand pounds',[1] by 1902 the value of goods imported into Rarotonga for the Cook Islands had averaged for the past six years the sum of almost £23,000 while the exports through Rarotonga had averaged for the same period almost £22,000. The nature of saleable native produce had also changed from the 1850 products of vegetables, livestock,

[1] W. Gill, *Autobiography, op. cit.* p. 252.

fruit and firewood to the 1902 principal products of copra (33 per cent. of exports), fruit (33 per cent.), coffee (30 per cent.), cotton and other goods (4 per cent.).[1] Thus by 1900 small but quite significant economic wealth was being produced in the islands and enough foreigners were making a good living from the islands to wish for a better living, much more power in the organization and control of political affairs, much less control from what they thought of as a sometimes corrupt and inefficient, always a too smugly moral, native administration.

Strategic pressures have already been mentioned. They were steadily exerted in the south Pacific throughout the later part of the nineteenth century. They were directed towards securing possession or control of island groups as a whole. The Cook Islands voluntarily agreed to accept control, but had not the islands thus volunteered they would doubtless have been controlled by New Zealand anyway, and sooner rather than later, or perhaps by a European power interested in picking up almost forgotten scraps from the nineteenth-century Pacific meal.

Idealistic pressures were also significant, perhaps as a rationalizing veneer, possibly as an underlying motivation, in determining New Zealand's interest in the Islands. In the New Zealand House of Parliament debates on the Resolution of Annexation, 1900, and the Cook Islands and Other Islands Government Act, 1901, one theme in debates that ranged from Matabele Land to Liberia, from Haiti to the East Indies, occurs on several occasions. This theme is the simple statement that annexation would be for the Islanders' own good since they would be governed as well as they ever could be. As the Premier, Mr. Seddon, in the Resolution debate, phrased the matter: 'I say it is our duty to help preserve the Polynesian race ... if we are to work out our destinies as a nation, by all that is good and holy, we have a duty to perform and I ask Parliament to perform that duty'. (At the end of this debate, when the Speaker announced that the motion had been carried, members rose in their places and sang the chorus of 'Rule Britannia' and a verse of the National Anthem. Seddon's political opponents later claimed that he had pre-arranged this spontaneous outburst of patriotic feeling, and sourly enquired why he had not included 'The Wearing of the Green' in the choral

[1] *New Zealand Official Year-Book* (1902), pp. 563-564. Coffee production was as high as 264,952 lb. in 1891, but fell to 62,600 lb. in 1901-2 owing to introduced blights affecting the fertility of the coffee bushes.

proceedings!) In any case, said another member, since the islanders were 'first cousins, or cousins a very short distance removed, from the Maori of New Zealand', it was only 'right and proper that the Maori race should, so to speak, be brought into one connection under the Government of this Colony'.[1] New Zealanders, more particularly, perhaps, their politicians, are capable at times of vivid flights of idealistic imagination, and more interestingly, they are capable of believing their fantasy. Thus idealistic pressures, exerted from without, coincided with strategic motives to produce significant political, if not broadly social, change at the end of the nineteenth century.

7. *Effective contact.* Association between islander on the one hand, missionaries, traders and other foreigners on the other, continued to be free and easy. The missionaries, with their knowledge of native language and custom, their knowledge also of the intimate lives of church members, were able to meet and mingle with the natives on the basis of cordiality and understanding, the few white missionaries as much as the many by now exclusively Cook Island native teachers and pastors. Traders and foreigners were intermarrying, despite laws against intermarriage, and acquiring some land by lease. To be a successful island trader means knowing much about the lives of the people and equally importantly, being accepted by them. Thus whether it was by supplying spirits or calico, fish hooks or kerosene, the trader continued to act as a channel through which the all-important material wants of the people were satisfied and in many instances new wants introduced to, and nurtured among, the people. The increasing mixed-blood population was quite freely and unthinkingly accepted by native and white alike. The free association between missionaries, traders and people put neither block nor roller under the runners of social change, but such association made possible either change or resistance to change, as other psychological or social pressures reinforced or resisted each other in their manifold effect upon the social system.

[1] From a speech by the Hon. Mr. W. C. Walker on the second reading of the Cook and Other Islands Government Bill in the Legislative Council, November 4, 1901, *New Zealand Parliamentary Debates*, vol. 119 (1901), p. 1076. The quotation from Seddon will be found in the *Debates*, vol. 114 (1900), p. 329. The same reasoning of course could be used to justify complete New Zealand control of every island group within the Polynesian triangle—no parliamentarian, however, seems to have pushed his logic or his imagination, even in the heat of debate, to cover this consequence of the 'cousinship' argument, although Seddon undoubtedly thought that it would be a good idea if New Zealand were allowed to govern Fiji and Tonga as well as the Society Islands.

8. *Adaptability*. For most of the period native society was locked pretty tightly within the confines of the evangelical-theocratic system. Evangelism had given the people a way of life which the missionaries believed to be self-sufficient, all-embracing and almost perfect. Missionary endeavour was therefore directed towards supporting this rigid system rather than allowing native society to adapt, according to its own cultural logic, to external pressures. Society was rigid and not adaptable, whereas in the earliest period and during the present day, native society appears more adaptable than rigid. Hence whether a native society may properly be thought of as adaptable or rigid must be partly a function of the balance of pressures acting from within and without on the society at any given period. That native society was gripped at this time in an 'unnatural' rigidity is probably indicated by the craving of many for alcohol. The illegal importation and consumption of alcohol during the later years of the period certainly constitute the major social problem of the period and of the people, and is probably best explained as an index of the anxieties generated in the people by the intense and un-Polynesian-like moral repressions of the theocracy. Both the adaptability of the culture and its relative compatability with European values were therefore masked during this period by the missionary policy of cultural insulation and isolation.

9. *Prestige factors*. It has never been clear that factors of prestige operated strongly during the whole of the nineteenth-century society in materially affecting the course of social change. The islander, in this respect, has been unlike the Maori of New Zealand, who has clung so rigorously in his sentimental attachment to the mellow and hazy values of old-time Maori society. If, however, the islander has rarely bothered to consider whether he is the equal, inferior or superior of the foreigners, he has possessed a hidden psychological strength in his own easy-going personality. The measure of missionary failure, as has already been mentioned, was the failure to develop an independent native polity. The measure of missionary success was the ability of missionaries to impose on the lives of the natives a consistent moral order; they had touched the hearts of the people with enthusiasm. Ignorance and fanaticism, hardness and intolerance made the moral order imperfect, sometimes mean and superficial, but at all times the moral order had a sense and a purposiveness behind and beyond it which appealed to that side of island character which is compounded of aggressiveness, emotionalism and

fanaticism. But, and this seems to be important, the Little Bethels and Barbican Chapels with their stark, massive, blinding-white exteriors, their austere varnished interiors,[1] did not produce faithful replicas in the South Seas of the serious and solid shopkeepers and artisans of Tottenham High Cross or City Road. The chapels, the hymns, the theology were all the same. The only difference, and the all-important difference, was due to the fact that the islander has another side to his complex personality. He is easy-going, he enjoys the simple sensuous pleasures of life without guilt, regret or foreboding; he likes, in sum, to flaunt hibiscus blossom just because the moon is high and life is as fresh and cool as the trade wind that steadily but gently bends coconut frond on shore or sail across the lagoon. Easy-goingness saved the islander from the dark cold drabness of his chapel. It gave him a moral order that became a blend of the evangelical and the Polynesian. It also gave him a flexibility of response, a capacity to adjust to change without becoming a convert to change which became the stabilizing conserving factor in his life that prestige and a sense of cultural pride have performed for other Polynesians or for native peoples of other cultures elsewhere in the world. The analysis of island personality is therefore one key to the understanding of island social change, but since this character is complex and the analysis should draw on all available information, both sociological and psychological, the analysis may well be left aside until the present situation in the islands has been discussed.

Throughout the whole consideration of nineteenth-century social change little influence has been ascribed to specifically economic factors influencing social change. Yet one major modern philosophy argues quite positively and definitely that the one significant major cause of social change is economic. Changes in the production relations determine changes in the social, political and intellectual aspects of both society and the individual. In the Cook Islands during the nineteenth century, however, it is evident that social change occurred without any important change in the production relations of these islands. The impulse to change came from foreigners

---

[1] Many visitors here found the Rarotongan chapels very ugly. Of the chapel in Avarua, for instance, Pembroke and Kingsley cry: 'That vile black and white stone abomination, paralyzing one of the most beautiful bits of scenery in the world' (*op. cit.* p. 155) and even Wragge, more scientist than esthete, pauses to refer to 'a massive repulsive-looking building looking like . . . some French prison' (*The Romance of the South Seas* (London, 1906), p. 131). It is a safe inference that all three visitors were romantics, strongly anti-missionary and completely blind to the large amounts of good in the evangelical world-order.

bringing with them new ideas and new items of material culture. The impulse was transmitted through aboriginal society, new ideas accepted, new moral standards imposed, some institutions lost, others redefined, but no significant change in production relations took place until well past the middle of the century, and then only minor ones, themselves developments in response to prior moral and spiritual changes. The changes towards the end of the period were mainly political and they may be loosely thought of as changes partly due to economic influences—but these economic influences were rather drives for power among persons wishing to make money as middlemen, rather than economic influences in the Marxian sense of changes in the basic production relations in the society.

In order realistically to summarize the process of social change one can adopt an insight of Freud's and say that social change, like most human behaviour, is over-determined. Just as the tic of one person or the phobia of a second, the altruism of a third, are all conditioned or determined by a variety of factors, causes and influences acting within each person and between one person and another, so social change is never due to one factor or another. Many factors and influences determine how people learn, how they change and how therefore the process of social change is initiated, continues or is blocked. Factors relating to production relations are one set of influences affecting the person, but only one among many. They appear to be insignificant or even absent in the Cook Islands in the period under review.

25
Coda

Throughout the preceding pages the process of social change has been analysed in some detail. The metaphorical base line was aboriginal society in Rarotonga and Aitutaki in the years 1821 to 1823. The other end of the time sequence has been Rarotonga in 1901–2. Throughout the period a tangled skein of influences and pressures has brought about now change, now resistance to change. Some of these influences have been more nearly sociological, others of them psychological. But it has become apparent, as the analysis has proceeded, that psychological factors hold an important clue to the problem of how change has come about. Not only such psychological factors as are involved in the learning process, however, but other psychological influences that go towards the determination of the personalities of the islanders, and those personality responses which each islander shares with every other by virtue of socialization and participation in the same culture.

In the second part of this study, therefore, the focus is shifted in time by almost fifty years and in place mainly to Aitutaki. Just as almost all that has been said so far about Rarotonga can be applied to Aitutaki (and Rarotonga has been the focus in the first part because of the richness of documentation applying to Rarotonga), so, in this second part, what is said about Aitutaki, its social life, its character structure, its administrative and welfare problems applies with almost equal force to conditions in Rarotonga.

The changes in time from the beginning to the middle of the twentieth century make it possible to present a detailed analysis of contemporary social conditions which, on the one hand, will stand out by contrast with those in 1900, and on the other hand will bring into clear focus the results of change. Continuing study of some aspects of the process of change during the first fifty years of this century would have been possible by constant reference to the only documentary evidence available, that is, official annual reports of the Cook Islands administration, but the results of such study would tend to be somewhat superficial and might blur the picture of social change that this investigation seeks to delineate. By comparing contemporary conditions with those in 1900 and again with the conditions prevailing at the time of first missionary penetration, a searchlight can be played upon the process of social change at three widely separated time intervals. From a comparison of the stabilities and changes apparent at these intervals it should be possible to determine the sequence and course of change and resistance to change. It may also be possible to assess the significance of the hypothesis that the character structure of a people is one of the more important influences which determines what a people adopts and what it refuses to adopt from another culture and what therefore will be the course of social change within the native culture itself.

PART III
CONTEMPORARY SOCIAL LIFE

26
Population

WITHIN the last half-century the population of Aitutaki, Rarotonga and the Cook Islands as a whole has been steadily increasing. The movement of native population during the past one hundred and twenty-five years is well indicated by changes in the population of Rarotonga (Table 2), and the changes indicated in this Table may be

TABLE 2

NATIVE POPULATION, RAROTONGA, 1827–1956

1827 estimate	6,000	1901 census	2,105
1828 ,,	7,000	1906 ,,	2,334
1831 ,,	7,000	1945 ,,	5,307
1847 ,,	2,000	1949 estimate	5,537
1867 ,,	1,856	1951 census	6,048
1889 ,,	1,800	1956 estimate	6,417
1895 census	2,307		

Source: Early estimates until 1889 are from Pitman, Buzacott, Gill, Chalmers, Exham and Bourke. Estimate for 1949 is from Cook Islands, *Annual Report*, 1949, and includes 260 non-indigenous native residents; that for 1956 is from the *Annual Report*, 1956, and includes 354 non-indigenous residents.
Census figures for 1895 and 1901 are from New Zealand House of Representatives, *Appendices to the Journals*, 1896, vol. 1, A-3, and *ibid*, 1902, vol. 1, A-3; for these two years the total Rarotonga native population, excluding other Cook Island and Pacific natives, was 1,623 and 1,509 respectively.

typical in their extent for many other islands of the Cook Group. Buzacott estimated the population of Rarotonga in 1828 and 1831 (at the time of the founding of the Mission) as about 7,000. This population was probably a stationary population, kept to approximately this figure by warfare and infanticide, the latter being generally confined to female children when there were already two or three in the family. Gill, however, is of the opinion that there was a marked decrease of population in Rarotonga in the fifty years before the coming of the missionaries and that 'actual births were then, as subsequently, fewer than the deaths'. As evidence for his opinion he talks vaguely of 'districts depopulated in heathenism' and of 'the well-authenticated accounts of the people'. It seems most probable, however, that if there was a decrease it was only a cyclical fluctuation, and it is more likely that Gill's remarks are special pleading, an attempt that is, in 1853 to excuse the early missionaries and others for their failure to prevent introduced diseases from killing off the population. A guilty conscience rather than a clear head is thus responsible for Gill's judgment.[1]

In the sixteen years after 1831, 5,000 people died of disease, and the drop in population continued after 1847 when whooping cough was introduced (1848), mumps (1850), influenza (1851) and measles (1854), this last proving 'fatal to an extraordinary extent'.[2] In 1853, again according to Buzacott, births exceeded deaths for the first time in twenty years, by one, and in 1854 the population was so seriously unbalanced that it contained 150 men for each 100 women.[3] It is probable that the native Rarotongan population of Rarotonga reached its lowest numbers about 1900 with a Census return of 1,509, so that with the exception of the apparent increase noted in 1895, it was only by 1911 that the significant increase, noted between the Census of 1906 and 1911, could be taken as indicating a definite upward trend.[4]

Changes in the sex ratio of the native population of Rarotonga are given in Table 3. In the century between 1854 and 1956 the ratio

TABLE 3

NATIVE MALES FOR EACH 100 FEMALES, RAROTONGA

	Total Native Population	Rarotonga Population 20-50 years	16-40 years	Population Cook Islands
1854	150			
1895	122	117		
1901	111		122	
1936	110			104
1945	106			101
1956	113			108

Source: As for Table 2.

of males to each 100 females has first declined from 150 to 106 and then risen to 113. For the Cook Islands as a whole, the ratio is lower still, averaging about 104 for the last twenty years. No plausible

[1] See W. Gill, *Gems*, p. 13 (for infanticide) and p. 123 for views on pre-European population trends.
[2] Sunderland and Buzacott, *Mission Life*, p. 108.
[3] W. Gill, in his *Gems*, p. 120 gives the annual statistics for births and deaths on Rarotonga between 1843 and 1853. The total number of deaths for this eleven-year period was 1,843, the total of births only 937, half the number of deaths.
[4] Further data on the history of population change are to be found in the recently issued report by Dr. Norma McArthur, *The Populations of the Pacific Islands*, Pt. 11: *Cook Islands and Niue*, Australian National University, Department of Demography (cyclostyled, no date).

POPULATION

reason can be advanced to account for the extremely large differential sex mortality of early years, nor for the gradual evening-up over the century. The assumption can only be made that the introduced diseases had a more lethal effect on males than on females, but that gradually a roughly similar immunity has been acquired.

Population changes since the commencement of reliable censuses are indicated in Tables 4, 5 and 6.

TABLE 4

POPULATION INCREASE, 1906–1956

	Aitutaki		Rarotonga	
	N	% increase	N	% increase
1906	1,154		2,334	
1911	1,221	5·8	2,626	12·2
1916	1,277	4·6	2,853	8·9
1921	1,343	5·1	3,287	15·2
1926	1,417	5·5	3,731	13·5
1936	1,707	20·4	4,818	29·1
1945	2,332	37·06	5,307	10·27
1949	2,590	11·0	5,537	4·3
1956	2,590	0	6,417	13·7

Source: Population Census, 1945, and *Annual Reports* on the Cook Islands, 1949, 1956.

TABLE 5

AITUTAKI AND RAROTONGA

AVERAGE ANNUAL PER CENT. INCREASE

	1911	1916	1921	1926	1936	1945	1949	1956
Aitutaki	1·1	0·9	1·0	1·1	4·0	4·1	2·7	0·9*
Rarotonga	2·4	1·7	3·0	2·7	2·9	1·1	1·0	5·0

* Population decline between estimates of March 31, 1955 and 1956 was 22 persons.

Source: Population Census, 1945, and *Annual Reports* on the Cook Islands, 1949, 1955, 1956.

From Tables 4 and 5 it is evident that both Rarotonga and Aitutaki, Aitutaki certainly, but with some doubt about Rarotonga because of the sudden spurt between 1949 and 1956, have probably passed through a stage where population increase was most rapid, Rarotonga between the years 1921 and 1936, Aitutaki (a step behind) between the years 1936 and 1949. Until the year 1949 the average annual percentage increase of population was decreasing for both islands. Between 1955 and 1956, Aitutaki showed a population decrease of twenty-two persons. This decrease may be only temporary. It can be expected, therefore, that the population of Aitutaki will probably

TABLE 6
AITUTAKI AND RAROTONGA POPULATION

	Aitutaki	Rarotonga
1956 (*Estimate*)		
Other than native	18	354
Native	2,572	6,063
Total	2,590	6,417
Per cent.*	0·7	5·8
1949 (*Estimate*)		
Other than native	11	260
Native	2,579	5,277
Total	2,590	5,537
Per cent.*	0·42	4·8
1945 (*Census*)		
Other than native	24	266
Native	2,332	5,307
Total	2,356	5,573
Per cent.*	1·02	4·7
1936 (*Census*)		
Other than native	12	236
Native	1,707	4,818
Total	1,719	5,054
Per cent.*	0·7	4·6

* Per cent=Percentage of other than Native to Native. In 1895 and 1901 the percentage of Europeans to Natives in Rarotonga was 4·1 and 4·0 respectively; that of the Chinese was about 0·5 in both census returns.

Source: Population Census, 1945, and *Annual Reports* on the Cook Islands, 1949, 1956; New Zealand House of Representatives, *Appendices to the Journals*, 1896, vol. 1, A-Z, p. 3, and *ibid.* 1902, vol. 1, A-Z, p. 16.

increase very slowly (an increase of 1 per cent. per year in the population of any group is sufficient to double the population of this group in seventy years), that of Rarotonga much more rapidly, perhaps as fast as the New Zealand Maori population which had an average annual increase of 2·89 per cent. during the inter-censal period 1945 to 1951.[1]

In Table 6 changes in native and non-native populations are given for the years 1936 to 1956. In Rarotonga the percentage of non-native to natives has remained relatively stable, ranging from 4·6 to 5·8 per cent. In Aitutaki there has been no fluctuation, with a range

[1] The present Rarotongan rate places the growth of population in this island as among the highest in the world, higher even than India, 1921–41, the Philippine Islands, 1920–45, or Western Samoa, 1921–45. In Western Samoa the average annual increase for the years mentioned was 2·5 per cent. The birth rate for the Cook Islands is about the same as, the death rate significantly higher than, the rates for Western Samoa. See United Nations Department of Social Affairs, Reports on the Populations of Trust Territories, *The Population of Western Samoa* (New York, 1948).

POPULATION

from 0·7 in 1936 to 1·02 in 1945, the higher figure in 1945 being presumably a temporary influence of war-time garrisoning.

The 'racial' composition of the two populations of Aitutaki and Rarotonga in 1945 is suggested by Table 7. Comparable data have

TABLE 7

AITUTAKI AND RAROTONGA, 1945
FULL BLOOD AND MIXED BLOOD POPULATION

	Aitutaki		Rarotonga	
	Males	Females	Males	Females
Full	1,065	1,007	2,350	2,172
Three-quarter	98	108	247	271
Half	28	26	138	129
Total	1,191	1,141	2,735	2,572
% Full blood	89·4	88·2	85·9	84·4

Source: Population Census, 1945.

not been collected in the 1951 and 1956 censuses. Almost 90 per cent. of the males and females in Aitutaki claim to be of full Polynesian blood compared with approximately 85 per cent. of the population of Rarotonga. The Census Report for 1945 states, however, that these figures may 'be accepted only with serious reservations. From reports received it is clear that the number of Natives of part European descent is considerably understated, while the contrary is true for the numbers of Natives of full blood recorded. The division into three heads is, in any case, merely an approximation. The Island Native has had contact with Europeans over a period equal to several generations and the fraction indicating the descent extends to thirty-seconds.'[1] People in fact no longer remember their racial ancestry, not because of shame or race prejudice, but from reasons of simple human forgetfulness, and equally simply, unless there has been recent intermarriage with non-Polynesians, the only thing that people can think themselves to be is full-blood Cook Islanders. Race bears no relation to culture in the Cook Islands as elsewhere, when the contact of races has been going on for many generations. The Polynesian has always been a mixed race, and today the Polynesian is just a little more mixed than he was before white contacts. It is not improbable that with the exception of small isolated island communities most island populations are composed dominantly of mixed blood groups, with the full blood in a very distinct minority.[2]

[1] Population Census, 1945, Vol. 2, *Island Territories* (Wellington, 1947), p. 3.
[2] See E. Beaglehole, 'The Mixed Blood in Polynesia', *Journal Polynesian Society* (1949), 58: 51-57.

The age composition of the populations of Aitutaki and Rarotonga suggests that although the rate of increase may be slowing down, none the less the increase of population will go on steadily for several generations. Table 8 gives the percentage of the two populations in

TABLE 8

AITUTAKI AND RAROTONGA, PER CENT. POPULATION AGE DISTRIBUTION, 1945, 1951

	Pre-reproductive		Reproductive			Post-reproductive		
	0-14 years		15-49 years	15-44 years		50+ years	45+ years	
	1945	1951	1945	1951		1945	1951	
		M F		M	F		M	F
Aitutaki	47·2	50·6 50·0	45·2	37·4	40·3	7·6	12·0	8·7
Rarotonga	45·6	43·6 45·9	43·7	42·8	40·2	10·7	13·6	13·9
New Zealand (excluding Maoris)	25·79		49·87			24·34		
New Zealand (including Maoris)		29·54		48·08			22·47	
New Zealand Maoris†		46·5		45·0*			8·5*	

* Maori percentages are for the 14-59 and the 50+ year groups.
† These 1951 figures include males and females and are therefore directly comparable with New Zealand figures for 1945.
Source: The figures on which the computations are based are from the Population Census, 1945, 1951.

three major age groupings. The population of Rarotonga is slightly weighted in the older age groups as compared with that of Aitutaki. Both populations are much younger than that of New Zealand where in 1945 and again in 1951 there were fewer children and many more older persons than in the two Cook Islands. The situation in these islands is much more similar to the New Zealand Maori population and the two populations, Maori and Island, can be expected to increase at comparable speeds. Education, housing and health services in the Cook Islands will need to face a considerable expansion in the next generations to meet the population's demands likely to be made upon these services.

Kinetics of population growth can also be indicated by what is known as a generative index which indicates the number of persons in the pre-reproductive phase of the life cycle (the future producers of population) for each 1,000 persons in the productive phase at the same time (the present producers of population).[1] Generative indices indicate that in the Cook Islands a steady and very substantial

[1] R. Pearl, 'The Aging of Populations', *Journal, American Statistical Association* (1940), 35: 287-288.

increase of population may be expected over the next decades, all the more so because the masculinity index and the sex ratio for children for the population as a whole appear to be normal.

27

Mortality and Fertility

The crude death rate for each thousand of the population in Aitutaki averaged 15·1 for the years 1952-55; the rate for the Cook Islands as a whole for the period 1950 to 1956 was 17·34.[1] The crude birth rate for each thousand of population is about fifty in Aitutaki whereas the comparable figure for the Cook Islands (average for 1950-56) is 42·30. Thus the death rate for Aitutaki is lower and the birth rate higher than for all the Cook Islands. This differential rate is one reason why the population of Aitutaki would be growing rather quickly at present, but for the check of high infantile mortality. By way of further comparison, the crude death rate for the New Zealand European population was 15·92 per 1,000 as far back as 1875, dropping to and remaining between 11 and 9 for the years from 1895 to 1925. In 1880 the crude birth rate for the New Zealand European population was 41 per 1,000 dropping to 25·12 in 1899. The New Zealand Maori crude birth rate rose from 34 per 1,000 in 1913 to 43·64 per 1,000 in 1955. Compared, therefore, with the mortality and fertility of European New Zealand, Aitutaki is where New Zealand was some seventy to eighty years ago. Its death rate and birth rates are at present slightly higher than those of the New Zealand Maori.

Infantile mortality still remains the principal check on Cook Islands expanding population. Data for Aitutaki over a fifteen-year cycle and for the Cook Islands over the past sixteen years indicate that infantile mortality under the age of one year has fluctuated from a low figure of 33 to a high figure of 210 per 1,000 live births in Aitutaki and has ranged in the Cook Islands from 73 to 269. This

[1] For the Cook Islands as a whole, Andrews, working from Moss's estimates for 1892 (which were probably too high for the total population though exact for number of births), gives the crude birth rate as 25·92 per 1,000 and the death rate as 20 per 1,000, comparing these figures with those for England and Wales, which were in 1885: death rate, 19 per 1,000 and birth rate 32·5 per 1,000. Andrews, *op. cit.* pp. 18-20.

fluctuation has been presumably due to the influence of special epidemics and has sent the infantile mortality figure up and down round the average of 120 to 130. Again for comparison, the New Zealand European infantile mortality rate was only as high as 81·1 in 1903 and since that date has become progressively lower to reach its present (1955) figure of about 20·09. The New Zealand Maori rate has dropped from 109·2 in 1935 to 62·51 in 1955.

Continuing improvements in the public health services in the Cook Islands will sooner rather than later result in lower crude death rates and lower infantile mortality rates. The result will be to speed up population growth unless other factors intervene to slow down the inevitable increase.

28

Public Health

Although Rarotonga and Aitutaki are both tropical islands, major true tropical diseases are not prevalent. Both islands are beyond the Pacific malaria zone, but filarial infections and yaws are common. A major cause of death at present is tuberculosis. In Rarotonga the death rate from tuberculosis for 1948–49 was 32·7 per cent.; in 1954–1955, 36 per cent.; in 1955–56 32·67 per cent. of the total deaths. The Aitutaki rate is a little less but still substantial: in 1944 the percentage was 32·5, in 1945 19·3, in 1946 approximately 19 and in 1947, 20. Although modern treatment facilities are available for some, isolation of patients is difficult, and crowded living conditions together with poor housing tend to spread the disease. A successful attack upon island tuberculosis will require a good deal of education and will cost much money. Results may be distressingly long in coming, but the attack itself is badly needed. It is a good sign that the tempo of this attack is increasing.

Filarial infection is also a disease that may be slow in yielding to public health measures. In 1946, about 74 per cent. of all the school children showed positive indications of being infected with microfilaria. Mosquito control measures do not always appear to be very effectively carried out by the people of Aitutaki, largely perhaps because of the easy-going nature of the Aitutakian. Much public health education will be required before the people become thoroughly enough aware of the dangers of mosquito infection that they will vigorously and efficiently bestir themselves to stamp out mosquito breeding places.

Leprosy is endemic in Aitutaki and during 1948 ten suspects were sent to Makogai; in 1955–56 thirty-one new cases were found on the island.

The cost of all the health services in the Cook Islands has risen from £1 2s. 4d. per head in 1944–45 to approximately £4 11s. per head in 1955–56. Almost 23 per cent. of the total recurring expenditure of the Islands' budget is now being spent on public health. With a continually increasing population and with a continuing serious incidence of filaria, intestinal helminthiasis, tuberculosis, pneumonia and other diseases, it is probable that the health services must be substantially increased still further before significant improvements in the health of the people will be apparent. The high infantile mortality rate will also require an expansion of education, child welfare work and medical care before infantile wastage can be satisfactorily controlled.

29

Migration

Changes in population structure or in numbers of population are affected also by migration out of the Cook Islands. This migration has so far been relatively small but it is increasing. Minor population movements go on from the less fertile northern atolls to the more favourable southerly islands.

Migratory labour is recruited from some of the southerly islands for work on the phosphate deposits at Makatea in the Society Islands. Recruitment of workers is for one-year terms and is supervised by the Cook Islands Administration. In March 1949 no men from Aitutaki were employed at Makatea, but 157 men from Rarotonga, about 5·8 per cent. of the total male population, were so employed. During 1955, however, the government of Tahiti decided to discontinue recruitment from the Cook Islands.

Migration to New Zealand is increasingly popular. Women leave their island homes to learn trades or to undertake domestic duties and men accompany their wives or go alone for adventure, new scenes or the excitements of city life.[1] Exit permits issued by the Administration are required by natives leaving the islands and as the 1955 Annual Report for the Cook Islands phrases the matter, 'persons desiring to leave the islands are subject to examinations for health and character'. The number of Cook Islanders in New Zealand has increased substantially from 103 persons in 1936 to about 1,000 or more in 1951, and the number increases year by year as the arrival of Cook Islanders in New Zealand exceeds the departures from New Zealand. In 1937–39 twenty-three more persons arrived in New Zealand from the Cook Islands than left for the islands. By 1954–55 this number had increased to 340. Assuming for the moment that all those residing in New Zealand originally migrated from the Cook Islands then the number of these islanders compared with the total Cook Island population increased from 0·84 per cent. in 1936 to just over 7 per cent. in 1951. If some of the Cook Islanders in New Zealand, however, are children of mixed marriages contracted in New Zealand, then the percentage of migrants would be decreased for each of the two censuses.

The prospect of living in New Zealand for long temporary periods, or permanently, is undoubtedly an attractive one for many Cook Islanders. It is probable that the number of migrants will increase with the passing years. If and when population pressure in the islands becomes acute, migration may well be a temporary expedient that can be used from time to time to relieve this pressure, and at the same time a method for increasing the labour force in the Dominion. It is no more than historical fantasy, but it is pleasant to think of the contemporary Cook Islander helping to increase New Zealand's population and productivity as did his ancestors of 500 years or more ago.

As islanders leave Rarotonga for New Zealand, the northern atolls people and some of the southern islanders drift to Rarotonga for temporary visits or permanent residence. This drift has been going on for many years, though its present extent is not clearly known. In 1895 other Cook Islanders constituted 18 per cent. of the total population of Rarotonga, other Pacific islanders (most from Tahiti

[1] Some of the trends in migration and the social life of migrants in New Zealand have been analysed by R. L. Challis, 'Social Problems of Non-Maori Polynesians in New Zealand', *South Pacific Commission, Technical Paper* 41 (Sydney, 1953).

and the Society Islands) making up a further 9 per cent. of the population. The percentages for these two groups in the 1901 Census are 20 and 7·6 respectively. The present percentage for all other Cook Islanders residing in Rarotonga, permanently or temporarily, is probably about the figure of 13·2 noted in the 1951 Census, but the percentage of other Pacific islanders has probably dropped greatly at the present time presumably because the modern demand for passports and travel permits has now made the Pacific as much a nationalist ocean as the Atlantic or the Indian. The early drift to Rarotonga was brought about by the disinclination of native Rarotongans to work for wages on plantations. Mangaians and others were perfectly willing to be wage-earners if in addition they had all the small fun and excitement of living in Rarotonga (the hub, after all, of their universe). Since the outer islanders migrating to Rarotonga become landless wage-earners their standard of living is dependent on seasonal and other work, their diet largely dependent upon imported European foods. For these reasons, the resident migrant constitutes at least a nutritional problem, and in some instances a social problem as well.[1]

The total result of migration out of the Cook Islands to New Zealand against migration from outliers into Rarotonga may be such as to give a relative balance to the effect of migration on Rarotonga's population. Only a great increase in migration to New Zealand would constitute by itself a temporary relief to growing population pressure in Rarotonga.

30

Population Density

Assuming, in the absence of soil and land utilization surveys, that all the land of Aitutaki is cultivable, then the over-all population density of this island in 1956 was about 430 persons to each square mile. The 1920 Trade Commission estimated that of the 16,500 acres of Rarotonga about 8,000 acres only were cultivable. Accepting this figure in default of any other, then the population density of Rarotonga in

---

[1] Some of these nutritional problems have been noted in a recent report. See Susan Holmes, 'Nutritional Survey of the Cook Islands', *South Pacific Health Survey* (cyclostyled), 1954.

1956 calculated according to the amount of cultivable land was over 500 persons to each square mile. The population densities of such islands as the Gilbert and Ellice, Carolines, Marianas, Marshalls and American Samoa, often believed to be among the most heavily populated in the Pacific, were in 1940 between 160 and 180 persons to each square mile. The over-all density of Western Samoa in 1945 was 60 persons to the square mile, the density calculated according to the amount of cultivable land was 130 to each square mile. According to these standards the population density of both Rarotonga and Aitutaki is alarmingly high.[1]

Because most Polynesian communities now live close to lagoon and beach, depending extensively upon fishing for a major part of their food supply, a more exact measure of population density may be obtained by calculating the average number of persons for each linear mile of coast line. The circumferences of Rarotonga and of Aitutaki are roughly 20 and 12 miles. The 1956 populations were 6,417 and 2,590. Thus the average number of persons for each linear mile is 320 and 220. Again by this measure, population densities in the two islands are already high. Comparable figures for Samoa in 1945 are 320 persons on the island of Upolu and 130 persons on Savaii (figures for 1921: 160 and 90 respectively). Population density on Upolu is among the heaviest in the Polynesian Pacific.[2] Rarotonga and Aitutaki are thus approaching a high saturation. The 1949 Cook Islands report warns that 'in the absence of exact information regarding the area of arable land, statistics of this nature are apt to be misleading', but it is not improbable that the figures given above are exact enough to indicate the sort of population density present in the Cook Islands.

The average population density for Oceania, excluding Australia, New Zealand and New Guinea, is about 29 persons for each square mile; the density of New Zealand, according to the 1951 Census may be taken as 18·70 persons to each square mile, with a range in the various provincial districts from 3·72 to 35·94 persons to the square mile. The average world figure for population density is 40 persons per square mile. There are four major human regions in the world where the average density of population far exceeds the world average. These regions are the Far East with a density of 292, India

[1] See United Nations Department of Social Affairs, *Population of Western Samoa* (New York, 1948), pp. 28-29.
[2] United Nations, *Population of Western Samoa, op. cit.* p. 31.

and Ceylon, density 400, Europe, density 186 and Eastern North America, density 52.[1] Thus two of the Cook Islands have population densities that far exceed those of the four major regions of the world, being greater even than the density of India and Ceylon. When to this already high population density is added the fact that the population of the Cook Islands constitutes technically an unstable population with a very high growth potential,[2] then it is clear that great increases can be expected in the next decades, that every improvement in public health technique will help to accelerate this increase and that the time may very soon come when increased economic productivity will be imperative, increased migration desirable and the use of contraceptives as a necessary control will require public and official advocacy.

Over the past five generations, a short 125 years, the population of Rarotonga has dropped from 7,000 to about 2,000 or less and has leapt forward again to almost 6,500. Disease has taken tremendous toll, but the population has at last secured immunity to some of what were once lethal diseases. What was formerly a dying population is now a young, vigorous, rapidly increasing population.[3] Problems of education and health change in magnitude and difficulty with this change in population trend. Basic to the future social adjustment of the Cook Islander is the biological future of his population, and there seems to be no doubt that population pressures will soon become acutely entangled in the social, economic, health and political policies that must be worked out if future progress is to be steadily directed towards the goal of a full and happy life for all those bred and born in the Cook Islands.

[1] S. K. Reed, 'World Population Trends', in R. Linton (ed.), *Most of The World* (New York, 1949), pp. 94-155.
[2] Reed, *op. cit.* pp. 112-115.
[3] By borrowing an insight from Furnas, one may say with a good deal of truth that it was the easy-going eroticism of the islanders, which the missionaries sought so hard unsuccessfully to eradicate that made possible the physical survival and increase of the population. Had the missionaries been more successful in their attacks on 'sin' there would have been few islanders left today to be virtuous. See J. C. Furnas, *Anatomy of Paradise* (London, 1950), p. 196. By somewhat curious logic Surgeon Andrews argued in 1893 that debilitation due to 'excessive venery' was an important cause in the high island death rate. One would have thought that the result of excessive venery would be a high birth rate. Andrews, *op. cit.* p. 20.

31

Economic Organization

Aitutaki is essentially a subsistence economy island, with a necessary development of a cash economy dovetailed in with subsistence activities. Subsistence farming produces the basic foods. Cash farming produces the crops that are sold to buy additional, but necessary foods, clothing, kerosene, tools, soap and all the other small objects used in a simple island life. The principal cash crops raised are copra, arrowroot and oranges. Copra and arrowroot are staples that bring in a steady annual income. Orange crops are more uncertain, being largely dependent on weather, shipping and blights. The total cash crop income for a year on Aitutaki varies greatly therefore from one year to another. In 1947 the total crop income from copra and arrowroot, was about £10,000. No oranges were exported during the season.[1] Additional island income came from airport wages, stevedoring and excess of Savings Bank withdrawals over deposits, making in all a total of about £17,000 for the year. A well-qualified informant has estimated that the minimum necessary annual cash income for each household is about £60. For the approximate number of 250 households on Aitutaki the total necessary household income is therefore about £15,000. Thus in 1947 island income was just about sufficient to cover minimum household cash needs.[2] No significant amount was available, however, to support education, administration, health and economic development had these social and public services been a charge on island revenue. By and large, therefore, Aitutaki is a fairly heavily subsidized island, with the people producing only enough to feed and support themselves at

[1] Typical of a tropical island economy is the great fluctuation in Aitutaki fruit exports. Thus the average number of cases of oranges exported from 1951 to 1955 was about 2,500, but the range was from 300 to 6,000 cases. Tomatoes ranged from 3,000 to 11,000 cases for export. Only copra remained a fairly stable export with an average of about 260 tons each year.

[2] According to island standards this figure for Aitutaki is fairly high. For instance, during the years 1921–40 the average per capita income of Western Samoa has been less than £2 annually. The income from bananas and cocoa beans has been smaller though increasing in recent years. Assuming that the average size of Samoan households approaches the Aitutaki figure, the comparable Samoan figure for annual household income from all sources would not appear to be higher than £40. See United Nations, *Population of Western Samoa, op. cit.* p. 35.

their accepted standards of living, but with no surplus income to finance social and welfare services, which they are accustomed to and desire to see extended.

32
Foods

The main vegetables and fruits grown and eaten on Aitutaki are as follows:

1. Arrowroot. The tubers are generally reduced to starch, and the starch and residue mixed into puddings in combination with other vegetables and fruit.

2. Coconut. The liquid is used for drinking, and raw flesh eaten, and the expressed cream used for mixing with puddings or fish or used with salt water to make a food relish.

3. Breadfruit. Widely used when cooked.

4. Kumara (the Sweet Potato). Cooked and eaten regularly.

5. Taro. Cooked, but not in great amounts as only small plots of taro are grown.

6. Bananas. Cooked or eaten raw according to variety.

7. Citrus Fruits, pineapples and papaia. Very commonly eaten when the fruits are in season. Mangos, chestnuts, a few avocado pears and some yams are also eaten by those who have fruit trees on their plantations or are prepared to set land aside for the yams. A few people grow tomatoes, cabbages and other European root vegetables, but these are not a general part of the diet.

The main source of protein on Aitutaki is fish from lagoon or deep sea, eaten cooked or raw. Poultry, pork and goat's meat are reserved mainly for feasts or for special occasions. Pigs are highly valued. A small suckling pig is worth about 10s. 6d. Large pigs suitable for wedding feasts are valued as high as £12. The many goats on the island are kept tethered on the household lots and used mainly to eat up the grass. Some people profess to a strong revulsion against eating goat meat. Others eat it readily, but a fairly high value is placed on each animal. Canned beef bought from the store and occasionally canned fish are both greatly enjoyed. They are the usual protein foods if for any reason fish is not available.

Drinking water comes from iron roof catchment or from wells. Kava was formerly drunk, though banned by the missionaries, but it had no ceremonial associations. Today fermented orange beer is widely consumed. Sugar is necessary to make this beer. When sugar is in short supply, some have substituted boiled-down canned jam, and as a last resort sweets re-boiled to a sticky fluid. Some coffee imported from Mangaia is drunk occasionally, tea more often.

White flour and sugar have become basic foods for the people. If through seasonal shortage flour and sugar are not available in the stores the people say, only partly in joke, 'The people on this island are starving just now'. If tobacco is also difficult to get, then the joke is no longer a joke. Life has suddenly become hard and serious. No one thought it extraordinary that a church camp for the Boys' Brigade should be cancelled one year because island supplies of tea, sugar and flour were exhausted, even though full supplies of native food were readily available from the plantations. This extreme reliance on flour made into bread is a good example of the cycle which starts with an emphasis on cash crops, leads to dependence on store foods, then to a use of cheap food, poor in quality, and so to a minor food anxiety when the cheap food is unobtainable or income insufficient to purchase as much of the poor cheap food as is desired.[1]

Although certain foods such as breadfruit are seasonal and therefore eaten in greater quantities at some times of the year it is probable that with the additional exception of flour and sugar which are dependent upon vagaries of import, the average daily diet of the Aitutakian is much the same in quality and quantity all the year round. The nature of this diet is indicated by Table 9 originally prepared in 1947 by Tau Cowan, then Cook Islands Medical Practitioner stationed on Aitutaki.

According to this tabulation the average consumption of each household member for each day is about 1 lb. of staple carbohydrates, about 7 oz. of proteins, about 6 oz. of grated coconut and the same amount of drinking nut flesh and liquid. It is not improbable, though the data are too scanty to make definite decision, that this amount of food is providing a relatively satisfactory diet as far as amounts of food are concerned.[2] The food situation in Rarotonga is generally

---

[1] The same cycle has been noticed in other colonial areas. See J. S. Furnivall, *Colonial Theory and Practice* (Cambridge, 1948), p. 369.

[2] Details of satisfactory island diets are given in J. C. R. Buchanan, *A Guide to Pacific Island Dietaries*, South Pacific Board of Health (Suva, 1947).

TABLE 9

FOOD CONSUMPTION—NORMAL CONSUMPTION FOR TWO DAYS IN EIGHT HOUSEHOLDS, SEPTEMBER 1947

No. in House	Arrowroot	Breadfruit (Off-season)	Banana	Bread	Sugar	Kumara	Meat or Fish	Coconut	Sauce	Papaia	Taro
3 Adults 5 Children	2 lb. powder 7 lb. root (cooked and eaten)	5 lb.	8 lb. green matured	—	—	5 lb.	8 lb. fish	12 lb. grated	1 litre	—	—
4 Adults 7 Children	1 lb. powder 4 lb. root	—	6 lb. ripe	4 lb.	2 lb.	4 lb.	6 lb. fish	6 lb. green drinking	1 litre	—	—
6 Adults 2 Children	10 lb. root	2 lb.	—	—	—	12 lb.	8 lb. fish	6 lb. grated 6 lb. drinking	1 litre	—	—
5 Adults 5 Children	8 lb. powder	—	4 lb. ripe	6 lb.	2 lb.	—	8 lb. fish	6 lb. grated 12 lb. drinking	2 litres	—	—
6 Adults 5 Children	5 lb. powder	—	6 lb. green matured	—	—	—	6 lb. fish	6 lb. grated 9 lb. drinking	—	2 lb.	—
4 Adults 3 Children	2 lb. powder 4 lb. residue	4 lb.	6 lb. ripe	—	—	—	8 lb. fish 2 lb. canned beef	8 lb. grated 8 lb. drinking	—	—	—
2 Adults 1 Child	1 lb. powder	2 lb.	3 lb. ripe	—	—	—	4 lb. shell-fish	2 lb. grated 6 lb. drinking	½ litre	—	4 lb.
3 Adults 4 Children	—	5 lb.	—	—	—	5 lb.	3 lb. canned beef	8 lb. grated 6 lb. drinking	1 litre	—	—

poor as compared with Aitutaki, so that at the moment few generalizations can be made about the Cook Islands as a whole.[1]

The main meal each day is generally eaten at midday or in the early afternoon, but much depends upon fishing conditions and whether food has been brought in from the plantations on the previous day. Food remaining uneaten from the main cooking will be generally consumed later in the day, in the evening or even on the following morning. This main cooking will often be supplemented by an early morning snack of tea, bread and jam. School children very often set off in the morning after a meal of tea and bread. If bread is not available then they will find fruit and breadfruit or some other staple with which to start the day, eating more seriously on their return home in the early afternoon. On Sundays the cooking oven is always prepared early in the morning from food collected the previous day. The oven is opened and the main Sunday meal eaten after the return from church later in the day. Since no rigid time schedule is ever adhered to by the Aitutakian, the time for meals is judged from the sun mainly and secondly from internal feelings of hunger.

33
Land Tenure

Practically all the land on Aitutaki is held under one or other of two common titles. The first type is native customary tenure, whereby land is held under Aitutaki custom by lineage or family groups without any legal determination or registration of the groups concerned. The second type is native freehold which is land held according to custom but for which ownership has been determined by the Native Land Court. Alienation of land is prohibited by law. Few sections of land are vested in individual native owners. A very small area of land in Aitutaki has been leased to the Crown or to Europeans; in addition small areas are owned by the Crown or vested in religious organizations. In the whole of the Cook Islands no more than about 7·5 per cent. of all the land is included in leasehold, Crown land or religious land; excluding the leases of Manuae, Te Auo Tu (leased to Europeans) and the Crown ownership of uninhabited Nassau and

[1] Present-day Rarotongan diet has been studied by M. Abraham, *Food Conditions in Rarotonga—Cook Islands* (typescript report) (September 1947).

Suwarrow, the total percentage of land not included under native customary or freehold titles is about 3·8. This figure is very low and indicates that the people of Aitutaki still control the major portions of their lands according to native custom. The average acreage for each person on Aitutaki is about 1·5. In the absence of adequate land classification statistics, however, it is impossible to know whether this figure is high or low (though the figures on the density of population, given earlier, suggest that the figure is low), nor is it possible to tell how great a population the island will support at the present or at a higher standard of living.[1]

The present land tenure system on Aitutaki represents a satisfactory relationship between the islander and his land so long as the main emphasis of the island economy is placed on subsistence agriculture together with an additional, but minor, cash crop cultivation. Lineage land is divided by informal agreement among the family groups making up the lineage in such fashion that each household has sufficient cultivable land and is able to use sections of lineage land for coconuts and supplies of firewood and rough wood for building. Reallocations of land can be made from time to time to take care of changes in the size of the households.

If future increases in population demand a closer cultivation of land, and if future policy to increase cash crops in order to support social services is put into effect, then it is doubtful whether native customary tenure of land will be a flexible enough institution to support necessary changes in the economic structure of the island. At present it is difficult for Europeans with capital wishing to invest in the island to rent land, for the reason that where all the members of a lineage or family group have to agree to a lease before the lease can be approved by and registered with the Native Land Court, native approval is rarely, if ever, forthcoming because family members can rarely come to agreement with Europeans about the advisability of renting or the merits of the lease offered them. This inability to come to agreement with Europeans is no recent development, as some assume. Thirty years ago, the New Zealand Parliamentary Inspection Party to the Cook Islands was informed of the inability or the unwillingness of natives to lease land to Europeans,[2]

[1] The atoll of Pukapuka is believed to be over-populated with an average acreage for each inhabitant of about 1·8. But an atoll can support less population than a fertile volcanic-coral island such as Aitutaki.

[2] Visit of Parliamentary Inspection Party, New Zealand House of Representatives, *Appendices to the Journals* (1920), vol. 1, A-5, p. 69.

and the same unwillingness was remarked upon by Moss and by Gudgeon in the period 1895–1905.

Similarly under the present system of native customary tenure it is difficult for an Aitutakian, who wishes to secure native freehold for a portion of family land in order so to develop it that the products of the land will accrue to him only as return for his labour, either to secure this freehold if the rest of his family group are not in agreement with him or to be sure that the members of his family group will not claim a share of the produce of his land under customary ownership should he sell the produce of his portion for monetary return. Section 50 of the Cook Islands Amendment Act, 1946, now makes it possible for a person to be guaranteed security of tenure over a piece of land should he desire to plant on this land long-term crops. Increasing use will probably be made of this guarantee in the future. It is to be hoped in any case that individualization of land titles will not become an accepted solution to the problem of land utilization should larger measures of economic development be planned. Atomization of land units, with increasing population, in the end results in persons owning pieces of land too small for efficient economic use.

In order to avoid the twin economic difficulties caused by lineage ownership at one end of the scale and individual freehold at the other, some authorities have recommended the adoption in the Cook Islands of the Tongan system of making available to each male as he reaches the age of 16 years, up to $8\frac{1}{4}$ acres of land so that on marriage each man has available land to support a household. But the adoption of the Tongan system would only be, at best, a temporary measure. The growth of Tongan population is rendering it increasingly difficult in some parts of the Kingdom to make the customary acreage available and this position would sooner or later develop in the Cook Islands.[1]

One reform of the land tenure system that would prevent land atomization and at the same time encourage a more productive use of the land would be that of making it possible for an individual to rent lands for suitable periods from his own family corporation in which the lands of the lineage had been vested according to customary tenure. The rent paid would be some compensation to the family group and would prevent the family from seeking, in an incalculable and arbitrary fashion, a share of the wealth produced from the land.

[1] J. C. Furnas, *Anatomy of Paradise* (London, 1949), p. 383.

In so far as Section 50 of the Cook Islands Amendment Act, 1946, is working towards security of individual tenure based upon rent to a family corporation which still retains full title to its family lands, the amendment is likely to be a wise step towards the most satisfactory compromise between the individual's desire to increase the cash productivity of his land and the family's desire to retain a system which is flexible in its operation and shares out land according to individual need. Releasing land for productivity by individual renting from a family corporation has been a successful working policy in at least one African tribal group.[1]

34

Work Organization

Although there are some few Aitutakians who today would be happy working in a western European competitive money economy and although there are a few more who from time to time earn fair amounts of money working on an individual wage basis (for instance, at the island airport), the majority still rule their lives by motives and types of social control that derive entirely from the values of pre-European Polynesian Society. For this society, and for Aitutaki today, significant motives include not only the immediate needs for food, clothing and shelter, but also the need to fulfil ceremonial and kinship obligations with gifts of food and property, the need for personal prestige that comes from the rivalry of the skilled or the expert with fellow workers and the need for the satisfactions derived from working in and with a group. Similarly the social controls that ensure that work once started is completed include such morally felt obligations as the responsibility to help members of one's kin group, the responsibility to return goods and services which one has previously received as a member of a reciprocal gift or service exchange, the responsibilities of being involved in a group wherein leader and

[1] W. H. Macmillan, *Africa Emergent* (London, Penguin Books, 1949), pp. 80, 82. Gilson has demonstrated that it was Gudgeon's misunderstanding at the turn of the century of native land customs that has fixed for present-day Rarotonga a bilateral system of land inheritance that allows land-owning groups to increase so greatly in numbers with the result that co-operation over the use of land for cash crop purposes becomes more and more difficult to achieve. See R. P. Gilson, 'The Background of New Zealand's Early Land Policy in Rarotonga', *Journal Polynesian Society* (1955), 64: 267-280.

workers change their reciprocal and reversible status and role on successive work occasions and finally the responsibility involved in a realization that security for one can only come from security for all.[1] Work for the Aitutakian, therefore, is not something that one does with one bit of one's life for a part of as many days as one has to. Work is an activity caught up inextricably into a web of social and personal needs and obligations; and the activity is inherently satisfying to the sort of person one has become through being bred from birth onwards in Aitutaki society.

Because of the dominant social phrasing of work activities it is only to be expected that the Aitutakian will work well in a group. Much of his plantation work and his fishing will be done individually, but whenever he can, he likes to join or to organize a group of workers for a specific job. Equally, if he is working by himself at some laborious job like tidying his household lot he likes to feel that a group or committee (his projected social conscience, so to speak), is taking a personal interest in the progress of his work. Or again, money may not be of sufficient interest for him to undertake a laborious extra piece of work, but if the incentive is that of preventing a liked person from being ashamed because the work is not done, then the prevention of humiliation will become a strong driving force.

Instances of these types of social motivation come readily to mind. Thus an official of a commercial company asked Aitutaki women to quote him a price for making 100 mats, each 8 feet by 4 feet, required for office and hostel accommodation. The Aitutaki women thought that three to four pounds sterling a mat might be a likely price but were not particularly interested in making the mats even at that price. The mats were later made in Fiji at 7s. each. But all informants were agreed that had the official said that he was in a fix and did not wish to be ashamed, and would the women of Aitutaki help him, then the same women would have made the mats quickly and if necessary, free. They would have done so, one feels, because the official, being liked, would have stood in an as-if kinship relation to them and the obligation to help kinsfolk would have operated strongly and efficiently.

Working parties of different sizes according to the task to be accomplished are popular and common means of getting work done. Thus when new thatch roofing is required for a school building the

[1] See Raymond Firth's analysis 'The Anthropological Background to Work', *Occupational Psychology* (1948), 22: 94-98.

job may be offered to a village or to a community organization such as the Boys' Brigade—a church youth organization. Working parties will be organized and the work carried out. Payment for the work will be a lump sum of money which goes to swell the funds of the village or the organization. Again land requiring cultivation may be prepared for planting by groups of village men. A person who wishes group help notifies the village at its regular Sunday evening meeting. Time and place are arranged and a group of young men each with his own tools or implements assembles at the cultivations indicated on the proper day. After an opening prayer the group sets to with a will and continues to work until the job is done. Generally one morning each week is set aside for group work. One section of land measuring 20 fathoms square can be cleared by some fifty men in about two hours work. A payment of 12s. a section is made by owners otherwise employed (for instance, as school teachers), 8s. a section by those not wage-earners. This money goes to the village funds. The workers' group clears one section for each person until each who wishes has had an opportunity to profit by co-operative labour; only then will it undertake to work on a second section for those who still need help. The system has the obvious economic advantage of quickly clearing a relatively large area of land and thus making possible early planting. At the same time the workers get lots of fun out of their group activities and the village as a whole profits from the group work.

Smaller working parties on a kinship-neighbour, rather than village, basis are also commonly assembled for such jobs as the making of roof thatching sheets or the planting of arrowroot. For a roof thatching party five or six women with some old men and the inevitable gang of children assemble in the shade and have a very pleasant time shouting, laughing, talking and squabbling as they work. Sometimes a little feast will be served or else a food distribution will be made later to those who have assisted. A planting party may receive instead of food the opportunity to drink several gallons of strong orange beer. The problem of the host to the party is that of getting the maximum amount of work finished before increasing mellowness makes work inefficient or ineffective.

Parallel to the working group of village men there is also a group of village women which sometimes co-operates with household heads in sweeping and tidying up house lots, and at other times has a general supervisory control over village conditions. Thus if straying pigs are causing trouble the women's group may take it upon themselves to find the owner of the pigs and levy a small fine upon him; or else the women's group may be charged with the job of reprimanding a householder who has not, in their opinion, planted a great enough area to care for his probable household needs and then encouraging him to plant more land; or finally, the women's group is responsible for seeing that house lots are tidy and clean should a village inspection be threatened by health authorities. Though informants thought of the women's group as paralleling the men's working-party, it is clear that the women are more goaders and pushers rather than active doers, and the village is their kingdom rather than the outside cultivations in which women in general do little work and show little active interest apart from their vague interest in them as sources of food supply.[1]

It is most likely in fact that the women's committee represents the survival today of a sort of local body or municipal council called the *au* which was expected, at the turn of the century, to function under the immediate control of each island council as a community committee of elected members caring for the economic welfare of village and plantation. Under the Statute of Aitutaki, 1899,[2] for instance, the *au* could levy dog and other taxes for public works and could control the introduction of horses and other animals likely to injure the food supplies in this fenceless island. The major Act No. 2, also gave to the *au* on every island powers to plant coconuts on waste lands, to report to the judges those persons who neglected their lands, to declare economic prohibitions or *raui* over coconuts or other crops to prevent undue waste, and generally to protect the lands of the sick, infirm and inferior from the depredations of others. The women of Aitutaki today do not concern themselves with dog or horse taxes but they do think of themselves as having a general

[1] As evidence for his judgment that Cook Island men in general work harder at physical labour than women, Lambert adduces the high incidence of inguinal hernias among Cook Island men, and of obesity among the women. See S. M. Lambert, 'Health Survey of the Cook Islands', New Zealand House of Representatives, *Appendices to the Journals* (1926), vol. 1, A-3, pp. 27-40. But note that Andrews, visiting Rarotonga in 1893, reports specifically that 'hernia is less common among the native population than amongst Europeans'. Andrews, *op. cit.* p. 21.

[2] See New Zealand House of Representatives, *Appendices to the Journals* (1900), vol. 1, A-3, for this Statute revising the laws of Aitutaki, and *ibid.* pp. 4-5, for the text of the Cook Islands Federal Parliament Act No. 2, 1899, *To Provide for the Institution of Local Government within the Islands of the Cook Group*.

prodding power in order to make sure that villages are tidy and that families have reasonably sufficient areas of food crops under cultivation. The men, on the other hand, think of their *au* as being mainly a co-operative working group, though doubtless from time to time they co-operate with the women by keeping an eye on others' plantations and report the depredations of straying animals.

35
Organization for Visitors

A characteristic development of the Polynesian interest in social activities is to be found in the institution that the Aitutakians call *tere*. The *tere* parties are groups of men, women and children who visit from one island to another for social or sporting purposes. The visitors come loaded with gifts and return to their homes loaded with gifts received from their hosts. Reciprocal receiving of visits and going on visits are kept on record, and although a return visit may not take place for some years, the record between two islands is not straight until a visit received has been squared off against a visit given. Since the preparation for and organization of a *tere* party involves a great deal of additional economic activity, the parties act in fact as stimulators of economic life, helping the people to produce more food and wealth and ensuring that what is produced is spread more widely throughout the island community. The best way to show the economic role of the *tere* party is to describe briefly the cycle of *tere* activities in Aitutaki for the year 1947.

Three major organized groups of visitors came to Aitutaki in this year. A sports group from Atiu stayed for six weeks. A group of New Zealand Maoris under the leadership of Princess Te Puea visited for one week for mixed social and political purposes. The third group was composed of village committee women from Rarotonga; this group stayed on the island for four weeks and its purpose was of a general social nature. Most *tere* parties are official in the sense that a particular village or the whole island act as hosts; occasionally, however, a private person may organize relatives into a group to visit a particular village perhaps the village of her birth, in another island, but this type of *tere* does not involve any overall village activity at the giving or receiving end.

About a month or so before a party of visitors is expected, the receiving village begins to plan for the reception. There will be frequent singing and dancing practices. At a village meeting, a decision will be made as to the amount of food and wealth each household is expected to contribute to the common village fund: perhaps one mat from each woman, or possibly two from each household; so many plaited hats and baskets from each household; one pig, four chickens and so many baskets of root vegetables; a levy of money for tea, sugar, flour and perhaps twine to make a new village fishing net (if village funds are low—or again, a series of village dances are organized at a charge of three or six pennies a person to raise village money). As the day of arrival comes near, village activity accelerates in a dizzy fashion until all is ready and the visitors welcomed at the host village. This village is mainly responsible for the board and keep of the visitors but other villages, after the first few days, take turns in inviting the visitors to share a feast with them, thus relieving the host village for a while of its major food responsibilities. A sporting *tere* party will, of course, find much of its time taken up with a round of football or cricket matches, but all visitors make plenty of time for sociable gossiping. Generally, the visitors arrive dressed in fairly uniform clothing, the women, at any rate, all in dresses and hats of the same colour and fashion. The first Sunday after arrival is the occasion for a spectacular dress parade for both visitors and hosts as all wend their way with excited demureness and over-emphasized gravity to the island church service. The visitors are often billeted in a large village meeting house or else in private houses out of which the owners move completely, leaving the guests sole occupiers for the length of their stay. All meals, however, will be eaten together in some communal place.

About the middle of the visit a meeting of hosts and visitors takes place at which gifts are exchanged. The visitors give their gifts first: perhaps £50 to the host village, then £1 to the village representative on the Island Council, and £1 to the village chief, a further £5 to the Boys' Brigade and to the school funds; perhaps several sets of china dishware, four or five dozen bolts of piece goods (enough, most likely, for a *pareu* for each man, a dress length for each woman). These would be the typical gifts from Rarotonga, which is known all over the Cook Islands to be poor in food and natural resources but thought to be wealthy enough in money and the store goods that money can buy. From other islands, native foods and products would be expected and welcomed.

After the visitors' gift-giving songs are sung and dances performed. Many of the songs composed for the occasion name prominent local persons—the person thus honoured throws coins to the singers and dancers—or else the songs make honoured reference to the host village, in which case the villagers throw coins to the singers (anything from a penny piece to a florin is considered an appropriate gift). Later the host village divides the grand money-gift to their village among village organizations or representatives—£10 to the local women's committee, £5 to each church and to each village policeman, and the like. Then the host village gives its gifts to the visitors and after a final display of dancing and singing and much good fellowship helped by sporting encounters or beer drinking, the visitors board schooner for home; one more *tere* party has been welcomed and farewelled and the honour of village or island has once more been vindicated.

Sporting visitors are not expected to make a lavish display of their gifts. The people of Atiu, for instance, brought gifts of appropriate amounts of mats, hats, coffee and honey, receiving in return from Aitutaki arrowroot and the salted shellfish called *paua*. Aitutaki gave to Rarotonga mats, salted *paua*, kapok and arrowroot, but over the year 1947, the amount of arrowroot distributed to visitors' groups was considerable, one estimate placing the amount at least at 1,000 lb. weight. At a buying price of almost sixpence a pound, this arrowroot would be worth about £25. For a *tere* party from Aitutaki to Rarotonga arranged almost ten months in advance, each person proposing to join the party was expected to have £5 in cash, five copra sacks of arrowroot (buying value £1 8s. a sack), two large mats, two plaited hats and two large plaited baskets.

Aitutaki has always been proud of the fact that the island has never defaulted in its duties as *tere* hosts, and has always been able to match gift for gift. According to some, however, this very hospitality of the island has been taken advantage of and Aitutaki has thus received more visits than the island has been able to return. Although the economic gift exchange is kept under careful scrutiny so that it is unlikely that the visits represent a drain on the hosts, none the less the feeding for significant periods of time of large bodies of visitors who are simply for the time being parasites on island economy, must represent a strain on island food resources, which no amount of careful planning can completely withstand. Thus although there may be a case for the regulation of the frequency of inter-island visiting groups, the visits themselves, if kept within moderation, undoubtedly play a part in stimulating production and at the same time provide new, exciting and satisfying social relationships and esthetic experiences for large numbers of people, who might otherwise be frustrated by the unrelieved and constantly recurring routine relationships of everyday life.

36

Work Habits

The people of Aitutaki work hard when necessary, but because they are mostly working as peasant cultivators and more importantly because their culture does not build into their personalities any set of obsessive-compulsive, perfectionist drives, they do not often feel any necessity to work hard, as hard work is understood by the European. There is a happy-go-lucky casualness about the Aitutakian when working, which some condemn as laziness and others are merely content to note as evidence of a characteristically Polynesian personality make-up that has been barely affected by a century of European pressure.

One aspect of the casualness to work is seen in the 'approximately-correct' attitude which governs the relationship between a man or woman working and the job being done. Whether the job is housework or tidying up a household lot or taking care of clothes, whether the worker is working in Aitutaki or in a European family in New Zealand, a casual carelessness seems to dominate the attitude to the job on hand. Anything is good enough that just works, or that looks right on the surface: the dust in the corner behind the chair, the untidiness under the bed, the heap of rubbish only partially out of sight, the woodwork joining that more or less fits together—these approximately correct jobs are good enough. Indifference is the attitude to one who wants perfection. It would be hard to find another group of people than the Polynesian whose basic drives are so far apart from the value attitudes that have formed the perfectionist drives of the European.

WORK HABITS

Many examples can be mentioned of the Aitutaki attitude: employees in a store are just as honest as their employer is prepared to insist they should be: unless the employer checks and re-checks stock and cash receipts at very frequent intervals the Aitutaki employee assumes that the employer is indifferent and so the employee himself becomes careless and casual about what he keeps for himself and what he recognizes as his employer's property. The employee can be made to be honest by a recognition of externally imposed checks and punishments—but as far as internal controls are concerned he generally lacks them in his personality make-up. Since his super-ego is largely a projected super-ego, lodged in the group and its standards, reinforced by ridicule and shame and public approval, this external super-ego operates in matters of honesty as much as in matters of good workmanship. In the same way workers take a cue from a foreman or leader. If the leader sets high standards, works along with the workers, then his group will respond. If the leader relaxes his vigilance and lets the workers go ahead at their own rate and in their own way then standards of work drop rapidly, ideals of thoroughness disappear, and systematic organization just does not count as important.[1]

Attitudes to property tend to reflect casualness. Money, for instance, is what you spend not what you save. One old woman, hearing that a contemporary of hers had died leaving money in the Savings Bank, was very sorry for the old man. 'This will never happen to me,' she said, as she arranged to withdraw her inconsequential savings from the bank and spend them on a trip to Rarotonga, 'if I have money, I'll spend it and enjoy it now.' Clothing similarly is what you wear, not what you save up for this special occasion or that. If a new dress is required for some event a woman will buy the material, sew up the dress and wear it, but as likely as not she will wear it next day for fishing on the reef or as she huddles over the smoky cooking fire. Then when the dress is dirty and in rags she will throw it away and start the cycle again. As long as one dress is presentable for Sunday church most women are quite happy in dilapidated clothes for the rest of the day and the week. Dilapidation is not due to poverty. Money could be earned to buy clothes. Dilapidation therefore is due to casualness, the very casualness that occasionally strikes a responsive note in the European who finds

[1] One recalls here the cynical statement of an old schooner skipper about his crew, 'First you tell 'em, then you show 'em, then you do the job yourself.'

life unnecessarily complicated by a wardrobe of clothes, the casualness that appeals to the beachcomber rebelling against the rigid perfectionism of his own society, the casualness about the moral code that so often worried the early missionaries when the apparently safely converted slipped by the wayside and relapsed into easygoing ways of life.

Casualness in regard to one's own personal property is not, of course, incompatible with an interest in preserving what is one's own from casual use of this property by others. Thus stealing is universally condemned. By stealing is meant the use or consumption without permission of wealth belonging to another, by a person not closely related to the owner of the property. Among the kin group property is freely usable or borrowed with prior permission or mention after the event. Among others, however, stealing refers either to the appropriation of food or of personal goods. A person steals food because he is too lazy to get it from his own, more distant plantations, or because he is hungry and wants food quickly or from a desire to outwit the owner. Very often, however, stealing of food is hard to detect and difficult to condemn because the 'thief' may be able to claim some right to a piece of cultivated land through distant though obscure genealogical descent, or else allege that last season some related person gave permission to plant food on the land: excuses and subtleties of explanation have no limit so that stealing of food is always disapproved though sometimes impossible to establish. On the other hand the stealing of property, such as pigs, goats, clothing or tools, to which one has undisputed sole right because one made the object or bought it with money personally earned, is universally condemned, and public ridicule or in extreme cases complaints to the police, are considered the only just punishment for such anti-social behaviour. What one earns as the fruit of one's own toil is one's own private property to be as casual about as one wishes: this is the universal Aitutaki rule. But since kinship relationships, widely extended, and lineage descent, deviously traceable, both produce obligations to help one's closer relatives and to recognize the special case of even the most distant relative, the operation of the rule is often subjected to a vague penumbra of doubt which leads the Aitutakian to condemn but not always to seek punishment or restitution.

The basic structure of Aitutaki economic life has not been greatly affected by years of European contact. Economic values are still embedded in a matrix of wider social values, so that for this culture one cannot reasonably think of a separate set of economic values. Work habits are still intimately related to the general cultural attitudes and therefore stem from a basic group psychology that is naturally and naïvely Polynesian. The relationship of the Aitutakian to his major source of wealth, the land, is still a relationship appropriate to a peasant subsistence economy, largely unaffected by such individualistic values as personal thrift, private economic power, individual responsibility for one's own success or misfortune. The relationship to the land is flexible enough to take care of the small interest in cash economy and the small need for money to purchase a minimum of imported goods. To increase the economic wealth of the community and thus to support, even partially, a welfare and planning superstructure, will require a long-term reorganization of the land-tenure system and a basic change in the psychology of the people and therefore in their cultural patterns.

37

Houses

The people of Aitutaki today live in seven villages, ranging in size from just over 200 people to 450 people. Formerly house sites were located on or near to family planting lands. According to Buzacott 'each tribe [household?] herded and slept in one large shed', and since this way of life led, in the missionary judgment, 'to the most reckless and licentious habits of life',[1] the chiefs were persuaded, once the missionaries were settled among them, to make the people live in a township in separate houses. Grouped together in this fashion the people could be more efficiently taught, more effectively persuaded to attend chapel and the deacons could more easily keep the population under surveillance to check moral backsliding. The village houses were either built on land owned by each family or on land rented from owners at a peppercorn rental of 1s. each year. Houses were, and remain to this day, irregularly sited on small or large plots of land, running beachwards or inland from the central roadway that cuts through the village. The only exception to the

[1] Sunderland and Buzacott, *op. cit.* pp. 210-211.

old practice of living near plantations occurred in times of war. Gill, for instance, notes that at times the people lived in fixed settlements either near the sea or in the mountains, 'of more or less concentration, as circumstances rendered expedient for their safety'.[1]

Today, many houses in the villages have coral-lime walls and floors, with roofs of galvanized iron or of coconut thatch. A large number of roofless, uninhabited coral-lime houses are to be found everywhere, some of them partially overgrown with tropical vegetation. These houses have been unroofed in hurricanes and the iron blown away. Shortage of iron and lack of money have prevented the houses from being repaired. Native thatching has not been possible because the native thatch cannot be safely used for a house of width greater than about sixteen feet. The dilapidated houses have generally been allowed to remain on the front of the house lot. To the rear the family has built a wooden frame building with walls made of wooden battens and a thatched roof. Some few families, where the household head has been permanently employed as a storekeeper, for example, or as a teacher, live in European-style houses built on cement foundations with wooden or lime walls and iron roofs. If window glass has not been available, wooden shutters are used to close window spaces in times of high wind. The orthodox design for lime houses has been handed down from early missionary plans. It is not suitable for the climate because window spaces are small and interiors become dark, sunless and airless. Native-style houses are expendable in the sense that they require a good deal of attention and are fragile in hurricanes, even though they may be cool and pleasant to sleep in. A satisfactorily designed house for native peoples that could be built of easily procurable and cheap materials, that would also be relatively secure in bad weather and yet open to sun and air in good weather is urgently needed in most Polynesian islands.

Most houses today are kept clean and simply furnished. A table, one or two chairs and at least one double bed with mattresses and pillows are considered necessary if one is to preserve one's minimum social status in the community. The bed is very often very elaborately dressed with fancy pillow cases, embroidered coverings and padded quilts. It is, however, rarely slept in, since most people prefer to sleep on a mattress placed on the floor. With the increasing use of mattresses, mat making has declined as a home craft. Mats are still

[1] Gill, *Gems*, p. 11.

used as floor coverings but no longer are piles of them required to make adequate beds. Bark cloth manufacture has long vanished before the simplicity and usefulness of cotton piece-goods. Sewing machines are both objects of prestige and widely used. Almost all women's clothes are made by amateur dressmakers using the household machine.

All households still follow the common Polynesian pattern of building and using a separate cooking house. The typical cooking house is a small, low, native-style hut with thatched roof and low walls. An open fireplace is at one end, a few cooking utensils are in a box and baskets of coconuts, bananas and taro lie at the other end. Food is eaten in the hut or on the grass outside. A bore-hole latrine surrounded by a shelter, often in extreme dilapidation, and a shelter for bathing, complete the household lot. For the most part the surroundings of the houses are kept clean and tidy, specially when a rumour spreads that an official is threatening to carry out a public inspection of the village.

38

Clothing

Both men and women wear the *pareu* (the local equivalent to the Malayan sarong) for informal, about-the-household, close-to-the-beach wear. For the rest, women wear dresses, with specially expensive dresses for Sunday church-going. Men wear trousers, occasionally shorts, for working, and in addition, shirts for dress-up occasions. Boys wear shorts and shirts to church, shorts only for everyday occasions and school; little boys below the age of 5 years often wear no clothes at all. Girls wear dresses for all occasions; little girls below 5 years may wear no clothes about the beach or in the house, but will always put on a dress if they leave the house to make a visit. Boys and men have their hair cut short, women and girls let their hair grow. A favourite women's and girls' occupation for Sunday after the return from church and the eating of food is to put on old clothes and spend a useful and pleasant time de-lousing one's partner.

39

The Village Day

After the hustle of getting up in the morning and the children's leaving for their walk to school the village settles down to routine. The women tidy the houses and then drift together for talk, dressmaking, mat-making, other domestic or economic activities. The men go fishing or spend the day at their plantations. Towards the later afternoon, village bustle begins again. Cooking fires are lighted and meals prepared. Children romp and play about the houses, often in laughing, shouting gangs. By sunset many people have found their way to the sheltered lagoon beach. To get a supply of fresh water large holes have been dug out of the beach, or 40-gallon oil drums, open at each end, have been firmly embedded in the sea bottom over a fresh water spring bubbling up through the sea. Horses are brought to drink from these drums. Mothers and young children wash themselves and their clothes in the sea and then rinse with the fresh water. Boys are fishing, elders gossiping. Pigs and ducks are wandering up and down the beach rooting about and snatching food where they can. Other pigs in their enclosures (and officially pigs should not be anywhere else than enclosed) fight and squeal as they struggle for their evening's ration of scraps and coconut meat. Up and down the beach, latecomers are making their way home from plantations, fishermen are mending nets or lines or taking a last fine chip with their adze from a new canoe hull. Darkness sets in and the dark of the moon soon means quietness throughout the village. A full moon and cool evening air mean longer village gossiping. But by nine o'clock the wooden gong booms out curfew. The more devout say family prayers before going to bed. The road and beaches are now deserted. No one may be about after this hour without a torch or light, and then only with valid excuse: calling the doctor to attend a sudden sickness, visiting a dying relative. Those without excuses slip from one house to another, by devious routes that lead from the shadow of trees to the shelter of near-by bushes. At what hour the curfew ends is a matter for dispute. At or before dawn only a known and respected fisherman is allowed to be out and about. Young lads will hurry home with caution and with guile since only the most easy-going village policeman would accept a fisherman's excuse were he to meet them on highway or beach.

40
Households

With the aid of specially knowledgeable informants, a census was taken of twenty-nine households with a total membership of 281 persons. This number is about 12 per cent. of the households on Aitutaki, over 60 per cent. of the households in the village of Amuri. The average number of persons in each household is 9·7, a little higher (almost 10 a household) if one anomalous household is omitted which by chance, at the time of census, contained only an elderly couple. Of this number in each household, little less than half are adults, little more than half (5·3 persons) are children of preschool and school age. About 12 children, or 18 per cent. of the total, are children of unmarried daughters in various households; a further 18 persons are members of the households because they stand in a 'feeding' relationship (the Polynesian form of adoption) to the head of the household. Although the usual Polynesian household is larger than a comparable European group, the figure for Aitutaki is larger than the common Polynesian pattern in other island groups. Whereas the Polynesian household usually ranges from 6·5 to 8 persons, the Aitutakian figure is well above the previously noted highest figure.

The households show wide variation in their composition. About 55 per cent. of them are made up of a two-generation descent group consisting of mother, father and children. A further 14 per cent. includes three generations of mother, father, young children and grandchildren. Of the remaining 31 per cent. of households, the composition falls into no neat scheme. The range is from one household consisting of an elderly couple to another household made up of two adult unmarried children, three school children, one married son and his wife together with the married son's wife's brother, his wife and baby child.

Informants stress the fact that formerly married sons would normally bring their wives to live in the father's household. Thus the expected household would normally be an enlarged household of three generations. This type is today found in only 30 per cent. of the households. Instead, therefore, of forming enlarged households, the island household today seems to be changing to a more European pattern where married sons bring their wives to their father's village, but not necessarily to their father's household, finding it more convenient perhaps to build another house with separate cookhouse, possibly on the father's house lot, possibly elsewhere in the village. This hiving-off may have been initiated by missionary teaching emphasizing both European family patterns as the ideal ones to follow and small households as being better morally than large aggregations. Because of a continuing tenacious Polynesian valuing of descent and descent-group lineage, the hiving-off has not so far resulted in any apparent atomization of families, though it may be of significance that Aitutaki people today talk of their *pamili*—the Aitutaki translation of the word *family*—and mean by this term all immediate close blood members of the two parents, as opposed to the enlarged household of two or three generations, still known as the *kopu tangata*.

Thus the smallest household group is today the *pamili*. These small groups of related persons make up the enlarged group of *kopu tangata* which may include one or more related households. Each *kopu tangata* may be said to constitute a lineage. Each lineage is known by the term *ngati* prefixed to the senior person's name. The same term *ngati* is also used, as will be indicated later, to indicate larger aggregations corresponding to tribal or sub-tribal groups.

The customary form of marriage is today monogamous, though the monogamy may at times be easily breakable. Formerly, according to Gill, the household of chief or sub-chief would contain from three to ten wives 'according to rank or property or renown' of the household head.[1] It is likely, therefore, that aboriginal households would contain many more members than even the enlarged monogamous household of today.

41
Adoption

Adoption of children is common in Aitutaki and follows the widespread Polynesian pattern that a child or infant taken into a household, fed and treated in all respects as a blood-child, is considered

[1] Gill, *Gems*, p. 12.

to be an as-if child of this household, inheriting land, property and status from the new household. Today with the superimposition of a European legal system upon customary usages and therefore with the possibilities open to a person, sometimes to follow the legal system and sometimes custom as best suits his purpose, confusion has been caused by doubt as to whether customary usage is sufficient to validate the inheritance of land by the adopted child. Hence the land courts generally rule that inheritance of property can be recognized only where the adopted child has been legally adopted. Since this ruling is not widely recognized, most households do not favour legal adoption, fearing perhaps that they may never know where matters will end once they get entangled in the complexities of enforceable law. Therefore most Aitutaki adoptions still conform to the customary practice that a child becomes an as-if child because he is fed and cared for, and this relationship should be sufficient to establish just claims to a share of property.

Generally, the adopted child is related by blood to the foster father. If the child is from another tribe or people he must, according to Moss, be formally admitted to his foster family.[1] Such a child, Moss adds, is known as a *tama 'ua*, a thigh child. Contemporary informants felt that unrelated children would only be adopted after much deliberation and with the full formal consent of the two families. Otherwise there might develop endless land claims and disputes. Informants also reserved the term *tama 'ua* for a specially favoured child, a child, in other words, to whom the foster parent shows his interest by constantly carrying him about in the normal Polynesian astride-the-hip fashion.

A child is adopted today for various reasons: because the foster parents are childless or children have become adult and gone to live elsewhere; because the foster parents wish to show affection and respect for close friends by adopting one of the friend's children; because of sorrow for a family in which one parent has died; from grief caused by the death of a blood infant and the desire to comfort the bereaved mother with another infant; finally from pity for an unmarried mother and thus the desire to provide a father for an otherwise fatherless child. Occasionally today a child may be bespoken before it is born, particularly from a mother who already has many children. The foster parents may take the infant at birth

[1] F. J. Moss, 'The Maori Polity in the Island of Rarotonga', *Journal Polynesian Society* (1894), 3: 20-26.

or wait for it until it is weaned. In either case they will provide the birth feast and name the child: a family name, a name associated with some happening at the time of birth, an ancestral name or the name of any object. Many families are very strict about their exclusive rights to family names, and another family may be asked to change a given name if it is felt that the name in question does not rightfully belong to the family concerned. If the foster child is left with its blood parents until weaning the foster parents are expected to provide the blood mother with foods of good quality and with gifts until such time as the child is removed to its new home. Formerly a child bespoken before birth and brought up continuously by foster parents would expect to inherit as would any normal blood child.

42

Kinship

The system of terms used in Aitutaki to classify relatives and kinsmen follows the common Polynesian pattern of being a classificatory system with stratum differences, and additional sex-linked seniority terms for brothers and sisters in one's own generation. Thus the general term for grandparents is *tupuna*, the descriptive terms *tane* and *va'ine* distinguishing grandfather from grandmother. For the parental generation the term *metua* is used, again with the sex descriptive terms of *tane* and *va'ine*.

In ego's own generation a man calls his older brother *tuakana*, a woman her older brother *tungane mua*; a man calls his younger brother *teina*, a woman her younger brother *tungane muri*. A man or a woman will call an older sister *tua'ine tuakana*, a younger sister *tua'ine teina*. A son is called *tamaroa*, a daughter *tama'ine*, a grandson *mokopuna tamaroa* and a granddaughter *mokopuna'ine*. Collateral relatives on both the father's and the mother's side are called by the same kinship terms as are applied to the different stratum levels. Thus a father's sister will be called *metua va'ine*, a mother's brother *metua tane*; one's cross and parallel cousins will be given the same kinship terms as are applied to members of one's own generation in one's own family.

The kinship group functions psychologically in providing for members of the group a warm matrix of personal relations, the majority of them positively loaded with emotion into which the individual is able to fit with security and certainty. Economically the group provides support through its control of land and thus the basis for the food supply; since food and gifts are the important means of validating status security, the kinship group stands behind the individual in all those activities upon which his respect and security in the community at large depend.

Within the group the two important organizing principles are seniority in age and respect for the male from the females. Seniority, age and sex combine to give a person his standing in the kinship group. Of these three factors, seniority as determined by the principle of primogeniture and sex are the more important. In fact Aitutaki is basically a 'seniority' society, not a social-class society as all Polynesian communities are often thought to be.

43

Tribal Organization

The formal structure of tribal organization is clear in its main outlines. Household groups either singly or combined with closely related household groups form lineages; lineages combine with related lineages to form sub-tribes; sub-tribes combine to form a tribe or *vaka* under a supreme chief or *ariki*. The tribe is generally known by the name of the first male ancestor who led the ancestral group to Aitutaki or Rarotonga or to other islands. In Rarotonga there were in 1823, and still are today, three such tribal groups, each group being thought of as owners of different districts in the island.[1] Moss has noted the manner in which the *ariki*, normally the supreme chief of his tribe, depends for his installation in office upon the *mataiapo* or sub-chiefs of the tribe, and in his decisions and activities is largely controlled by the *mataiapo*.[2] This control of the controller by a group of sub-chiefs probably represents a Polynesian pattern for preventing, in some islands at least, the absolute corruption that

[1] J. T. Large reported in 1892 that the Makea, Tinomanu and Tangiia tribes of Rarotonga were made up of twelve, eight and twenty-eight sub-tribes respectively, making a total of three major tribal groups and forty-eight sub-tribal groups. See, in this connection, H. Nicholas (translator), 'Genealogies and Historical Notes from Rarotonga', *Journal Polynesian Society* (1892), 1: 20-29, 65-75 and *ibid.* (1893), 2: 271-279.   [2] Moss, *op. cit.*

comes from absolute power. The Tikopian system of using complementary officials or sub-chiefs to act as adjustors between men of high rank and their people is an obvious parallel to the Rarotongan and Aitutakian pattern.[1]

In Aitutaki there are four principal tribal groups. According to tradition the original migration that settled Aitutaki had one supreme *ariki*, Te Tupu o Rongo. After settlement and the spreading out of the population into districts, the three first-born sons of the *ariki* by his first three wives were allotted chieftainship over three of these districts, the fourth chieftainship being assumed by a Rarotongan chief who married the oldest daughter of the supreme chief and who returned from Rarotonga to lend his support in some island fighting. Thus today four villages and four districts are headed by *ariki* chiefs descended from the original lineage lines. The supreme chief today is the senior member of the lineage derived from the first-born son of the principal wife.[2] Gudgeon notes that each tribal group formerly possessed a special tattoo mark that was tattooed on the body, occasionally on neck, wrist or legs (but never on the face), often on tribal ornaments and on garments, the purpose of which was 'to preserve the descent of each family by giving each member thereof the proof of his descent on his own person'.[3] These tribal descent marks are unknown today, and it is rather unique for any Polynesian tribesman to be so unsure about his tribal descent that he should need tribal symbols tattooed on his person to remind him of the tribe to which he belongs.

According to Rarotongan authorities each Rarotongan tribe consisted of four defined social classes. The simplest exposition of this system is probably that given by the Rarotongan chief Pa Ariki, in explaining the relation of chief to land, to a group of visiting New Zealand legislators (April 28, 1903). Pa Ariki said in effect: The

---

[1] Raymond Firth, 'Authority and Public Opinion in Tikopia', in M. Fortes (ed.), *Social Structure* (Oxford, 1949), pp. 168-188.

[2] The traditional history of Aitutaki is briefly summarized by P. H. Buck, *Vikings of the Sunrise* (New York, 1938), pp. 97-106. According to another authority, the *mataiapo* of Aitutaki trace their descent back to twenty chieftainesses who came to the island with its first discoverer Ru, sometime before A.D. 1000, while the *ariki* trace back their descent to the chief Ruatapu who lived about A.D. 1350. See D. Low, 'Traditional History of Aitutaki', *Journal Polynesian Society* (1934), 43: 17-24, 73-84, 171-186, 258-266 and *ibid.* (1935), 44: 26-31.

[3] W. E. Gudgeon, 'Origin of the Ta-tatau or Heraldic Marks at Aitutaki Island', *Journal Polynesian Society* (1905), 14: 217-218.

ariki owns his land. Under him are the younger members and cadet branches of the kingly family called *rangatira*, with their own subdivisions of land. The power over the *rangatira* is with the *ariki*. The *mataiapo* are the younger cadet members of the *mataiapo* family who are called *komono* (or sub-chief), owning land under the *mataiapo*, and again *kiato*. The *mataiapo* controls both *komono* and *kiato*. The 'small people', the *unga*, stay on the lands and acknowledge the over-lordship of the chief or sub-chief by making food, and other, contributions to the chiefs whenever these are called for. The 'small people' were the rank and file of tribal fighting, now the fishermen and cultivators of the soil. If the contributions are not forwarded after a period of three years of asking then the tenant is assumed by the chief to have vacated the land and another tenant can be given the land to cultivate. Tenants' land will be divided into blocks that range in size from two to five acres depending upon the situation and boundaries of the various divisions and subdivisions. In sum, the supreme district chief is the *ariki*, the *rangatira* owing allegiance to him by blood. The *mataiapo* are independent chiefs, owing traditional allegiance to, and responsible for the choice of, the *ariki* of their district. Sub-chiefs of *komono* and *kiato* status owe direct blood allegiance to the *mataiapo*, indirect traditional allegiance to the supreme *ariki* of their district.[1] The fact that chiefs of *mataiapo* status possessed lands in their own right and were not dependent as tenant chiefs upon the supreme chief gave them much power in Rarotongan society, even the power to elect and control to a large extent the supreme chief of the district in which the *mataiapo* owned lands. It is not improbable that the Rarotongan *ariki* was the Cook Islands version of the more generalized Polynesian type of sacred or divine chief, the *mataiapo* thus being the secular or executive chief, corresponding in status and in some functions to the Samoan talking chief.

Aitutaki informants believe that aboriginal Aitutakian society was not marked by a class system as rigid as that of Rarotonga. They are of the opinion that, functionally at least, the Aitutaki system was so tempered by a widespread knowledge of kinship relationships, that land ownership became associated with every branch of

---

[1] Pa Ariki's exposition is to be found in New Zealand House of Representatives, *Appendices to the Journals* (1903), vol. 1, A-3B, pp. 9-10. See also Appendix B to this report on *Social Distinctions, Rarotonga, ibid.* p. 42; Moss, *op. cit.* p. 21, may also be consulted together with Nicholas, *op. cit.*

the Aitutaki *mataiapo* families (both senior and cadet) and that therefore there were no landless commoners or tenant cultivators on the island, but only groupings of lineages in which each person considered himself the social equal of other tribal members, though on occasions the senior members of the group would receive specially large food distributions, for instance, out of respect for their seniority in descent.

It is not improbable that Polynesian social-class structure was blurred in its outlines not only on Aitutaki but elsewhere in Polynesia where smallish populations on small islands intermarried continuously from one generation to the next and where the result was, if not one happy family, one band of brothers, at least a group in which everyone was so intricately related to everyone else that patterns of functioning equality were more believed in than ideals of class structure. Even the happy Polynesian facility of forgetting, on the small islands, some of the kinship relationships more than three generations back in order to avoid infringing any incest or other tapus, did no more under the circumstances than make marriage possible—it would do little to break down both the idea and the fact that all members of the island group were really so closely related to the chiefly lineages that a rigid social-class structure became impossible to sustain.

This interpretation of Aitutaki society is also born out by a remark of Moss about Rarotongan feudalism. After defining rigid social classes Moss adds, 'but intercourse between persons of all classes was, and still is, marked by the most perfect freedom'.[1] Perhaps confusion over the nature of a Cook Islands class system is partly a matter of focus and therefore of emphasis. If one studies the problem by approaching it from the point of view of chiefly status and feudalism one ends with the impression of a rigidly structured social system. If, on the other hand, one asks how the system can operate, one notes the Aitutaki insistence on the fact that there were and are no commoners on the island and no family ever paid tribute to a chiefly group. Thus theoretically the Cook Island system was one that conformed in ideal pattern to the system prevalent in Tahiti or Hawaii or in New Zealand. Practically, however, in the Cook Islands, status could not be sustained and seniority society, not a class society, became the society that actually operated on a day-to-day basis.

[1] Moss, *op. cit.* p. 21.

44
Warfare

In the high islands of Polynesia with their concentrations of wealth and population, warfare was endemic; elsewhere on the low islands and the atolls, where material resources were poor and population pressure only at times acute, warfare was epidemic, almost cyclical, with the major function of releasing pent-up aggression. In Rarotonga early authorities all mention the fact that up to the time of European contact war to the people 'either offensive or defensive, was their continual employment and delight'.[1] The principal causes of war, again according to Gill, were: trespassing over tribal land boundaries; trying to recapture absconding wives; stealing from plantations; trying to revenge former wrongs and insults; the desire for human flesh to supplement a monotonous chiefly diet. Although it is hard, at this date, to form a judicious opinion as to the actual amount of fighting that went on, since one has to rely almost exclusively on missionary accounts which, being written by persons with a natural and normal desire to magnify their own success in turning the people from ways of darkness to those of light, tend to be biased in favour of increasing the intensity and amount of warfare, none the less it is probable that warfare had become by the time of missionary contact so onerous and fear-producing that the people were glad of excuses to divest themselves of an institution that weighed so heavily on their psychic shoulders. All the more so because of the martial metaphor and imagery of much Christian teaching, which offered a substitute satisfaction to the early converts to Christianity. Warfare was originally organized on a tribal district basis. With the gradual elimination of warfare, tribal importance was decreased. The sporadic fighting between Christians and pagans that marked the penultimate phase of group conversion was organized more on an ideological than a tribal basis. Subsequent Christian fanaticism, another substitute for aboriginal aggressiveness, was also ideological. Thus the final triumph of Christianity was marked by a decay of tribal importance. Today, village organization of activity on Aitutaki is stronger than appeal to tribal sentiment as a motivating force in social integration whether for work or for play.

[1] Gill, *Gems*, pp. 12-13.

45

Village Activities

The Aitutakian is no exception to this generalization that can be made about all Polynesians: they are never so happy as they are when sharing the satisfactions and psychological support that come from group membership. The Aitutakian likes to rub shoulders, quite literally, with other people in a group. The physical contact that comes from being closely packed in a crowd, leaning closely against other persons, walking with arms round another person's shoulders, whether the other person is of the same or opposite sex, amounts almost to a craving, if frustrated. Thus village-organized activities, either for work or for play, provide major satisfactions for the Aitutakian, male or female, young or old. Work organization has been noticed in another section of this report. Here mention can be made of a village organization for play that fits into this general pattern of the importance of village, as opposed to tribal, activity.

The principal type of village-organized play may be termed circuit dancing, and occurs each Christmas Day and for one or two days at New Year. May Day circuit dancing is church organized. Sometimes the several villages on the eastern side of Aitutaki combine to provide a dancing team and then alternate their dancing circuits with villages from the western side, so that one group dances on one day, the other group on the next day. The dancing team consists of about fifty young women and ten men. The women are all dressed in frocks of the same colour. Men and women wear flower leis round their heads. Each group is accompanied by a deacon or other elderly leader good at speech-making, village elders and old women, together with a percussion band of young men. The dancers proceed from village to village, forming a dance group in each village, either on a cleared open space, or in the middle of the village road. Dancing goes on for an hour or more. The dance rhythms are very fast, the songs sung being specially composed for the occasion. The dance will last for half a minute or so, then there will follow a minute's rest, then the dance again, the whole being repeated time and time again. The home folk dance in a confused mass in front of, and facing the lines of visiting dancers, so that there is a maximum of physical

VILLAGE ACTIVITIES

contact, pushing and shoving at the end of each excited spasm of activity, together with wild shouting and noise-making.[1]

In the rest pauses between dances home folk contribute money by throwing small coins on the ground before the elderly 'treasurer' of the dancers' group. Occasional large contributions of, say, a one-pound note will be made only after a short speech enables both visitors and home people to realize who the generous person is. At the conclusion of the whole dance the local leader formally thanks the visitors for their display and hands over a further money gift. Then the visiting leader makes a speech of thanks, which is followed by hymn-singing and praying before the visitors organize themselves to move on to the next village. As much as £12 may be collected from one village, up to £50 collected on the circuit, the amount varying with the prosperity of the island and the novelty of the dances, the skill of the dancers and their capacity to whip up the local folk into a frenzy of excitement in which pockets are emptied of money freely and quickly. At Christmas and New Year the collected money augments the funds of the village sports' association and will be later used by this association to build or repair a village hall or to entertain visitors to the village from another island.

Throughout the dancing older home people sit about placidly on the grass or stand gossiping idly. Infants sleep peacefully in their mothers' arms. Older children romp and play about on the outskirts of the dancers. An occasional broadly sexual allusion in the dancing will cause amusement to the onlookers. A half-drunken husband tries to kiss another woman and speech-making is punctuated with the verbal abuse by his wife. Above all is the rattling insistent goading rhythm of wooden gong and high-pitched tin. The dancers sweat in the heat and the dust rises from their stamping feet, but none relaxes and the excitement is relished by a people that easily explodes into emotional outbursts that can be intensified to a high degree by noise, rhythm and physical closeness. Hymn-singing and prayer at the end provide a sort of safety valve that slowly brings the people back to an everyday level of feeling. The finish of the day finds everyone tired, relaxed and happy. The collected moneys become a tribute to

[1] Belcher's description of the Tahitian dance applies equally well to the Aitutaki technique of dancing: 'It is merely a display of extraordinary activity, the acme of which is an instantaneous and simultaneous stop when at the highest pitch of exertion. It is what may be termed a romping dance '. . . but the dancers of Aitutaki do not chase about or break ranks, they dance all the time in lines and files. E. Belcher, *Narrative of a Voyage Round the World*, 1836–1842 (London, 1843), vol. 2, p. 9.

the prestige of the dancing village and further increase this prestige when used later for building or for entertainments.

During certain seasons of the year inter-village sporting events are a characteristic feature of island life. As part of New Year celebrations village competes against village in canoe racing on the lagoon. At other times cricket, football and the game of throwing wooden discs called *pua* not only absorb village interests but are means for working off internal and inter-village tensions. Such tensions are always latent in a Polynesian island, due partly to the close physical and social contact involved in village life, partly to the fact that, until recently for most islands, isolation from the outside world tends to magnify the importance of social frustration to a greater degree than it does social satisfactions, and partly to the fact that the intense emotional life of the islander, held in check mainly by a projected social, and not a deeply internalized, super-ego, tends easily to flood over into outbursts of activity if tension fails to be kept in check by continuing social satisfactions. Thus village organized sports lower tension by providing frequent and approved means of emotional catharsis.[1] If internal tension is not lowered the result will be a proliferation of internal village disputes or squabbles between villages that sometimes result in institutional schisms. Thus, about thirty years ago, the people of Amuri village were involved in controversy over whether their wishes were being given due weight in the building of a new island church. They also thought they were being asked to contribute more than their fair share of money to church funds. The controversy could only be resolved by Amuri people withdrawing from island church organization and setting up their own Free Church of Amuri, financed by 1s. a month levy on each Amuri household, with their own pastor (self-trained) and church building. At about the same period other tensions within the island church led to the establishment of Roman Catholic and Seventh Day Adventist churches. Neither of these two churches, however, is on a village basis and in neither of them is membership

[1] One is reminded in this connection of an observation made by Gudgeon at the turn of the century. Writing of the people of Aitutaki he says: 'Their chief employment ... would seem to be chronic disputes over the succession of intestate estates and the appropriation of coconuts and other produce from the more energetic portion of the population, who in order to better their condition, have attempted to cultivate the land ... the tribes of Aitutaki are worth looking after, though exceedingly turbulent.' W. E. Gudgeon, 'Report on Trade and Social Condition, 1901–1902', New Zealand House of Representatives, *Appendices to the Journals* (1902), vol. 1, A.-3, p. 49.

at present very large. Formerly it is probable that such disputes and tensions would have become involved in personal insults and slights, chiefly prestige and village honour and would have been resolved only after desultory island warfare.

46
Village Leadership

In aboriginal times chiefs and *mataiapo* sub-chiefs were the natural leaders of tribal and village groups. This pattern of leadership has continued throughout the period of contact, but has gradually become attenuated and weaker. Chiefly leadership in Aitutaki has gradually given way to the leadership of village and island pastors in spiritual and moral matters (though the Cook Island development has never given the extreme secular and religious power to island pastors enjoyed by the pastors of village churches in Samoa), and to the leadership of elective officials in most political matters. Thus, each Sunday evening village meeting on Aitutaki is generally 'presided' over not by the tribal chief associated with the four *ariki* villages, but by the person elected to serve on the island council. These island council representatives can be elected for all seven villages from either chiefly or commoner families. Again in the recent controversies that led to the formation of the Cook Islands Progressive Association (an indigenous political movement with a vague programme of welfare and reform), two elected representatives to the Association were, one of them, a person with an unclear claim to be the next supreme chief of one island, the other a New Zealand Maori, of no rank, not long domiciled in the Cook Islands. Both the representatives, however, were men of frustrated ambition, both by personality make-up were of the 'against-all-authority' type (except naturally their own authority), and both therefore the sort of leader normally chosen in times of controversy and agitation. None the less the people were seemingly quite content with non-chiefly leadership in a way that would seem quite impossible to a people like the New Zealand Maori with their continuing strong tradition of chiefly control over tribal affairs.

The present acceptable type of island leadership in Aitutaki therefore is the inevitable result of missionary policy operating over many years on a relatively small island population. Early missionary effort in Rarotonga and Aitutaki was devoted to controlling the power of the chief so that it could be used for spreading Christian morality and theology. With subsequent dethronement of the Church from supreme control to a position of one institution among many in the island social system the power of the chiefs tended to be whittled down in a similar degree. If present trends continue, Aitutaki chiefs will be sentimentally regarded only. Effective power will have been transferred to an electorate for some occasions choosing its own leaders, and at other times having its leaders chosen by a distant Administration.[1]

47
Marriage

Marriage has two social functions in Aitutaki. First, it marks an end to the previous period of post-adolescent premarital experimentation. After a thorough exploration of the cultural gamut of free sociosexual intimacies, a young man takes what an informant called 'a real fancy to a girl and decides to settle down'. Second, marriage initiates a series of gift exchanges which become both the incentive to economic production and the social validation of new kinship relationships and obligations. When parents think vaguely of their desire for grandchildren they are likely to take the first step towards arranging a marriage for their son.

There are thus two socially approved ways of starting a marriage relationship. A boy will ask his parents to approach the parents of the girl he wishes to marry. The parents will do this willingly if they approve of the girl, unwillingly if they yield in the end to the importunities of their son, though they disapprove of the girl. On the other hand, an older social practice is followed by parents: they decide on a suitable time for the marriage of their son and on a suitable partner. The matter is discussed with the girl's parents and the marriage arranged. Dutiful sons and daughters accept the arrangement. Others revolt against the choice to be forced on them or against having to make any choice at all when they are still too reckless to

[1] Note that the summary just given refers particularly to Aitutaki. As will be suggested later, the status of superior chiefs on Rarotonga is much more secure and firmly established than that of the Aitutaki chiefs.

wish to settle down with a single partner. The rebel then marries the parents' choice, but makes no pretence of being faithful to his wife, or else he elopes with a girl he prefers to his parents' choice. Though the term elopement is often used by informants in referring to these unapproved marriages, the actual eloping is more metaphorical than a literal 'running away' or absconding. The eloping couple are pretty well thrown on their own resources and have to start a new household, without the respect, acceptance or help of either set of parents. Such marriages often prove extremely brittle and are cracked by divorce in a short time. A civil registry marriage is most likely with eloping couples. Such a ceremony is recognized today as legally binding but is not generally approved as a basis for marriage.

An approved marriage always takes place in church. The wedding day will be one suitable for both sets of parents. Three or four days before the ceremony the groom sends a gift of one or two cooked pigs, together with a sack of flour or loaves of bread and biscuits to the bride's parents. This gift is a contribution towards feeding helpers who are called on to prepare the wedding feast. Generally the community is expected to help the young couple as well. On the day before or sometimes on the morning of the marriage the groom hires or borrows a truck, loads it up with friends and the bride, a drum and tin cans and then drives slowly through each village with much shouting, drumming and noise-making. The people of each village come to their doors and throw money gifts into the back of the truck, generally sixpenny and shilling pieces. The amount of money thus collected depends on the popularity of the young couple and the relative prosperity of the times. Somewhere between £2 to £12 would be a usual collection. Since Aitutaki economics can now not function except on a part-money base, money collections of this kind are made at deaths and on village-organized occasions. The collections both enable large groups of kinsmen or the community to help bear a private burden and also help symbolize the close-knit integration of the individual with the structure of community life.

After the church marriage, the groom returns with his bride to his own household, since marriage is by custom patrilocal and descent patrilineal. The marriage feast is provided by the groom's family. His relatives bring gifts to be included in the formal marriage gift exchange and in return take away pieces of pig, loaves of bread, and baskets of food after relatives of both groom and bride have eaten the marriage feast of pig, chicken, fish, yams, breadfruit, soft drinks and cake. For the gift exchange, the groom's family provides such gifts as frocks, food, money, dress lengths, whereas the bride's family provides plaited mats, fancy bedspreads, mattress, pillows, shirts and other male clothing. The majority of these more personal gifts are retained by the young couple but some of them will be shared out between the relatives on both sides. This 'spreading out of gifts' as the Aitutakian phrase goes, will take place at the time of the marriage feast or writ for some days or weeks. Everything depends on when the exchange gifts are ready, but no family could retain community respect if it failed to go through with a gift exchange and distribution. The lavishness of the marriage feast and the number of exchanged gifts will depend on the prosperity and status of the family groups concerned. Informants believed that an ordinary wedding might cost the two parties from £30 to £40. To put this amount in perspective it has to be remembered that the average yearly household income for Aitutaki in 1947 was about £60.

The pattern of marriage has changed little, if at all, over the past 100 years. Thus Gill describing Rarotongan practices of the 1850's notes that at that time proposals of marriage were made by letter, by confidential friend or in person to the parents of the girl. The marriage feast varied in amount and variety 'according to the stations and subsequent property of the parties'. Somewhere between 100 to 1,000 each of coconuts, bananas, breadfruit, from 20 to 100 fish and from 2 to 200 pigs would be displayed, eaten and divided among assembled guests together with appropriate amounts of bark cloth, mats, baskets, piece goods, bowls, stools and cloth-beating mallets. Food and durable goods would be exchanged between the two parties, the bride ordering her gifts to be distributed among her relatives, the groom the gifts he received among his kinship group.[1] Thus the marriage pattern is unchanged, only some of the objects themselves have changed to those more appropriate to present-day life.

48
Sex Relations in Marriage

The pattern of sex relations in marriage is probably very similar to middle-class European practices. The prone-supine position with the man above is normal. Newly married couples have frequent sex

[1] Gill, *Gems*, p. 54.

SEX RELATIONS IN MARRIAGE

relations, older married people tend to have sex relations about three times each week or perhaps more frequently in the first week after menstruation, thereafter less frequently during the rest of the inter-menstrual period. Married sex relations take place in the sleeping house at night. It is against principle that children should observe or listen, hence children are expected to be asleep at this time and other adults sleeping in the same room are expected politely to pay no attention.

Informants believe that physical sex incompatibility is very rare among Aitutakians. On the other hand, some believed that Aitutaki marriage is characterized by a patterned lack of faithfulness that has increased over the past fifty years. Marriage relations are accompanied by much jealousy. If men wander to other women because of a desire for novelty, then wives will often be unfaithful in order to spite a wandering husband or to teach him a lesson. Whereas formerly a marriage was customarily broken by one partner leaving the household and living with someone else, today a legal divorce is increasingly sought from the Courts if money can be scraped together to pay legal charges. Formerly also children of a broken marriage customarily remained with the husband's family. Today bargaining about the children may often result in a division between mother's and father's families. The chief causes of divorce are unfaithfulness and pronounced social incompatibility. The Aitutakian is likely to flare up easily with an emotional outburst if close and continuous social relations result in frustration. Thus physical brawls and violence are far from being unknown among married couples. They occur most commonly when a wife refuses to obey a command from her husband—the only resort left to the husband seems to be physically beating his wife with a hope that thus he will secure compliance. Certain families in some villages are well known in the community because of the frequent use by their men of violence to their wives. As two children phrased the matter to their mother after casually enumerating the names of all the married couples in the village who were known occasionally to fight each other, 'You and Dad are really the only married people in this village who don't fight with each other'. When married couples find more frustration than satisfaction in marriage, a break will readily occur, all the more readily because no stigma, beyond mild disapproval at the most, is attached to those who fail to make a success of marriage. So complaisant is the community to those who fail to live happily married that informants merely metaphorically shrug their shoulders when mentioning the two instances known to them of 'married couples' consisting of father and daughter. Incest is of course not approved, but the Aitutakian would just rather save himself the trouble involved in determined social disapproval which might lead to someone having to do something. As long as the surface of the pool is smooth the Aitutakian sees no point in fishing for trouble in the depths.

49
Pregnancy

Marriage in Aitutaki is almost inevitably followed by pregnancy. Contraceptives are not used and many dislike using them. Thus, when the United States Armed Forces evacuated their garrison from the island at the end of the second World War, the medical department left behind boxes of sheaths. These were given freely to older married women who complained of having too many children and wished for a rest from child-bearing. The women reported that their husbands refused to use the contraceptives, giving as their own additional justification: 'Why, in any case, should my man waste his seed?'

Natural abortions are not uncommon among elderly married women, especially towards the end of their child-bearing years. Criminal abortions are uncommon. They occur very rarely among unmarried girls, and only occasionally among married women tired of continual pregnancies. The only methods used are prolonged massage and reliance upon folk gossip about the efficacy of this medicine or that. It is believed that formerly native medical experts possessed a knowledge of drugs or herbs which were capable of contracting the uterus, but this knowledge is now lost or highly secret since it is a criminal offence in the Cook Islands to practise native medicine and no one will openly prepare or prescribe herbal remedies for fear of prosecution.

The usual signs to diagnose pregnancy are the failure of the menstrual period for two to three months, morning sickness and a general feeling of being unwell. Personal distaste for certain foods previously liked and cravings for other foods, in particular raw shell fish, are signs of a well-advanced pregnancy. Few know how many months have passed since conception and no one worries about fixing a probable birth date. When the baby begins to fall then a guess is made that birth will occur within a week or so. No preparations are made for the birth of the child. The reason given is that the baby might be born dead and therefore it is a mistake to prepare for an event that may end in disaster.

The local Cook Islands medical practitioner sees only about 50 per cent. of the pregnant women and he attends a delivery only if complications are suspected or evident. The majority of deliveries are quite natural, no help being required other than that provided by local native midwives, either men or women. Sometimes the husband assists; or else a man who has a reputation in the community for skill and knowledge. The man's job is to sit behind the parturient woman and provide physical support; whereas the woman kneels in front and helps with massage. Four to five women of the family sit round to give moral support, words of good cheer and miscellaneous bits of advice. Knowing that something of interest is about to happen, children hover around. They may be chased away because they are in the way, but they come back to peer through cracks in the wall or through the door. As one girl aged six years expressed herself off-handedly: 'A cat having a baby is just like a woman—there is blood and a mess everywhere.'

Delivery takes place inside the living house, in any convenient room that is cleared of bedding or furniture. If it is thought that the delivery is proving difficult, the midwife will massage the patient's abdomen with coconut oil. This oil is also applied frequently during the pregnancy months because it is believed to prevent the skin becoming too taut. Most women worry if labour pains last longer than twenty-four hours, even though this may often happen with a first-born, and will therefore often try to force a birth under these circumstances by the use of oil massages and intermittent pressure on the fundus. The cord is not tied until after the placenta is delivered. Therefore the midwife is concerned to force an immediate delivery of the placenta, and to this end will often apply extreme manual pressure, sometimes causing great pain and bleeding. After the placenta is delivered the cord is tied with thread and cut with any instrument available. The placenta will be buried anywhere, occasionally a stone being placed to mark the spot, or else it will be thrown into the sea. In Rarotonga, among the chiefly families, the placenta is buried in the garden in front of the house and a small stone (like a miniature gravestone) is set up on the spot. In weeding or digging these front gardens informants remarked, one continually knocks against these placenta stones, but the old people remembering whose placenta the stone marks, object to the stones being removed. They are thought still to be highly tapu.

The midwife rubs the baby gently with oil and then wraps it in clean rags. The mother is cleaned up and immediately or a few hours later is bathed with hot water in which guava leaves have been steeped. This water has an astringent effect. Fish, baked or cooked in coconut cream, is considered the ideal food for the nursing mother since it is believed to help the flow of milk, and she will be fed this dish very frequently. The mother is allowed to take things easy for a month or more, though this practice is more honoured with first children than with later children.

Colostrum is thought to be bad for an infant so the child is given water or a laxative mixture until milk comes. Thereafter the child is allowed to suckle whenever and wherever it wishes. The nursing mother is supposed to avoid highly flavoured foods like pork, shell food, taro leaves and pineapples, and to concentrate on a bland diet which it is thought avoids upsetting the infant's digestion. A mother is never given cold water to drink, always warm water, to avoid an attack of chills.

In a brief note on Aitutaki birth customs Low records several customs not known to my informants: draping the shoulders of a girl just married and during pregnancy with bark cloth 'marked in a certain way', so that the girl would be observed at public meetings and her condition known—according to Low, 'a form of showing off by the parents of the girl'; holding a special feast for the first-born boy or girl who, known as a *mataiapo*, is looked up to by the members of its own generation as the head of the family group—a feast for a first-born is common today, with the gift-givers rewarded by a food-distribution; and on the fourth night after the birth of a first-born, the husband should have sex relations with his wife in order to help her make a quick return to full strength. Low also says that a baby, 'in olden times', was never fed more than 'three times a day and once at night—never more than four times' in each twenty-four hours.[1] But this last statement is highly doubtful, since the practice of restricted feeding would run counter to widespread Polynesian attitudes and would be construed as a form of cruelty.

[1] D. Low, 'Birth and allied customs in Aitutaki, Cook Islands', *Journal Polynesian Society* (1943), 52: 199-201.

50
Infancy

A child is suckled as long as it wants to, up to a year or well past a year as the child feels inclined. An older child may wish to suckle early in the morning or at bedtime or on other occasions when it sees its mother's breasts—as may happen frequently in the informalities of an Aitutaki household. Neither child nor mother will be embarrassed by a long-continued suckling period. If the health of the mother is not good, or another pregnancy occurs during infancy, then the child will be fed by a wet nurse or artificially fed with canned milk or custard apple juice or more recently with goat-milk. As soon as a child shows interest in solid foods, perhaps by the age of six months, it is given such food as sweet potatoes or fish cooked with coconut cream, but it will continue to rely on its mother's milk at least for a night and morning meal. By the age of one year most children have weaned themselves through the natural process of growing up. A child may continue to suckle occasionally just for comfort, or a mother may encourage a child to suckle, just because it gives her pleasure. Or again, an older child jealous of an infant sibling, may seek love and affection from its mother's breast. In this last instance the older child may be mildly teased or ridiculed, but it will be allowed its satisfaction and comfort notwithstanding. A well-qualified informant could recall no instance of a native child being a finger- or thumb-sucker, nor was thumb-sucking recognized by mothers as being a behaviour problem; the same informant had seen thumb-sucking in mixed-blood families and is inclined to interpret the habit as being due to the practice of the European father's insisting that the native mother limit the suckling of the child to adult-fixed intervals and rhythms.

All Aitutaki infants are handled, petted, nursed, carried around for much of each day. The crying infant is picked up, suckled and carried until crying ceases. Any clean rags are used as diaper-like wrappings, or else the infant is allowed to sleep on a pile of cloth or rags. Fathers take a good deal of responsibility for their infant children, particularly for a month or two after birth or when an old woman is not a household member. Thus the father will not only assume responsibility for getting the right foods for his wife, he will also often attend to the infant at night, soothing it if it cries, changing its bedding and the like.

There is no toilet training, in the accepted meaning of the term training, for the Aitutaki child. The adult attitude is one of complete permissiveness to the crawler and partly to the toddler who are allowed to relieve themselves in or around the house as inclination moves. If bedding is wet by the child up to three years, it is put outside in the sun to dry, without comment. Enuresis in older children is unknown. By the age of three or so, the child has learnt control largely through the natural process of development and later developmental crises do not disturb the reflex control thus securely established.

51
Age Grades

The process of growing up in Aitutaki means a slow passage from one age grade to another. From birth to old age the people recognize eight age rankings. In order these are: infants, *pepe*; the very young, 'toddlers', *pepe varevare* ('lacking reason'); little children, *tamariki rikiriki*—from two to five years; children, *tamariki*—from five to ten years; big children, *tamariki lalai*—about ten to fourteen years; young men and women, *mapu*—after male circumcision at the age of fourteen years; people in middle years, *mapu pakari*; older people, *tangata metua rua'ine*.

In each age grade the principle of primogeniture operates in Aitutaki, as elsewhere in Polynesia, to give special status to the first-born in a family or household group, and extra-special status to a first-born male. Low has recorded that formerly, for a first-born of a family of rank, the mother and father, child and close relatives proceeded to the family religious structure, the *marae*, six days after the birth of the child. Mother and child were carried on a wooden seat carved from a solid block of *tamanu* wood. After setting down the mother and child in the centre of the *marae*, the father made a speech recounting the family history, illustrating his theme by a number of family chants, and promising so to train the child that it would be fit to carry on the family traditions. The father then named the child and those assembled ate food.[1] Today *marae* meetings are

[1] Low, *op. cit.* p. 200—presumably the food being *noa* or common, would be eaten away from the tapu *marae*. Informants were aware of the family ownership but added that today the *marae* were no longer sacred, and few, but the very old, would hesitate about lighting fires or eating food on old *marae* sites.

of course no longer held and no church celebration has been substituted. But the status of the first-born is still validated by a family feast, and this feast will often be repeated for the second-born, if the first-born is a girl, and the second a boy. Similarly through the growing-up period, the eldest born boy will be accepted as the natural leader of a children's group; he is given preferences and privileges above the other children in the family; he will get most of everything for his marriage, the remaining children being treated with lesser effort.

Today also, special attention is given by the father to the naming of his first child. This naming takes place at the church baptism. The name is generally chosen from the father's family; only if the mother is of especially high status would she be allowed to suggest a name from her own family, and more often this would occur for later children rather than for first-born.

One further sign of status is still occasionally attached to first-born boys. The father may decide not to allow a first-born boy's hair to be cut until somewhere between the ages of 14 to 20 years. When his hair grows uncomfortably long, the boy will put it into plaits. His school fellows and friends will respect him for the honour being done him even if they remain secretly glad that they themselves are just ordinary boys. A large feast is planned, and the materials accumulated over a long period, for the day when the hair is formally cut off. Relatives and friends assemble each with scissors and they take turns in clipping off pieces of hair. The clipped pieces are kept as souvenirs of the occasion and the feast eaten and distributed among those present. The length of the boy's hair and the size of the feast are both taken as signs of the family's status in the community. Informants were unclear as to the significance of this custom apart from the fact that it was related to the status of the family and its first-born son. But the dynamics must derive partly from the common Polynesian attitude of thinking the head sacred, and partly perhaps from the fact that the father, through this custom, may be symbolically thinking of his first-born favourite son as a girl, since a boy with his long hair in plaits is sometimes outwardly difficult to distinguish from a girl.[1]

[1] Possibly he is unconsciously following the custom of confusing the appearance of a boy with that of a girl in order to ward off the influence of malignant spirits —a custom known both in contemporary Baghdad and shown in some eighteenth-century Windsor portraits of the children of Frederick, Prince of Wales. See *Times Literary Supplement*, no. 2857, November 30, 1956, p. 717.

52

Growing Up

Soon after the child reaches the age of one year, it will be passed over to the care of grandparents if it is a first child, thus enabling the parents to devote more time to domestic duties, gardening, fishing and social activities. The grandparents continue a permissive system of discipline in which great freedom is allowed the growing child. Sometimes the infant has spent most of its time with grandparents from a very early age onwards. In both cases the birth of a second child to its parents will cause little or no jealousy in the first-born. On the other hand, if the first-born is brought up by its parents then the birth of a second child will arouse aggressive jealousy. The older sibling will often smack the younger child or push it aside and try to take the mother's breast for itself. Parents are likely to show both amusement and annoyance at the behaviour of the older child. They will respond with laughter and ridicule, perhaps tease the aggressive child by appearing to show more affection for the baby. Alternately and intermittently they will coddle the older child with large amounts of affection. It is unlikely, however, that the older child will be seriously distressed for very long by jealousy nor will he feel forsaken and dispossessed. Soon he will be a member of a children's gang and will be ranging far and wide from beach to gardens and back again, thus living a life of pretty free and fascinating independence.

Parents agree that whether sibling jealousy becomes acute depends also partly on the preferences that parents themselves show towards their children. A child will more readily identify with its father, for example, if the father takes a fancy to his child, because this will mean that the father will handle the child more than usual, caring for it, playing with it and carrying it about. If, on the other hand, the father shows little interest in his child then the mother becomes the central figure in the child's life and close identification with the mother will be important until the child's gang claims the child's activities. In general, parents discipline their children by threats of beatings (but threats are rarely carried out) and what informants call 'tongue lashings'. Occasionally, however, the rather thin self-control of the Aitutaki parent breaks down under continued disobedience by the child and then the parent is liable to resort to rather severe physical beatings in order to enforce his commands. A wife who tries to shelter or protect a child at this time or who interferes with advice often receives a physical beating as well—as if anger, once broken loose, knows no restraint until exhausted by violent physical attack on any or all frustrating persons in the immediate environment.

In already established families the toddler normally passes on to the care of the older children of the family. Both boys and girls from the age of 5 or 6 onwards act as nursemaids. The younger child sits or plays near the older children as they engage in their group fun; or else the younger child is carried on the hip and the older goes from one part of the village to another. The mother, either casually or conscientiously depending on her temperament, sees that the toddler gets food and a daily fresh-water bath. Otherwise most supervision falls on the older children. Sometimes frustrated older children will mildly slap a toddler for disobedience, but generally they use ridicule and shaming in order to secure obedience to their wishes. The Aitutaki child therefore in the years between 2 and 5 sleeps when it likes, plays when it likes, eats when and where it likes (sometimes in its own home, often at a relative's house if food is being served and the child is hungry), goes to concerts, parties or the occasional cinema if it wishes to. The day is golden and the night too and childhood has its own freedoms and only its simplest disciplines, because the controlling thought on the part of both parents and older children is that if a child wants anything badly enough to make a fuss and if what it wants is not, broadly speaking, harmful, then let the child have what it wants: food, or sweets from the store, or visiting when the parents visit. A child crying for something that is not 'harmful' will readily break most parents' resistance. The sort of ego that is built into the child under these conditions is one that results in much basic security though not a great measure of self-control; emotions are intense, though not deep and are liable to break through into overt behaviour if frustration is long continued or impulse becomes strong; anxiety induced by frustration is close to the surface and can be readily drained off by aggressiveness or, later in life, by the use of alcohol; the opinions of one's peers as expressed in ridicule or contempt carry great weight, so that being ashamed or the avoidance of shame becomes a crucial factor in making decisions; authority is looked upon as benign and as controllable if one is persistent enough with supplications or bequests.

53
The Middle Years

The middle years of childhood and onwards to the period of early adolescence are marked by a continuation of the slow natural process of growing up. Today, the child from 5 onwards spends a good part of each day at formal schooling, but the sudden curbing of a previous life of careless freedom and independence is cushioned by the knowledge that schooling is what older boys and girls naturally have to do, and by listening in on the fringes of schoolboy groups to interesting stories of school life. Having built up favourable expectations the child is thus better able to adjust to the frustrations of routine school work.

Outside of school the child is still allowed much freedom, but he gradually participates more and more in adult activities: fishing, gardening, bringing food to the home from distant gardens, household activities and the like. These tasks are always carried out in association with older boys or girls, with relatives or parents and they are often both exciting and interesting.

For the boy the middle years come to an end rather abruptly with the operation of circumcision, carried out at about the age of 14 years, often on a group of age mates from the same village. Formerly, according to Low[1] the age of circumcision was 18 years or after; the instruments were of shell and coconut shell; after the operation the boys were treated each day for three weeks by the application of a hot stone and bandages of bark cloth soaked in coconut oil together with leaves of the *rau-pipi* plant; two weeks after the operation the boy had intercourse in the belief that this would help the wound to heal rapidly and cleanly. Today, a much more matter-of-fact attitude prevails. A community expert operates with a knife or razor blade, the boys then bathe in the sea and afterwards go to the hospital nurse or dispenser for regular dressings. No boy in Aitutaki could today easily bear the shame of being known to his friends or to the girls as an uncircumcised youth.

The sex education of the Aitutaki child is largely directed to two ends: one of these is to teach the child modesty, the other is to frown upon overt heterosexual activity in children of the middle years. Grandparents or parents often in their play with infants or

[1] Low, *op. cit.* pp. 200-201.

very small children lightly kiss the child on the genitals—but this is thought of objectively as just part of the fun of playing with a baby. Except when playing on the beach or in the lagoon older boys habitually wear short pants; girls wear at least a dress even if swimming and even if it has more holes in it than material. Thus boys and girls will be taught the minimum amount of modesty for mixed groups by ridicule: a boy appearing without pants in a mixed play group (not a swimming group) will be ridiculed about his black scrotum or warned to keep his genitals covered for fear of something biting his scrotum. The occasional child who plays with his own genitals is mildly reprimanded by his parents, but without fuss or anxiety.

Heterosexual experimentation by boys and girls of school age is generally disapproved by parents and teachers, and if persisted in would be punished. Yet children of this age are fully cognizant of the physiological facts about sex through study of animals and through their interest in older girls who are visited clandestinely in the house by boys. The general attitude of parents seems to be one of disapproval for precocious sex activity, whereas during and after adolescence nature is expected to take its own course. In general, adolescence is a period of low pressure and little difficulty as far as adjustment to the maturation of the body is concerned.

There is a somewhat conventional double standard of sex morality for adolescent boys and girls in Aitutaki today that is believed in by parents but little followed by the boys and girls concerned. This double standard is supported by the Church although it is most probable that in old-time society less experimentation was allowed girls of chiefly status than was permitted young people of common families. Today parents say that they wish their adolescent daughters to remain chaste until marriage. They may beat their daughter if they discover her with a boy whom they dislike, but if they approve of the boy then they generally pay no attention to the affair and will privately confide to friends that it is good for a girl to have experience before she settles down to marry. The girl may finally marry her fifth or her eighth or her tenth boy; so long as the daughter's affairs are not complicated by pregnancy, they are thought of as private and not public business. Pregnancy in unmarried girls of the 12 to 15 years of age group is rare—partly due to natural adolescent sterility reinforced by anxiety—and is likely to occur only when after a period of experimentation, the girl settles down to a steady partner. If a girl becomes pregnant, however, her parents are likely to fuss, particularly if the father occupies some prominent position in the Church, a deacon's position, for instance, or is noted for his assiduous professions of piety. A lapse in the moral standards of his family reflects upon his own status and in endeavouring to bolster up his status, the father is likely to take extreme measures. These are usually directed towards persuading the parents of the boy to force him to marry the girl or else, if the boy's parents do not agree, then informing the police that the boy is guilty of a crime of cohabitation with the expectation that the Court will fine and imprison the boy.

Forced marriages generally turn out to be unhappy marriages, since the boy feels that he has been trapped and does not alter his ways just because he is legally tied to one girl. Thus his married life is punctuated by affairs with other young girls, and by violent quarrels with his wife or her parents. Perhaps in his early thirties such a boy may finally settle down and come to terms with his fate.

From boys a different standard is expected and it is just assumed by parents and the community that the boy will sow a largish crop of wild oats. He is the unlucky one if he gets involved in a premature marriage or in a court cohabitation case. Most boys are lucky, however. A girl known or said to be a virgin will prove irresistible to the majority, and the boy who first associates with such a girl is able to boast of his trickery or skill or good luck among his fellows. A girl will generally make a fuss if a boy or gangs of boys whom she does not like try to have sexual relations with her (thus she may acquire a boomerang reputation for being virtuous). Perhaps a boy will try to hide himself in the girl's sleeping room or else skulk in the bush near to the house, hoping to sneak into her room after the household is quiet. Most girls dislike the midnight intruder, since his actions may sometimes be indistinguishable from rape and as one informant added, 'It is so easy for the raper to steal other property as well as he fades away in the darkness'. Incidentally a young man caught hiding near a house with a presumed intent to enter a girl's room will not only be frightened by police interest, he will also be publicly named and ridiculed at a Sunday evening village meeting. Girls naturally have many opportunities to meet boys whom they like: coming home from the beach, at singing meetings or parties. Once a girl accepts a boy as a steady partner and this fact is known to the girl's parents, the boy will often visit the girl's house at night, leaving early the next morning before the household is astir. Or else the two will meet regularly at a friend's house.

Adolescent sex customs may be summarized by saying that there are cultural contradictions between a desire to keep girls chaste and a feeling that not only must young boys be allowed freely to experiment (and this in a society where prostitution is normally unknown) but also the young man who does not experiment is subject to much suspicion and expected to become an unfortunate woman-hunter in later middle-age. It cannot be said that many young people feel the contradictions very keenly, however much parents strive to preserve an outward semblance of morality. Young people assume that sex relations are interesting, exciting and satisfying—perhaps more exciting because there are parents and police to be outwitted. Thus pre-marital relations are normal for all young people. It is doubtful whether this freedom makes for more happy marriages. Only statistical tests could indicate whether informants' opinions about the high incidence of unfaithfulness among married couples are correct judgments and if so, whether there is a significant relationship to be analysed between Aitutaki adolescent freedoms and later behaviour in marriage.

Homosexuality is an unknown practice in Aitutaki. Only two instances of berdache-like behaviour could be recalled by informants. Two adolescent boys gave up fishing and gardening in favour of women's work and acquired a high reputation in the community for their skills at housework, embroidery and mat-making. One boy ultimately married and adjusted to a man's role, the other left the island and settled elsewhere.

54
Sickness and Death

The ancient native ideology of sickness was based on a belief that most sickness was due either to an avenging god or else to the curse of one's enemy. There were certain exceptions. Thus yaws, the only indigenous infection, was believed, according to Lambert, to have been originally an inherited disease, limited to certain families who were notorious eaters of human flesh, but later disseminated through the population by intermarriage. Again tuberculosis, dysentery, typhoid and gonorrhoea were simply accepted as inevitable and given no accepted native explanation. Of leprosy and filaria, however, Lambert notes that there were formerly two generally believed theories. One, that these two diseases were sent by gods because the patient had broken the tapu against lighting fires on one's own family *marae* or else one had desecrated the *marae* of another family. Two, that these diseases could be willed upon the patient by a person himself infected through contact with the patient's clothes, utensils or food, and this willing or cursing was often motivated by revenge or punishment: revenge upon a rival in love or upon an unfaithful wife, punishment by a father for laziness or disobedience in a son or sexual immorality in a daughter.[1] Early authorities also note the use of sorcery to cause diseases or death. Thus Buzacott describes a technique where a sorcerer is employed, by a person who has been robbed, to burn the spirit of the thief in the hot embers of an oven. The sorcerer was paid for his services, the thief either died or became seriously ill. Sometimes the sorcerer himself was speared to death before he completed his job by the person against whom the sorcery was supposed to be directed.[2]

Today there are significant differences between different age groups in beliefs about sickness. It is probable that in the over-50 age group, many still believe that sickness is caused by curses, whereas in the under-50 age group a very small number believe in a curse ideology, and this number would include those who for various reasons were closely identified with older people in the community. The majority in the younger age group to all intents and purposes believes in a simple theory of germ infection.

Informants are able to describe a case of curse infection in the following terms: 'A son of 30 quarrels with his father aged 50. The son strikes his father as the quarrel becomes heated. The father then curses his son: "I put this curse on you: you will get sick and die and you will not have any children by your wife." If at any later time the son suffers injury or sickness then this is caused by the curse.' So far as informants know, sorcery to implement such a curse is not practised today. The curse depends for its effect upon vague understandings about the efficacy of curses (probably always implemented by sorcery) in aboriginal society together with a feeling that if a son strikes his father then this is such an outrageous act that it ought to be punished psychically even if it is not legally punishable.

[1] S. M. Lambert, 'Some Polynesian Medical Superstitions encountered in the Cook Islands', *Journal Tropical Medicine and Hygiene* (1933), 36: 189-192.
[2] Sunderland and Buzacott, *op. cit.* pp. 55-56.

SICKNESS AND DEATH

Supporting a belief in the psychic causation of sickness is the practice of using confession as an auxiliary aid to the treatment of disease. Older persons often suggest to the Cook Islands medical practitioner that confessions be allowed as part of treatment. When no objection is raised the sick person is treated by both the principles of European medicine and a half-surviving native ideological practice. Relatives come together over the patient's sick bed and urge each other to confess sins of omission or commission. This confessional treatment is used as much for those in the under- as in the over-50 age group.

Considering the general ideology of sickness, over 100 years of contact have resulted in the majority of the community accepting for the most part a germ theory of infection. A spirit theory, however, is accepted by a community not only because it offers a plausible theory of sickness but because it also enables persons to displace onto a world of malevolent spirits much internal aggression. The problem of controlling this aggression is one reason why people have difficulty in learning to substitute a germ theory for a spirit ideology. It is not improbable that aggression which was once displaced onto spirits or mobilized and checked by fear of sorcery is in native society today being dissipated through substitute channels. Two channels that probably function in this way today are release of aggression through fermented bush beer and the unconscious use of petty and interminable family squabbles.

When sickness ends in death, it is the job of relatives, even of the village as a whole, to comfort the mourners by assembling with them until the corpse is buried and cheering them up by singing dances, songs and hymns. Formerly relatives would shout from the time of the death until the following morning, or as long as the body was in the house.[1] Today relatives and friends gather, each bringing a money gift of 1s. to 5s. which is pooled to pay for food for a feast to relatives, helpers, carpenters and grave diggers. For a small funeral, only relatives and friends wail and sing. For a mourner of status or

[1] Surgeon Andrews of H.M.S. *Ringdove*, who made the health survey of Rarotonga in August 1893, reports that the principal cause of the very prevalent chronic laryngitis ('it is rare to meet with a native whose voice is not hoarse, or peculiarly harsh and strident') was the custom at 'obsequious' (*sic*) and other ceremonies of young people singing for several nights on end 'with only short intermissions during which they take such refreshments as tea, coconut-water, or orange beer, and biscuits . . . it is after a death or some other important national event that the singing is conducted with most spirit and energy'. Andrews, *op. cit.* p. 19.

for the death of an important person, village-organized groups of singers come together. Two groups, perhaps, display themselves one on either side of the main door of the house. One group sings, then the other, and alternately a spokesman for the relatives gives a small money gift to each group-leader, thanking him and his group for their kindness in coming together and cheering up the waiting hours of the mourners. The money thus collected is later divided among the singers and may amount to sixpence a person. The amount of money that each singer receives is inconsequential. More important is the fact that although the mourners may be cheered, or even flattered by the attention, none the less they are placed under an obligation, on the pain of being ashamed if they disregard their obligation, of returning food for the attention. A modern money economy makes it possible on some occasions to compound food for money, but the amount of money still remains less important than the reciprocal filling of an obligation. Sometimes for an important funeral a feast may be given to all those who assemble. This feast is usually tea and bread, and the money collected is used to buy the store foods required. A pig or pigs are also killed and distributed as payment to carpenters and grave diggers.

Formerly a body was buried anywhere the survivors chose—in the household lot, in the bush, by the roadside. Small churchyards surrounding the island church were at one time popular but are now full to the limit with graves. Most roads between villages are lined with graves; the box-like coral lime tombs are in many cases half lost in overgrown vegetation. The administration today discourages house or roadside burials, but some still insist in having memorials of their dead close by. Others, however, bury on their plantations. Once the sand settles a tombstone is built on the grave. The completion of the tomb becomes an appropriate time to kill pigs and distribute the cooked meat to all those who brought money gifts at the time of death.

55
Religion

The numerical strength of the various religious groups on Aitutaki and Rarotonga in 1945 and 1951 is given in the accompanying Table 10. With the exception of those few persons in the two islands who belong to the Church of England and those few who object to state their religion, practically everyone on the two islands is a member of one of the four principal religious groups. As befits its historic role in the islands, the London Missionary Society church

TABLE 10

RELIGIOUS PROFESSIONS, 1945, 1951

	Rarotonga		Aitutaki	
	1945	1951	1945	1951
London Missionary Society	4,658	4,868	1,911	1,538
Roman Catholic	316	425	145	143
Seventh Day Adventists	292	358	189	299
Congregational	—	—	86	296
Latter Day Saints	29	137	—	73
Other	—	8	—	9

Source: Population Census, 1945, 1951.

claims the largest membership. The group on Aitutaki, known locally as the Amuri Free Church, are pure Congregational, a break-away group from the local L.M.S. congregation. The three later-coming groups, Roman Catholics (introduced into Rarotonga by the Picpus Fathers in 1894), the Seventh Day Adventists and the Church of the Latter Day Saints (established in Aitutaki in 1950), are all small but fast-growing church groups.

Church-going remains an absorbing Sabbath occupation for the people on both islands. Morning and afternoon services are well-attended by the people dressed in their best clothes. It is probable, however, that for most, religion has by now become a customary observance, an occasional stimulant to the emotions, and not a deeply felt practical guide to behaviour. Because the Cook Island missionaries did not adopt the Samoan practice of admitting to church membership only married people, but have always admitted adolescents, the problem of adolescent church members living the free-and-easy premarital life of the islands has always proved difficult to solve, except by suspension and consequent disgrace of the girl and her parents. Thus the London Missionary Society church while remaining a strong, socially integrative force in island life, has done this at the cost of unconsciously fostering a dual standard of morality, specially for the young. At the present time, only the Seventh Day Adventists carry their religion over into practical affairs to the extent of teaching such skills as home hygiene, English, improved planting and cultivation, carpentry, type-writing and sewing to their church members. The result is that whereas the London Missionary Society and Roman Catholic churches emphasize, in general, religious and moral training (with, of course, the inevitable associated schools on Rarotonga), Seventh Day Adventists try to improve the economic and social skills of their members, whether child or adult.

The churches on Aitutaki still continue to provide a status system within which the individual can gain status advancement, either by working up within the status system of the one church, or else by changing church membership, hoping to secure a higher status (even if only the status of novelty) in the new church than he possessed in the old. Historically, when the early missionaries put a stop to warfare, they froze the status system of each island. On Rarotonga, for instance, each tribe and sub-tribe had made use of warfare as a means of increasing, if possible, its own status by defeating other tribes and thus establishing a position of superiority in the island inter-tribal status system. Christianity, by forbidding warfare, made impossible any change in the relative positions that the tribes of Rarotonga had achieved for themselves in the 1820's. The status system within each tribe was very largely based on seniority and primogeniture. This system was not disturbed by the new religion, with this exception that whereas warfare had made it possible for an occasional warrior, if not of too lowly status, to increase his power and influence in the tribe by successful exploits and bravery in war, Christianity, by stopping war, at first, and for a time, blocked any possibility of a person achieving by his own skill and capacities a higher place in the internal tribal status system.

However, with the establishment of a church on each island, the way was immediately opened for a reorganization of the island status system. Thus, having initially blocked the operation of mechanisms of social change in aboriginal social life, the church as an institution offered a new series of mechanisms as a substitute for the old. The new system was composed of a hierarchy of statuses through which any person could laboriously try to push himself: from the status of pupil through those of candidate, member, senior member, deacon, native teacher, deacon-policemen, perhaps judge, with always the possibilities of being detected in 'sin' and thus falling quickly down and out of the hierarchy by being given the status of suspension or excommunication. Mobility in the new status system was open to all. In some respects the prizes—secular and spiritual power over one's

RELIGION

fellow islanders—were greater than in the old warfare system; the difficulties in the way of securing increased status were at least as great as in the old and the chances of defeat were many. The aspirant had against him a whole army of fellow church members banded together as policemen—as late as 1892, one police to each fourteen people in Aitutaki—with powers of 'snooping', searching, prosecution, fining, extorting confessions, that were almost unlimited. A person therefore who managed to secure high status in this church-state system was either a very good person, or constitutionally a very weak-impulsed individual, or else a very clever person, or finally a very lucky person. The stakes of the game were high, the play exciting, the fall of the person who lost very low. No wonder that the aggressive fanaticism of the Polynesian found plenty of delight in the system, which thus became almost a parody of William James' moral equivalent of warfare.

Although the relative status system of each tribe or village as compared with every other was pretty well frozen by the coming of the missionaries, survivals of former tribal struggles for increased status, or at least struggles to avoid lower status, occasionally broke through the otherwise frozen surface of the social pond. Thus in 1849 on Rarotonga Pitman had trouble with '20 or 30 unsteady youths led by an apostate years ago excommunicated for adultery and trying to divide the people so that another settlement might be formed away from the church' (L.M.S. B.22, F.2, J.A.). Amid great excitement, threats of war, brandishing of old weapons and violent words, the secessionists were finally allowed to move to a new district and build themselves their own church. Again, the villages of Vaipae and Tautu, on Aitutaki, were formed by secessionist groups which felt that they had been so bitterly aggrieved and disappointed in the struggle for those island offices of governor and police which gave power, financial wealth and marked social superiority that no recourse was left but to move as a group to another part of the island.

Those tribal groups on Rarotonga that had profited by the religiously motivated status-freezing were most loth, naturally, to allow any subsequent disturbance, whereas the tribes which believed themselves to have been unluckily treated in the new system were always likely to be the thorniest, most sensitive groups to deal with, and those finding it most difficult to co-operate in island government. Thus, following the trouble in Rarotonga in 1895 when the Takitumu tribe proposed to choose as their new chief a person not directly related by blood to the old chieftainess, the other Rarotongan chiefs saw this departure as a threat to the status system of the island and to their own positions as heads of this status system. Again there was collecting of weapons and rumours of war, only resolved in the end by the chiefs prevailing upon two wise old men to draw up a *Report on the Succession of Arikis: the Mode of Election and Installation.* This report clearly states that it is the job of the priests, the *mataiapo* and the *ariki* of Rarotonga as a whole to decide on succession to a vacant title, should the priests and *mataiapo* of the district concerned not have chosen from 'the nearest relations of the Ariki deceased'.[1] Thus, the position is established that any paramount chief of a particular district is only *primus inter pares* among the priests and *mataiapo* of that district, and that, secondly, any paramount chief must be acceptable to the other tribal chiefs of the island before his claim to chiefly power and status could be recognized by his equals on the Ariki Council of the Island. In this fashion inter-tribal status, as fixed by the Christian theocracy, was given the minor safety valve of secession and the final rule of succession to fix the system as a regulatory status system for the whole of Rarotonga.

The church-defined status system was a system that substituted for the war system, but on the other hand it was complementary to the ascribed status system defined by birth and primogeniture. It was an achievement system that paralleled the fixed chiefly status system. The Rarotongan missionaries appear to have supported this chiefly system, unlike John Williams in Rurutu, who seems deliberately to have tried to break down the chiefly status. Thus, in a letter to the London Missionary Society Directors of January 2, 1829, Williams writes: 'At ten o'clock we entered the chapel, taking care to avoid the common practice of allowing the king to enter first. This is a heathen custom founded on superstitious notions. They look on the place of worship, as they did on their maraes and canoes, as very sacred, and imagine that the king must enter first, to remove the great sacredness, before other persons dare go in.' Another point of contention in the Rurutu chapel was who should occupy the king's seat. Williams did not like the idea of a special seat being set aside for the person in authority, so he persuaded the king to sit among

---

[1] The report was adopted by the Ariki Council of Rarotonga, as a guide to the settlement of the 1895 and any subsequent disputes. It is given in full as an enclosure to Moss's despatch to the Governor, November 18, 1895, New Zealand House of Representatives, *Appendices to the Journals* (1896), vol. 1, A-3, p. 27.

the people and some of the under-chiefs to occupy the sacred seat of the king, Tamatoa the king being complaisant enough to accept all Williams' suggestions.[1] It is probable that Williams's Cook Islands brethren were less egalitarian and not at all social iconoclasts. A nobleman was to them a nobleman, a king remained a king, whatever his colour, only provided he be a Christian.

Although being a church deacon today no longer carries with it the perquisite of being a policeman, and therefore very little secular power, none the less the position of deacon is one of influence and respect in the community. Within the church therefore a status system still operates which appeals to the islander and enlists all his enthusiasms and energies. It may not be far from the truth to say that of the church's dual function, the status-serving function may be more alive today than the function of controlling, other than superficially, the religious and moral beliefs and practices of the island community.

[1] Prout, *Memoirs of the Life of Rev. John Williams, op. cit.* p. 285.

PART IV

WELFARE, PSYCHOLOGY AND SOCIAL CHANGE

56
Welfare and Development

IN considering problems of administration, welfare and development in Aitutaki one inevitably moves focus from the needs of one small island to the needs of the Cook Group as a whole. Aitutaki is part of the Cook Islands racially, economically, politically. Its needs and its development are, and must be, geared to those of the larger socio-political unit of which it is one small dependent member. Therefore in the present section of this monograph one must discuss the general social and political problems of the Cook Islands, knowing that the greater includes the less, and what applies to the group as a whole applies in great measure to Aitutaki itself.

Social and political problems are problems just because no ready-made solution to them is apparent. No ready-made solution by the application of rule-of-thumb empirical procedure is available (except by pure luck) because prior thought has not always been devoted to the question of ends. When policy is finally decided some problems can be readily solved, and for the more obstinate ones, a way of solution is at least indicated, even if the finished answer is not immediately available. Thus in evaluating present-day social, economic and political problems in the Cook Islands, the prior policy that must be first decided is quite simply: what is the political future of the Cook Islands, and what therefore is its economic and social future?

At present the Cook Islands are an integral, territorial part of New Zealand. Legally, therefore, the people of the Cook Islands are not dependent peoples in the sense that they occupy dependent or colonial areas, subject to the government and goodwill of a metropolitan power. Legally, it would seem that they are not wards of the New Zealand government, but citizens of New Zealand. Yet they are citizens with a difference, since, although in general the laws of the Cook Islands are the same laws as those that control the lives of New Zealanders, enactments of the Parliament of New Zealand do not automatically come into force in the Cook Islands unless specifically applied to the Islands. There is no representation of the Cook Islands in the New Zealand House of Parliament. The nearest analogue to the relationship between New Zealand and the Cook Islands is probably to be found in the relationship between France and her dependent peoples, though the analogy does not apply in all respects.[1]

The question of whether the Cook Islander was to enjoy all, or only some, of the benefits of New Zealand laws and conditions, since the islands were going to become part of the colony of New Zealand, was answered at one moment in the House of Representatives debate on Annexation by Seddon the Prime Minister, with the one word *No*, and a few minutes later by the one word *Conditionally*. No wonder a puzzled member interpreted Seddon's words as meaning that 'we are going to have within our realm a varying law—one law to suit one section, and another law to suit another section'. Seddon did not bother to clarify the matter in subsequent debate, so impatient was he to get the annexation settled. Something of this initial puzzlement and uncertainty has clung like a fog to all subsequent attempts to clarify the political relationship between the Cook Islands and New Zealand.[2]

Seddon always appears to have had in mind that after annexation the Cook Islands would be given representation in the New Zealand General Assembly. In his Memorandum to Ranfurly, Governor of the Colony, suggesting the extension of the boundaries of the colony, Seddon stated that 'provision could also be made, as in the case of the Maoris, for electing one or more of the natives from each group to the House of Representatives, and for one or more of the high chiefs being appointed to the Legislative Council of New Zealand'.[3] In the debate on Annexation the proposal was rephrased: 'I think we may reasonably concede them a representation in our Parliament . . . they should have one member representing these islands who would come to the House of Representatives and have one nominated, who would practically be a European [sic] and represent the European interests in another branch of our Legislature.'[4] Seddon concluded by remarking that this might be a debatable point. No member debated the question. It appears to

[1] See Lord Hailey's article on 'Britain's Future Colonial Policy', *Listener*, vol. xl, No. 1022 (1948), pp. 291-292 and E. Beaglehole, 'Good Government and Self-Government in the South Pacific', *Proceedings, Seventh Pacific Science Congress* (1953), 4: 77-83.
[2] New Zealand Parliamentary Debates (1900), vol. 114, p. 402.
[3] Seddon to Ranfurly, New Zealand House of Representatives, *Appendices to the Journals* (1901), vol. 1, A-1, pp. 5-6.
[4] New Zealand Parliamentary Debates, *op. cit.* p. 392.

have been quietly forgotten, though a watered-down version of the proposal appeared two years later in a report by C. H. Mills, Minister in Charge of the Cook and Other Islands Administration: 'As our social, fiscal and commercial relations become more closely interwoven, however, the cardinal principle that there should be no taxation without representation will have to be applied in the islands, and legislation passed to meet the case.'[1] No legislation has ever yet been passed to meet the case. When the Cook Islands Amendment, Act, 1946, was passed, however, suggestions were advanced in official quarters that maybe the time might arrive when further consideration would have to be given to the question of Cook Islands representation in the New Zealand General Assembly. But there, fifty years after Seddon's initial suggestion, the matter still lies.[2]

Whatever may be the legal technicalities of the present relationship of New Zealand to the Cook Islands the question still poses itself: What is the future political relationship? The future seems to hold at least three main possibilities. The first is represented by a policy whose main aim would be the gradual advancement of the Cook Islander in social and political affairs so that in the near future he would be fit to assume the rights, privileges and responsibilities and obligations of full citizenship in the New Zealand Commonwealth. A modification of this possibility would involve a continuation for a long period of the present semi-wardship status, without precluding but deferring, an ultimate citizenship status. The second possibility would be that of encouraging in the Cook Islands the development of a minority national group with fairly full political independence but bound by economic, strategic and political ties to New Zealand. As a third possibility there is the path which might lead to full economic and political independence, ultimately to an independent sovereign legislature, but always subjected to the protection of New Zealand—a 'protected state', in other words, on the model of Tonga, or as Samoa is likely soon to be. Of these three possibilities, it is not improbable that New Zealand will favour the first, the completer incorporation of the Cook Islands in the New Zealand state. Thinking Cook Islanders would probably agree that this is the most likely outcome of their own political and social development, but

[1] New Zealand House of Representatives, *Appendices to the Journals* (1903), vol. 1, A-3B, p. 34.
[2] E. Beaglehole, 'Government and Administration in Polynesia', in *Specialized Studies in Polynesian Anthropology*, B.P. Bishop Museum, Bulletin 193, Honolulu Hawaii (1947), pp. 62-64.

nostalgically, they would also probably cast a tear of regret into the wide Pacific that the second or third possibilities could not be realized. Assuming therefore that the first possibility of advancement and incorporation is realistic, how may present social and political trends in the Cook Islands be evaluated and what developments seem appropriate in order more quickly to turn a possibility into accomplished fact?

57

Administration

In aboriginal island culture there was no formal administration of island affairs. Social life was organized and regulated by patterns of culture and custom that everyone believed in and all explicitly followed. The forces of public opinion as expressed in ridicule and shaming and sheer personal inertia were sufficient to ensure a reasonable amount of conformity when individual desire came into conflict with accepted custom. Chiefs were accorded deference, power and respect. They were able to organize larger-scale enterprises such as warfare and their power, dependent as it was, on the goodwill of kinsmen and fellow tribespeople, was generally used to obtain the maximum social cohesion.

Into this culture came the missionary and the whaler and the trader, all purveying new ideas and new goods, all explicitly offering the challenge of a new way of life and standards of behaviour that conflicted radically with the old. The missionaries rapidly realized the need for an administrative organization that would protect their own interests as well as the interests of the natives, and at the same time act as an arbiter or umpire between the interests of the natives and those of the trader. The mission theocracy was the outcome of this need. Passing years have brought more complicated problems and the union of all the islands into the Cook Islands administrative unit has finally led to an administration that has four functions: a protector, an arbiter, a provider, a planner for future needs.

In Aitutaki, as on all the individual islands, these functions of administration are carried out by a Resident Agent, an administrative staff of medical practitioner, nurses, policemen, postal clerks, agricultural foremen and the like (assisted from time to time by

ADMINISTRATION

supervisory visits from professional personnel from Rarotonga) together with an elected island council. The majority of the senior administrative officers on Rarotonga and elsewhere are white New Zealanders, local islanders (and some few Europeans) being employed in subordinate positions. Broadly speaking, Aitutaki and the Cook Islands are administered by Europeans, islanders carrying out only local routine duties.

The island council of Aitutaki consists of a representative from each village, elected by a showing of hands from all adults, 18 years and over, at a public village meeting, and coming together at regular intervals under the chairmanship of the Resident Agent to discuss matters of concern to the island as a whole. Minor revenues are raised by the council with such taxes as a horse tax, a licence fee on all stores, a motor vehicles tax, an occasional motion picture exhibitor's licence fee and wharfage. The money thus raised is not great in amount. In 1946 the amount in the island exchequer was about £300, in 1947 about £170. The money is used for island affairs, for instance, in the provision of entertainment to the sailors from visiting warships, or in providing food for those working on the roads or to provide materials, at rare intervals, used in building a new village water tank.

The duties of the council are not onerous and it is doubtful whether the council makes any significant contribution to the political education of the islanders. According to some observers, the people of Aitutaki have lost the ability and interest to initiate and sustain what may be thought of, broadly, as welfare activities. They have become rather passively dependent on orders or policies, handed down to them from the administration; reserving to themselves the right to co-operate or to criticize as they think fit, but not often adopting enthusiastically as their own, projects which may be wise but which may require effort to carry out. The old-time chief probably acted as a galvanizer after securing the assent of his people to a proposed activity. With the loss of power by the chief no one nor any group has taken the place of the chief. The island pastor is interested in spiritual, not material welfare. The Resident Agent has a multitude of administrative duties. The powers and interests of the island council are hardly such as to fit the council to take an active and vigorous lead in, for instance, mosquito control or economic developments. In order to secure more lively interest by the islander in his own welfare it is probably necessary to start with the grass roots and organize producers associations and co-operatives—learning the responsibilities of group life by first learning how to be responsible members of organizations with limited objectives—and secondly to provide island administration with an executive assistant to the island council and Resident Agent—a trained islander with the capacity and the job to organize co-operatives and other groups so that policy can also be worked out at the bottom as well as being initiated from the top. If such an executive assistant were given, as part of his training, some of the basic skills involving modern techniques using group discussion and group decision as methods of removing resistance and barriers to change, if, in other words, he were keenly aware of the fact that you cannot do things to people, or for people, but only with people, then a basic training in political and social responsibility would be well under way. This training would serve the people well in their social and political advancement.[1]

In order to co-ordinate matters of relevance to the Cook Islands as a whole, the Government of New Zealand passed the Cook Islands Amendment Act, 1946, which provides for a Legislative Council of the Cook Islands, thus reviving the administrative body, but with a different composition, that functioned under the British Protectorate,[2] but which lapsed in 1912 when its administrative activities, though not its grass-roots educational function, were virtually absorbed by the Island Council of Rarotonga, the latter thus becoming in effect an Executive Council for the whole group. Membership of the present Legislative Council consists of ten unofficial members elected by the Island Councils (three islanders and one European from Rarotonga, one islander from each of Aitutaki, Mangaia, Penrhyn, Manihiki, Atiu and Mauke) and ten official members, namely, the directors of education, agriculture and health services, the treasurer of the administration, the Resident Agents from the above six islands, and finally the Resident Commissioner of the Cook Islands, who is the president of the Council and has a casting but not a deliberative vote. According to official records the second (1948) session, 'was very successful, and many

[1] Useful summaries of some successful modern techniques of initiating responsibility are to be found in the following articles: G. W. Allport, 'Psychology of Participation', *Psychological Review* (1945), 52: 117-132; K. Lewin, 'Group Decision and Social Change', in T. M. Newcomb and E. L. Hartley (eds.), *Readings in Social Psychology* (New York, 1947), pp. 330-344; E. Jaques, 'Field Theory and Occupational Psychology', *Occupational Psychology* (1948), 22: 126-133.

[2] See Moss, *op. cit.* pp. 25-26, and the previous account given in Part II.

useful and constructive recommendations were made. A notable feature was the active part taken by the unofficial members both in general debate and in submitting proposals for the general welfare of their islands. Two Ordinances, the Manufacture and Sale of Food Ordinance 1948 and the Building Ordinance 1948, were passed. The establishment of the Council is universally regarded as marking an important stage in the political development of the island',[1] a development, it would appear, that picks up the threads of the later nineteenth century and carries on after a lapse of forty or more years.

It would seem that important as this development has been, it could be made more important still were more courage and faith used in planning the composition and functions of a Cook Islands Legislative Council.[2] At the moment the Council may be thought of as a representative but not a democratic organization, whereas if the people are to make advances towards the goal of full New Zealand citizenship, they surely need prior training in being democratic citizens of the Cook Islands. This training could be partially secured by turning the Cook Islands Legislative Council into a democratic organization through allowing its members to be elected by an adult franchise. Since members of the Island Councils are already elected, there seems no reason why the people should not learn their responsibilities as voters in federal affairs by learning how to choose satisfactory federal representatives. If, in addition, federal representatives sat in the Legislative Council for a period of two or three years only, each member would learn some of the responsibilities of discussion and policy making. At the same time, by forcing a change of personnel

[1] Cook Islands Annual Report, 1949. The Annual Report, 1956, notes of the ninth annual session of the Legislative Council that it 'was the longest, most valuable and constructive session since the Legislative Council was established'. The Council decided to adopt a local income tax, recommended that local island councils be given control of roads, water supplies, harbours and reef passages, debated the establishment of standing committees and accepted in principle a broad programme for the economic development of the islands.

[2] Since this text was completed, the New Zealand Minister of Island Territories asked Professor C. C. Aikman to make a study of constitutional and administrative developments in the Cook Islands. Professor Aikman's *First Report on Constitutional Survey of the Cook Islands* (cyclostyled), presented to the New Zealand House of Representatives, October 1956, represents a fresh and imaginative approach to many difficult problems. Among other recommendations may be noted those suggesting an expansion in the function of island councils and in the powers of the Legislative Council, a reduction to four of the official members of the Council, an increase to twenty of the elected members and the establishment of an executive council charged with formulating and co-ordinating policy.

at set intervals, many persons would have the opportunity of learning the new ways of democratic government.

A further small change would also be helpful in this respect. At the moment, official and administrative members of the Council are evenly balanced against native members, with the presiding Resident Commissioner holding a decisive casting vote, even in policy discussions in which his own administration's policy may be under criticism. Long continued, this system might very well create attitudes of frustration in the native members, thus forcing them into attitudes of vehement, irresponsible and continued criticism, a characteristic feature of Crown Colony government which in this respect, Cook Islands administration resembles.[1] At best, the system prevents the native members making mistakes in policy making, and thus learning responsibilities from an analysis of mistaken, as much as from successful, decision. Finally, under the present arrangement, island resident agent members of the Legislative Council may find that in voting against the native members from their own islands (as conscience or prudence may dictate from time to time) they are weakening their own prestige in their own islands and again laying themselves open to the continual criticism of voting against the best interests of their own island people. To avoid these difficulties which are implicit in the Council set-up, if yet not explicit in Council deliberations, it would be a simple matter to change Council membership so that it is more nearly a native body, perhaps by dropping island resident agents from the body, though certainly leaving some departmental heads as members. In the give and take of discussion between natives and senior administrative officers much goodwill can be gained on both sides. Certain powers may be reserved for the time being to Resident Commissioner or cabinet minister in New Zealand (on the model of the present Samoan reservations), but on most matters there should be ample opportunity for native members to learn through taking responsibility for actions which they initiate what is actually involved in this responsibility. In no other way than by learning what responsibility means can one expect either the rank and file or the leaders of the community to learn quickly what membership in a democratic modern state really involves. To apply a well-known phrase from Lord Hailey to the present context one might say that New Zealand policy towards the furtherance of Cook

---

[1] See T. S. Simey, *Welfare and Planning in the West Indies* (Oxford University Press, 1946), p. 21.

Islands political advance 'is a matter not only of purpose but of performance and it must be judged by its operation in practice'. Changes to make possible improved practical operations directed towards realizing the ideals already discussed thus become a better criterion of policy than vaguely expressed good intentions.

58

Administrative Personnel

At some time in the future it is expected that more and more administrative posts will be filled by native islanders. The development of secondary education in the group, the provision of scholarships for pupils to advance their education in New Zealand are welcome signs that problems involved in the basic training of a future administrative staff are being thought about. In the meantime, however, senior administrative officials will continue to be recruited in New Zealand and it would again represent a sign of performance rather than purpose if there were evidence that problems of recruitment for senior posts were being seriously considered in New Zealand. The type of person most successful in island administration needs to be carefully studied, particularly the type of person most suited to help an island people making advances to full citizenship. The person with well-developed perfectionist tendencies will be unhappy in a situation in which there are few neat and tidy solutions, in which again, a people often obstinately prefers to follow its own judgment even though this judgment is mistaken. In this situation the perfectionist will either become unhappy and limit himself to the small niceties of well-established minor routines, or he will bruise his good intentions by vainly striving to clamp good solutions on a people learning in its own way. A more flexible, empirically-minded person has greater chances of being successful in his administration and of clashing less with the native peoples. He should be the sort of person chosen for Cook Islands field administration.

Training for the job to be done, not so much technical training but training for the work of getting on with native peoples (what for instance, are the relative values of 'self-control' and a 'balanced mind', an ability and a 'desire to show affection and to contribute to society', the capacity for self-insight and objectivity as compared with the ability emotionally to identify oneself with the emotional values and the habitual thought patterns of a given society?)[1]—this is a training that should not be lost sight of, either in the preliminary training of an administrative officer or in the latter stages of making available frequent refresher courses. A deliberate avoidance of situations or problems that are difficult to solve is a sign that both the tyro and the old-hand need help ('for God's sake don't tell me any more of your worries or I will get a nervous breakdown' said a visiting official to his island subordinate, and the worries were not personal but professional). Long continued, the avoidance can lead to the happy-go-lucky inertia, the pollyanna-ish attitude that everything is really fine so long as nothing positive is done. To overcome these personal blockages to efficient service, informed help is clearly necessary and should be readily available.

59

Economic Development

The present economic situation in the Cook Islands is indicated most vividly by the following figures. In the year 1955 each Cook Islander paid on an average about £35 for his imports, of which he spent almost 45 per cent. on food, piecegoods and apparel, and an additional amount on import duty (administration revenues are also obtained from income tax and stamp duties, both of which bear lightly on the islander, who pays no other direct taxation).

The same Cook Islander received on an average about £25 for his exports. His education for the same year cost £5 16s. 3d. a person, his health £5 7s. 5d. and his public works £3 14s. 6d. Island revenue was unable to bear the total cost of administration services, so the New Zealand Government subsidized each islander to the amount of £18 a person—more than enough to cover the cost of education, health services and public works. In other words Cook Islands economy is unable at the moment to pay the costs of its welfare and development services.

[1] Cf. Simey, *op. cit.* pp. 111-114, 246-248, for a brief discussion of the personal problems of administrators and the problems of selection and training. Margaret Mead in the 'Mountain Arapesh', *American Museum of Natural History, Anthropological Papers* (1949), 41: Pt. 3, pp. 299-301, argues persuasively that identification is a greater virtue than objectivity.

ECONOMIC DEVELOPMENT

That the Cook Islander enjoys a relatively high standard of education, health and public works services is indicated by Table 11, showing the comparative costs of these services in four other island groups.

TABLE 11
EXPENDITURE PER HEAD, PACIFIC ISLAND SERVICES
(in national currencies)

	Education	Health	Public Works
Tonga (1951)	£0 10 10	£0 13 10	(not shown)
Gilbert and Ellice Colony (1952–53)	£0 8 9	£1 8 1	£0 16 11
Fiji (1954)	£1 13 10	£1 15 1	(not shown)
Samoa (1955)	£2 0 1	£2 5 6	£2 2 10 (Econ. Develop.)
Cook Islands (1955–56)	£5 16 3	£5 7 5	£3 14 6

Source: Respective annual reports for years shown.

From this table it is evident that the Cook Islander enjoys a very favoured position in regard to per capita expenditures on social services and public health. This position is largely due to the generous subsidies provided by the New Zealand Government: subsidies and grants for all Cook Island services amounted to £18 per person in 1955–56; for Samoa, 1955, subsidies from the New Zealand Government amounted to about 18s. 3d. for each person (this amount includes profits from the New Zealand Reparation Estates in Samoa). Even though some grants from the Colonial Development and Welfare Fund are made to both Fiji and to the Gilbert and Ellice Islands Colony and again, even though the missions are responsible for much of the education in Tonga and the Gilbert and Ellice Colony, whereas education is the major responsibility of the government in Fiji, Samoa and the Cook Islands, none the less the figures indicate on the whole that it is going to be a far-off day before the Cook Islander will himself pay for his own services, farther off still before he would be able to embark on substantial expenditures for improvements and developments.

There is no reason why New Zealand should not continue to subsidize the Cook Islands administration. The Cook Islands are legally an integral part of the territory of New Zealand and therefore presumably just as entitled to be helped with social and public works services as the inhabitants of any part of the mainland of New Zealand. Hence judgments such as those put forward by the 1920 Trade Commission: 'the time has arrived when steps should be taken to adjust the finances so that the income of the Group may meet the expenditure and thus lighten the financial burden which has uncomplainingly been carried by the New Zealand taxpayer', seem increasingly remote and unrealistic, specially since they were supported by the curious reasoning that since the most virile nation in the world is the one which has to work hard, and since the most virile native in the South Seas is the one who has to labour most for the necessities of life, therefore the Cook Islander should be forced to meet all public expenditures, thus making him work hard, thus making him virile.[1] What 'virile' meant to the Commissioners they did not say, and on the problem of how to make islanders work hard, when the Commissioners had to admit that 'the wants of the natives are few; these wants are easily supplied', the Commissioners were singularly silent. There seem to be only two significant points to be kept in mind. One is that the Cook Islander is entitled to help; the second is that the islander should be given every opportunity, through economic and social development, of so increasing the wealth of his group that he has the possibility of sharing more fully in the cost of his administration and its associated services. The important danger to avoid is that of so enthusiastically developing the economic side of contemporary Cook Islands culture that the islander himself becomes dependent on cash crops for his standards of living and thus is at the mercy of world developments over which he has no control. The only valid policy to follow would seem to be one which still takes a subsistence economy as the basis for the island way of life but which seeks to raise the standard of living of the people by providing for more adequate housing, health, education through a greater, but still subsidiary, development of the economic resources of the community.

Assuming that the goal of social and political development is to be closer association with New Zealand, then the goal of economic development should be the closer integration of an island economy with a New Zealand economy in such fashion that the Cook Islands produce for New Zealand those products which by virtue of climate, soil and native work psychology they are pre-eminently fitted to produce on a scale that would represent a welcome widening of New Zealand's own economy.[2] The total acreage, surveyed and

[1] See *Report of the 1920 Trade Commission to the Cook Islands*, New Zealand House of Representatives, *Appendices to the Journals* (1920), vol. 1, A-4, pp. 49, 51.

See in this connection some parallel conclusions of G. G. Peron, *Agriculture of Samoa, Cook Islands and Fiji*. Massey Agricultural College, Bull. 20, n.d. Recommendations for improvements in agriculture are also contained in J. C. Gerlach, *Report on an Agricultural Survey of Rarotonga, Aitutaki and Atiu* (Cook Islands), n.d. (cyclostyled).

ECONOMIC DEVELOPMENT

unsurveyed, of the Cook Islands is 56,693. Of this total about half is suitable for annual or tree crops, the remainder being problem soils or coral rubble. For lack of detailed information agricultural policy for some time is likely to be empirically formed rather than scientifically founded, and in addition it is likely to be a policy of doing things for people, rather than a policy which aims at a public discussion of the aims underlying a public policy and then the use of voluntary associations, controlled by the producers, for carrying a policy into effect—two basic planks, for example, in a successful replanning of agriculture in Jamaica.[1]

It seems that a case can be convincingly argued in favour of the establishment of a Cook Islands Development Committee which might first make an inventory of available resources and then foster a vigorous development of agricultural products: whether forestry, pineapple or citrus fruits, bananas or copra, coffee or groundnuts, tobacco or cocoa, avocado pear or macadamia nuts.[2] Shipping, whether inter-island or between the Cook Islands and New Zealand, must be a first charge on such a Committee's attention—the same problem of regular and economical shipping that has time and time again been considered, without satisfactory solution, since R. J. Seddon pledged his attention to it in 1900,[3] yet which must be solved

[1] For details see Simey, *op. cit.* pp. 168 ff. Relevant comments on the Cook Island situation are also to be found in K. Cumberland, 'New Zealand's "Pacific Island Neighbourhood": The Post-War Agricultural Prospect', *N.Z. Geographer* (1949), 5: 1-18.

[2] Between 1891 and 1897, for instance, the average annual production of coffee in the Cook Islands, mostly from wild thickets of self-sewn seeds, was 225,245 lb., sufficient to provide about 15 per cent. of New Zealand's present annual coffee needs, filled at the moment almost entirely from Africa. Island production dropped rapidly after 1898 because of the introduction on imported young trees of Ceylon leaf blight. The average annual copra production for the years 1889 to 1902 was just over 700 tons, about 70 per cent. of the copra production in 1948–49. That the New Zealand Minister of Island Territories is aware of the many pressing economic problems in the Cook Islands is shown by the recent commissioning of two authorities to study and report on island conditions. See H. Belshaw and V. D. Stace, *A Programme for Economic Development in the Cook Islands* (cyclostyled, 1955). This extensive and comprehensive document has been adopted in principle both by the Legislative Council of the Cook Islands and by the New Zealand Cabinet as a broad approach to economic development in the Islands.

[3] *Rt. Hon. R. J. Seddon's visit to Tonga, Fiji, Savage Is. and the Cook Islands, May, 1900* (Wellington, 1900) p. 329. See also the following reports: *Trade between New Zealand and Fiji, Tonga, Western Samoa, and Cook Islands, Report of Commission*, New Zealand House of Representatives, *Appendices to the Journals* (1920), vol. 1, A-4, pp. 1-68; *Visit of Parliamentary Party to Pacific Islands, February-March, 1920, Minutes of Proceedings*, ibid. A-5, pp. 1-74;

before the full agricultural resources, particularly of perishable fruit, can be made freely available for New Zealand's almost unlimited home market.

Along with a consideration of agricultural policy, and intimately connected with it, must go the makings of a policy for cushioning island economy, as far as possible against wide swings in world markets. Price stabilization policies should be reviewed and perhaps initiated. Obvious possibilities for secondary industries are jammaking, copra processing for margarine and soap, coconut and manioka processing, a dried fruit industry and an energetic development of a tourist trade with New Zealand. Small industries of this kind would also encourage the growth of producers' co-operatives and further trade union organization which together with consumers' co-operatives would materially help the growth of a democratic social and political responsibility. The story of the co-operative movement in the Gilbert and Ellice Islands Colony and in Fiji has much to teach that should be of the utmost value to the Cook Islands administration.[1]

One important aspect of Cook Island life that will be carefully watched by the proposed Development Committee is the marked growth of population. Improvements in the public health service will inevitably be reflected in a lower death and infantile mortality rate (the infant mortality under one year per 1,000 live births for 1955 was 149·93—well above the figure for the infant mortality rate in white New Zealand for the years 1871–80) and thus in a still greater increase of population. There will be in a generation or so greater pressure on the land, therefore prudence would dictate the working out of a policy about land tenure and land utilization designed to cope with larger populations. Policies in regard to the planned migration of Cook Islanders to New Zealand and their settlement, and training for New Zealand industries, both primary

---

Cook Islands Fruit Industry, Report on, by Parliamentary Delegation. New Zealand House of Representatives, *Appendices to Journals* (1936), vol. 3, H-44A, pp. 1-12; *Cook Islands Annual Report*, Dept. Island Territories (1956), p. 21.

[1] H. E. Maude, 'Development of Co-operation in the Gilbert-Ellice Islands Colony', *South Pacific* (May, 1950, supplement), pp. 1-10. Since 1955, eight thrift, credit, loan and savings co-operative societies have been established, seven of them on Rarotonga, with a total membership of 656 persons, total deposits and assets being £584. An experienced Registrar of Co-operatives has also been appointed to encourage the development of such societies in the Cook Islands. From this small beginning producer and consumer co-operatives may well grow in the immediate future.

and secondary, should be a concern of the Development Committee as well as the planned migration, if necessary, of small populations within the Cook Group itself. Gilbert and Ellice Islands experience could be drawn on to make internal island migration efficient and successful.

60

Education

In Aitutaki there is a satisfactory physical plant at a central school for taking care of the education of the 675-odd pupils of the school. A number of island teachers provide the instruction which is closely related to an island milieu. For some subjects teaching is in the native language, in others English is used; again, for some studies, the pupils are taught translation or written expression in both languages. There is a marked wish in the community that children should be taught in English and thus learn adequate skills in the use of English. Since English is likely to be increasingly used in all contacts with Europeans this wish is understandable, even though, the native language being still the language of household and social life, instruction in the native language would probably be much more efficient and satisfactory. If the goal of social and political development is to be closer association with New Zealand then English should be taught so that children acquire at least a moderate facility in its use. The final standard of education acquired by the time of school leaving is not high, but probably adequate for the majority at the present time.

If there is one islands' educational policy that needs rethinking more than any other it is the policy which dictates the major use of island teachers in the schools. The island teacher is cheaply trained, but to a rather low standard. He is also paid considerably less for his work than his European colleague. On the score of cost then (and the per capita expenditure on education in the Cook Islands is already high—£5 16s. 3d. as compared with a New Zealand expenditure in 1955 of £12 2s. 10d. and a Tongan expenditure in 1951 of 10s. 10d.), the policy can be justified. From the educational viewpoint, however, it is probably true to say that money is saved at the expense of a kind of education peculiarly needed in the islands at the present time. Island teachers, with their present training, are able to instruct in the three R's and in health and needlework and the like, but it is very doubtful whether they have much capacity to educate if the purpose of education in the Cook Islands can be validly thought of as the task of giving school pupils some simple idea of the western world, its inter-relations with an island world and the islanders' place in island-western world system. Of native teachers asked to educate in this system and not merely to instruct, Furnivall has remarked that they are unsatisfactory because their knowledge of western scientific principles, and of the ideals and values of the western world are both inadequate since they are only in a marginal position on this world system. Therefore they cannot interpret the world to their pupils nor can they teach their pupils how to live in it.[1] If an understanding of the world-island system represents the aim of island education then only well-trained European teachers with an interest in island life are good enough for the challenges of island education. Otherwise the end of education becomes little more than the teaching of literacy in an island culture where books and reading matter other than the Bible are practically non-existent, the teaching of computation so that one can feel sure one is not being short-changed by a trader, and a little health and hygiene that may or may not make a permanent impression on one's life. The Bible may have been a satisfactory guide to life under the simplicities of a nineteenth-century mission theocracy. It is doubtful whether its former supremacy can remain unchallenged today. The incorporation of the administrative school system (in 1956 approximately 90 per cent. of Cook Islands children were instructed in administration schools, the remainder in London Missionary Society and Roman Catholic Mission Schools) in New Zealand's successful Maori School system, with a consequent staffing of the majority of island schools by highly trained Europeans (and equally highly trained islanders in due course) might very well go far towards changing instruction into a realistic education for an island-New Zealand-world system. The cost would be higher than present island educational costs, but perhaps costs should not be the sole determinant in discharging New Zealand's educational responsibilities to an island people.

[1] J. S. Furnivall, *Colonial Theory and Practice* (Cambridge, 1948), pp. 371-407.

61
Intellectual Capacity

In order to get some indication first of the level of intellectua capacity of Aitutaki children and second of the qualitative organization of their intellectual capacities, 176 children between the ages of 7 years 6 months and 15 years 11 months (about 27 per cent. of the 1947 school population) were tested with the Raven Matrix Test (1937), Koh's Block Design Test and the Goodenough Draw-a-Man Test. Numerical results are given in Table 12. The results

TABLE 12
AITUTAKI CHILDREN, TEST RESULTS

Age Range Years and Months	N=176		Matrix Percentile				Koh's Block I.Q.				Draw-a-Man mental age			
			Average		Median		Average		Median		Average		Median	
	M	F	M	F	M	F	M	F	M	F	M	F	M	F
7·6- 8·11	10	10	15	15	10	7·5	95	80	96	76	7·6	7·3	7	7
9 - 9·11	19	13	20	15	10	5	81	75	73	80	8·5	7·7	9	7
10 -10·11	16	12	20	20	25	5	73	69	70	53	9·2	7·3	9	7
11 -11·11	11	13	20	10	10	5	73	69	71	58	9·9	7·6	9	7
12 -12·11	10	8	15	5	10	5	81	62	86	58	10·1	8·1	10	8
13 -13·11	16	19	15	10	15	5	87	64	90	67	9·7	8·2	10	8
14 -14·11	6	7	20	25	18	25	95	68	94	64	10·4	10·0	11	10
15 -15·11	6	—	20	—	25	—	85	—	81	—	11·4	—	12	—
Average for Group	—	—	18	13·5	—	—	84	70	—	—	9·6	8·0	—	—
Median for Group	—	—	—	—	25	13	—	—	93	76	—	—	10	8

indicate that Aitutaki children score significantly lower on the three tests than do European children, and that Aitutaki girls score consistently lower than do Aitutaki boys. That these results are not peculiar to Aitutaki only is indicated by Table 13 which is a summary

TABLE 13
MATRIX TEST RESULTS, SAMOA

Age Range Years and Months	Samoan Average N=55		European-Samoan Average N=52	
	M	F	M	F (all ages)
6- 6·6	51	52·0		
7- 7·6	52	50·5		
8- 8·6	44	14·6		
9- 9·6	15	18·5	37·5	39·6
10-10·6	7·5		34·4	
11-11·6			57·6	
12-12·6			39·25	
Average for Group	29·5	28·8	45·8	39·6

of results of Matrix testing by Anne Lopdell of a small group of Samoan and European-Samoan children. The pure Samoan group scores much lower than do European children but European-Samoan boys do about as well, while European-Samoan girls are below European standards. Comparison of median results also indicates, in general, a greater variation in the boys' scores for both Aitutaki and pure Samoan children than for the comparable groups of girls.

Before these test results may be taken as a final evaluation of Aitutaki children's intellectual capacity, it is well to remember that the tests are probably highly saturated with European cultural influences. Although the tests appear on the surface to be relatively 'culture-free'—more so, at any rate, than some tests that might otherwise have been chosen—a capacity to do such tests demands among other things a culturally-formed appreciation of patterns and shapes, a childhood experience of block-building and manipulation of pieces of wood (whether of regular or jig-saw shapes), the habituation to the use of pencil and paper for drawing that only comes through uncounted childhood experiences. On all these counts the Aitutaki and Samoan children are deficient in their cultural and personal experiences. Hence we should expect them to do worse at tests which implicitly presuppose such experiences than middle-class European children. Even among European children, however, there is evidence that social class differences affect test results. Thus Kerr reports of the Mosaic test, similar to the Koh's test in that designs have to be built up from coloured shapes, that children and adults from comfortable homes make markedly different designs as compared with children and adults from poor homes. If economic circumstances within European culture result in differences in opportunity and practice for the manipulation of materials then cross-cultural differences are likely profoundly to affect test scores.[1]

The conclusion is reached therefore that the tests of intellectual capacity used with Aitutaki children reveal a rather low level of performance and a rather general sex difference within the group, but that one is unwise to interpret the results as indicating absolute intellectual inferiority. If it is assumed that the tests are tapping a

[1] See M. Kerr, 'Validity of the Mosaic Test', *Journal of Orthopsychiatry* (1939), 9: 232-236. A more recent study using the Goldstein-Scheerer Cube test with a group of adolescent boys from schools in or near Accra comes to the conclusion that tests of abstract ability are no more culture-free than tests of intelligence. See G. Jahoda, 'Assessment of Abstract Behaviour in a Non-Western Culture', *Journal Abnormal and Social Psychology* (1956), 53: 237-243.

INTELLECTUAL CAPACITY

'manifest' intellectual capacity, then it is also probably true to say that the 'latent' intellectual capacity is not being reached. Were suitable tests available, there is at present little reason to assume that a tapped latent capacity would not result in a higher manifest capacity score. The only piece of evidence against this view, and it is difficult without further research to know how much weight to give to the evidence, is the fact that Rorschach records of Aitutaki children suggest a level of intellectual capacity below that of normal European children.

In the cross-cultural measurement of intellectual capacity the psychologists' skill and techniques do not yet appear to be adequate to measure differences in quantitative amounts of latent intelligence. But test results are still valuable in so far as they can be used to indicate the existence of cross-cultural qualitative differences in intellectual or cognitive organization. Two aspects of Aitutaki cognitive organization seem to be suggested by the present results. The first concerns the fact that the culture itself does not place value on problem-solving. In its technological aspect Aitutaki culture is extremely simple. Results are achieved by the simple application of rules traditionally inherited. This is not to say that judgment is not required of the successful fisherman or cultivator, but the number of variables within his control are so few that complicated judgments are hardly ever required. Success in farming or fishing or even in many aspects of social life is more likely to be achieved by the application of rules learned by rote, rather than by the use of principles applied by reason. Cognitive organization, therefore, is likely to be rather simple in structure and largely formed by experience derived through the rote learning of repeated lessons. It is not without significance in this connection that island teachers noted with surprise that pupils whom they considered to be clever at school work often did poorly at the tests, while other pupils considered poor at school often did much more successfully. A probable explanation of this difference is to be found in the fact that school work is organized mainly on the basis of rote-memory instruction and thus sets little premium on the development of a latent capacity to think in terms of the abstract organization of relations.

Early missionary records also stress the capacity of the Cook Islander for rote-memorizing. Thus Buzacott writes: the people 'could repeat the whole of the sermons at the meetings for conversation on the subject of the Sabbath discourse, but there was an utter lack of impressions on the heart'; and again Buzacott notes: 'Under belief that the alphabet and the primary syllables . . . were a series of cabalistic sounds and signs peculiar to Christianity, many of the natives were wont to congregate together in the cool of the day and chant off the lessons they had learnt at school, just as they had been wont to chant their heathen songs. Some even imagined them to be forms of prayer, to be repeated in times of danger.'[1] Finally, John Williams's observation on the children of Atiu and Aitutaki is worth mentioning. Few of these children could read, but all of them, as well as the adults, could correctly recite 'a long and instructive catechism . . . which contained a comprehensive system of divinity, expressed in striking and beautiful language'.[2]

Since one of the principal functions of culture is that of presenting to the members of a given society a set of workable ready-made solutions to most of the problems of life that experience in a given environment suggests as being the crucial problems of that environment for those people, and since many of these cultural solutions can be most readily transmitted from one generation to the next by rote-learning, Aitutaki culture today is still fulfilling its age-old function. The rote-learning of ready-made solutions only becomes disadvantageous to a people when rapid social change produces new problems, sufficiently unlike the old that ready-made solutions are no longer effective. Western European culture has for some time shown this lag between traditional solution and new problems. Aitutaki people are more fortunate since traditional solutions mainly work, and for the most part, though for them, too, the time may soon come when a capacity to solve new problems in new ways is going to be more important than ready-made applications of the old.

The second characteristic aspect of Aitutaki thinking is the fact that it functions mainly at a perceptual, rarely at an abstract, level, and at a perceptual level which may be significantly different from the perceptual level thinking of the Western European. Nadel has already noticed that in East Africa, Samoa and Northern Nigeria where there are no cultural models available in the way of toys, pictures, blocks and photographs, abstract thinking proves to be difficult and a different mental orientation is evident towards selected perceptual material. Hence the way perceptual relations are noticed

[1] Sunderland and Buzacott, *Mission Life, op. cit.* pp. 53, 64.
[2] John Williams, *Missionary Enterprises, op. cit.* pp. 267, 287.

will be a function of a given culture.[1] How the relations, once noticed, will be abstracted and generalized about will also depend on the interests and training available in the culture concerned.[2] The children of Aitutaki have plenty of experience of coloured objects or variously shaped objects, but their culture teaches them to be interested mainly in the objects and not in their abstracted shapes, colours and patterns. Therefore the quality of their thinking will reflect this perceptual orientation, and imaginative thinking either of a controlled or a free fantasy type will be rare. This quality of Aitutaki thought again receives confirmation from the limited use of imagination in Rorschach records.

To these qualities of Aitutaki intellectual organization and perhaps more besides, John Williams, with his customary perspicacity, was probably referring when he wrote his classic passage about South Seas intellectual capacity. 'It will depend', Williams says, 'upon the standard by which we measure intellectual capacity, whether we pronounce the South Sea Islanders inferior to other races. If depth of thought and profundity of research be the only satisfactory evidences of superior mind, I will yield the point at once. But if wit, ingenuity, quickness of perception, a tenacious memory, a thirst for knowledge when its value is perceived, a clear discernment and high appreciation of the useful; readiness in acquiring new and valuable arts; great precision and force in the expression of their thoughts, and occasional bursts of eloquence of a high order, be evidence of intellect, I hesitate not to affirm, that, in these, the South Sea Islander does not rank below the European.'[3] Not all the characteristics that Williams mentions may be of equal value in inferring intellectual capacity, but the point he made in 1838 is still valid: Polynesian (and Aitutaki) thought is different from our own, but it is still not inferior to that of the European.

---

[1] S. F. Nadel, 'The Application of Intelligence Tests in the Anthropological Field' in Bartlett *et al.* (eds.), *The Study of Society* (New York, 1939), pp. 190-192. See also J. Blackburn, *Framework of Human Behaviour* (London, 1947), pp. 88-89.

[2] Anyone who has had the task of trying to explain an architect's plan for a radical redesigning of an old house to far from dull children of 12 or 14 years old —even a house in which the children have been living for some years—will realize that the capacity to abstract from familiar shapes and forms is difficult for children in our culture, even though our culture is, to a degree, shape and form conscious.

[3] J. Williams, *op. cit.* p. 516. For a general review of the cultural problems involved in the study of abstract thinking with particular reference to primitive peoples, see E. Cassirer, *An Essay on Man* (New Haven, 1944), pp. 44-46.

62

Character Structure

Two sets of material are available for an analysis of the character structure of the people of Aitutaki and Rarotonga. One set consists of the observations made by missionaries and anthropologists on the character of the people. The other set is made up of a series of contemporary Rorschach records of Aitutaki children. The material is thus complementary: on the one hand there are records of overt behaviour in a variety of situations: how the people behave and feel in various social situations; on the other hand there are records of underlying personality structure to be interpreted for cultural similarities rather than as protocols of unique personality differences. The theory of character structure based on these materials will then consist in a statement of dynamic relations that is thought to be adequate to account for both similarities of overt behaviour and of personality structure.

All observers of the people of Aitutaki and Rarotonga appear to agree on ascribing to them the following characteristics: the people were warlike and engaged in frequent tribal wars; in war they were somewhat cruel (though in peace as Sir Peter Buck observes, they are industrious, kindly and hospitable to the highest degree)[1]; easygoing for the most part and, as John Williams remarks, 'of warm temperament'; outgoing in social relations and friendly though given at times to outbursts of unrestrained enthusiasms; sociable, gregarious; noisy and demonstrative whenever excitement arouses enthusiasm; sensitive to group judgments, group-bound in moral standards, extremely responsive to feelings of shame; quick to perceive insults and injuries to self-esteem; given to brooding over insults and slights; aggressive at times, given to fanatical outbursts and to occasional violence in personal relations; in general, lacking in emotional control; concerned to a good degree with questions of prestige and status; interested in novelties but satisfied with the *status quo* and not concerned with questioning an accepted way of

[1] P. H. Buck (Te Rangi Hiroa), *Arts and Crafts of the Cook Islands*, B.P. Bishop Museum, Bull. 179, Honolulu Hawaii (1944), p. 8. R. L. Stevenson had the same contrast in mind when he fixed it with the adjectives 'sunshiny . . . and cruel'. But when he adds the word 'lewd' his choice is surely as inappropriate for the Polynesian as calling a Kinsey report 'obscene'.

CHARACTER STRUCTURE

life; extraverted and out-going but not introverted or given to philosophical speculations.

These generalizations may be supported by a variety of illustrations in order to give a feeling for cultural values:

1. *Easy-going nature.* Examples of the casual easy-going ways of the Aitutaki people have already been given in the previous discussion of what has been termed an 'approximately correct psychology'. A revealing instance of unrestrained enthusiasm is given by Buzacott in a brief account of his pastoral visit to Aitutaki in 1831 (and an illustration also of the Aitutaki interest in novelties). The people had been taught to sing hymns, and had become, says Buzacott, 'devotedly fond of singing, and seemed to have no sense of fatigue. Their urgent requests to be taught *new* tunes often deprived our brethren of their rest. . . . With this exercise, my throat has sometimes been so sore as to cause me to spit blood for several days.' Williams and Buzacott took turns sleeping and hymn-singing throughout the nights, though 'the singers made such a noise with their stentorian voices that sleep was impossible', and even Williams, whose endurance was greater than that of most men was 'completely exhausted'.[1] After such bouts of unrestrained enthusiasm the people generally sleep or rest from the extreme fatigue for several days, when a period of relaxation may slowly give rise to mounting tension until another outburst of hyperdynamic, Dionysian-like activity takes place.

2. *Sociable gregariousness.* This characteristic has also been illustrated in previous material. Noisy demonstrativeness is characteristic of group meetings, leave-takings—anything in fact from working parties to Sunday School gatherings and football matches. As Buzacott remarks, again of Aitutaki, the people are 'unaccustomed to restrain their feelings' and leave-takings or welcomes were always accompanied by wailings and tears, loud cryings and screamings increasing in tempo if temporary danger through capsizing boats led to additional excitement. Again, the way in which from an early date annual Sunday School prize-givings were caught up in village rivalries and noise-making is illustrated by a further example from Buzacott's records: On the occasions of special annual examinations and Sunday School festivals the scholars of the two Rarotongan villages of Avarua and Arorangi united and alternately entertained each other. 'The children formed gay processions on these occasions,

[1] Sunderland and Buzacott, *Mission Life*, p. 114.

each class headed by its teacher, bearing an ornamental flag of original design; the school coming from a distance entered the village with shouts and songs of joy, while their hosts drawn up in single file on either side of the high road, would greet their guests with shouts of welcome, and follow them into the house of God.' After a service, distribution of prizes, a feast and short speeches, there were 'farewell cheerings' and the return home.[1]

Crowd-excitement, to take another example, is characteristic of football matches and other sporting activities. Football games, particularly, are followed by spectators with noisy excitement. It is common practice for the women supporters of each team to dance a group dance each time their side scores and to boast in no measured term about the skill of their team and the abysmally poor quality of the opposing team. Such demonstrations inevitably give provocation to the women of the other team and provocation leads to fighting, so that village policemen are kept busy trying to restore order by separating the groups of milling women, all of them shouting and screaming, hair-pulling, punching and pushing each other. Temporary restorations of order inevitably collapse when further scores are made.

3. *Sensitivity to group judgments.* The most common reason given by the Aitutakian for doing or not doing something is that of avoiding shame, and shame here means being ashamed before the members of one's family, friendship group or village community. The acts for which one feels shame are, of course, many: they range all the way from being caught stealing to acting ungenerously. Thus the strongest incentive for acting in a truly Aitutaki-like manner comes from this fear of being ashamed. Children at school hate being shamed before other pupils or fear their parent's or teacher's response to their being shamed. During the dancing tours that take place at Christmas and New Year, the one motive that gives rise to the generous giving of money gifts is the desire not to be shamed when one's name is called for a money gift, so that in fact one gives at least as much as, and strives to give more than, the previous person whose name was called. In church, at the time of church collections, the pastor will sometimes say: 'X has given a one-pound note. Are you going to be

---

[1] Sunderland and Buzacott, *op. cit.* pp. 70-71. An engraving illustrating one such prize-giving and facing p. 63 of this book suggests a peaceful meeting of dark-skinned but otherwise white cloth-clad English angels, and hardly suggests the excited tension presently to burst forth when formalities of presentation would be finished with.

shamed?' All who do not wish to be shamed then contribute at least as much money. Again, one finds that in personal relations, one is shamed by not fulfilling obligations, or even expectations (however lightly the expectations are held). Thus if a request is made to which a person does not want to say *yes*, but cannot say *no* because of resulting shame, then he will do all he can to avoid the request-maker, hiding in the bushes beside the road, covering his face with his hands if personal association cannot be avoided. Conversely, to get a person to say *yes* to a request, it is necessary to manoeuvre the person into the position where he unwittingly accepts an obligation, and thus will be unable later to say *no* to the request because of shame.

Broadly speaking it is possible to classify cultures into those that cause the individual to feel shame if he violates moral standards and those that cause the individual to feel guilt. In the one culture the person is only likely to feel that he has done wrong when public discovery of his act brings inevitable public disapproval and thus feelings of shame; in the other culture, knowledge of having performed some wrong act is followed by the punishments of guilt-feeling, even if the act is not publicly known. A typical 'shame culture' tends to impose its disciplines by using the three techniques of physical punishment, the widespread use of punishment by members of an extended family or kin group (rather than concentrating the power to punish on the relatively few adult members of the biological family) and the use of such special disciplinary agents as spirits, ghosts, ogres, malicious 'familiars' and malevolent demons. Judged by these three criteria it is probable that Aitutaki culture was formerly a shame culture. Christianity taught the lessons and techniques of the guilt-culture. Today, therefore, shame-producing techniques survive alongside of guilt-producing mechanisms. Aitutaki people observe moral standards partly from shame and partly from guilt. Determining influences swaying a person more to one discipline than the other are to be found in such factors as age, generation level, degree of quasi-Europeanization, and amount of faith in, and practice of, Christian dogma and teaching.

That aboriginal culture tended to emphasize shame rather than guilt could be shown by many quotations from missionary records. The following quotation from Buzacott is typical. Writing in 1831 he remarks: 'It seems impossible to awaken in the minds of the natives any adequate conception of sin against God. Most of them considered that only sinful which was openly discovered to be such. There was no godly sorrow for sin. It was a long time before the mass of the people comprehended what sin was in the sight of a holy God. We had no reason to complain of want of attendance on the means of grace ... but there was an utter lack of impressions on the heart.'[1] Buzacott clearly has in mind in this passage the difference between intellectual comprehension of the new theory and a sense of guilt which would cause the theory to make emotional sense. It was only after many years of labour that he felt that some few were developing a satisfactory sense of sin and therefore responding to a guilt conscience. Today, as already suggested, an internalized super-ego of the guilt type[2] predominates in those brought up largely in European-like ways. For the remainder, the widespread use of shame as a sanction suggests that the shame conscience is still basic but that for some there has been a superimposed grafting of the western European guilt conscience.

4. *Aggressiveness.* Fanaticism, violence and aggressiveness have always been characteristic of the Cook Islander, though violence and aggressiveness, being relatively easy in the culture to dissipate, have tended to be of the rapid flaring-up, rapid dying-down type, whereas fanaticism and brooding over insults tend to occur where ready means of catharsis have not been available. Violence and aggressiveness received sanction in the older culture through institutionalized warfare, arbitrary chiefly cruelty and sorcery. That the institutional practices, with their concomitant cruelty, irresponsibility for human life, infanticide, cannibalism, ever-pervading fear and anxiety, had become too top-heavy for the amounts of intra-personal aggressiveness that needed to be dissipated is implied by the ready manner in which these practices were abolished. The Aitutakian clearly needs some outlet for his aggression, but the outlet, so to speak, does not need to be big, because the tension that exists can be rapidly drained off by the provision of minor permissive patterns of aggressive behaviour. Thus, the Cook Islander, as noted already, is prone to indulge in long drawn-out intra-family squabbles and disputes particularly over the disposal or use of land. Scandal-mongering and malicious gossip are common means of passing away an idle hour.

[1] Sunderland and Buzacott, *Mission Life*, p. 53.
[2] See G. Bateson, 'Cultural Determinants of Personality', in J. Mc. V. Hunt (ed.), *Personality and Behaviour Disorders* (New York, 1944), 2: 714-735. I am indebted to John Whiting, Harvard University Laboratory of Human Development, for insights into the differences between guilt and shame cultures.

CHARACTER STRUCTURE

Drinking fermented orange beer allows a man to work-off aggression in noisy outbursts of shouting and banging. So long as such a person is not frustrated he can be persuaded to go to sleep, but remonstrances or expostulations are likely to result in fighting and physical violence. Hardness and insensitivity to physical defects or inferiorities in other persons may also be a sign of mildly aggressive cruelty: a child suffering from *talipes*, for instance, will invariably be given a nickname stressing this deformity and the squint-eyed child will never be allowed to forget, because of his nickname, his unusual appearance (though habit naturally will always dull the first cruel impact of words).

Again, there are many instances in the missionary literature of converted Christians becoming extremely fanatical and even cruel in the pursuit of their judicial or disciplinary secular-sacred duties. Thus the preservation of church-supported law led, as has been already shown, to a police-like state in which the aggressive interference with other people's lives became for a time an almost insupportable tyranny—a tyranny imposed, one may well imagine, because of the violence in Aitutaki character and broken down in the end because of that easy-going characteristic which makes long-sustained violence 'just too much trouble'. However, at the height of the new interest in the new religion, conversion was popular, but none the less purchased at the cost of waging incessant internal warfare with impulses now outlawed by the new order. Hence it was characteristic of this period that fanaticism was often directed at the persons who did not play the game by being as steadfast as the more conscientious. As Henry Royle, missionary on Aitutaki, wrote in 1846: 'The current of popular feeling is so strongly against a mere profession of religion that it is hazardous for anyone to assume a character which he cannot consistently sustain.'[1] Today the most strongly fanatical in many of the Cook Islands are those given to the most extreme condemnations of other people's behaviour, but who appear at the same time to be fighting most intensely a battle between Christian principles and a desire to be no more moral than their more easy-going friends and kinsmen.

Since there are many opportunities normally available for working off aggression associated with injuries or insults, the Aitutakian is not normally a brooder over real or fancied wrongs. Formerly, however, when insults were normally avenged by recourse to armed

[1] Quoted in R. Lovett, *History of the London Missionary Society*, p. 366.

violence, one might have to wait for some time before the appropriate moment for revenge arose. Hence the custom, noted by Buzacott: 'On receiving an injury, if they could not at the moment be revenged, it would be recorded by a certain mark tatooed (*sic*) on the throat; and if the father died unavenged, the son would receive the mark on his throat, and thus it would go on from generation to generation, and nothing would obliterate the injury but the death of some one of the family by whom it had been inflicted. Some had two marks, others three, and some so many that their throats were covered.'[1] One suspects that these last were either craven-hearted, hyper-sensitive, or else aesthetically so interested in the pattern of tattoo marks that they had forgotten their mnemonic purpose: the use of sorcery should at least have afforded a simple technique of revenge. In any case, one is not told how the tattoo marks were erased after successful revenge!

5. *Prestige and Status.* The western European has strong impulses to compete with his fellow men for wealth, power and prestige. The Cook Islander was and is indifferent to wealth; he spends what he gains with little thought of thrifty saving for the morrow; he is unconcerned with justifying himself to himself or to society as a better man than the next because he possesses more wealth. But the Cook Islander is prepared to compete for power and prestige, mostly for prestige, secondarily for power. Although, as has already been noted, Aitutaki society was a status society, yet superior statuses tended to be blurred by the operation of kinship principles, even statuses otherwise fairly secure because firmly based on the first-born male support. The ideal pattern of the society was one of clearly distinct hierarchical statuses; the actual pattern was one of blurred distinctions, but this very blurring made it all the more necessary to strive, unsuccessfully always, to approximate the ideal. Thus the Aitutakian was sensitive to slights or insults due to a lack of proper recognition of his status, therefore of the proper amounts of power and prestige rightfully, so he thought, due to him. One high chief mournfully excused himself to John Williams when the missionary chided the chief for not exercising his power to protect from violence the native teacher Papeiha with the remark that he could do nothing, 'all heads being of equal height'.

Thus the statement of Moss about Rarotonga has the ring of truth about it: 'Pride of place and power are among the strongest passions

[1] Sunderland and Buzacott, *op. cit.* p. 244.

but find vent in a corporate instead of an individual form'[1]—not entirely so, however, because Moss goes on to remark about the frequency of status quarrels between individual members of the same household, as well as the existence of bitter feuds between different families. It is not improbable that one reason for the tyranny associated with the 'police state' of the mid-nineteenth century was the fact already discussed that those in power (police, deacons and judges) were implicitly using their power-position to preserve or increase their power and prestige by humbling or attempting to disgrace traditional or present rivals.

The position therefore in Aitutaki and to a great degree in Rarotonga is that status is ideally ascribed, but practically it has to be achieved or at least validated from time to time by humbling equals or rivals. The major technique employed for this job is competition, particularly group competition, because group competition makes possible an affirmation of both the values of group sociability and group membership as well as the values of the competitive justification of status. Competition also becomes the technique that the culture uses to prevent the easy-going, approximately-correct psychology from disintegrating group integrity and social life. Villages would become untidy if there was no check on the habit of throwing rubbish in the approximate direction of the household rubbish dump. Occasional inter-village competitions for the prestige of being the tidiest village make people willingly tidy up their household lots.

Mixed in proportion, the five major values that have been discussed display themselves according to the logical demands of different culturally defined situations to make up a characteristic Cook Islands character structure. Richard Seddon, Prime Minister of New Zealand toured the Cook Islands fifty years ago and said in effect in his public speeches to the people: 'You are an innocent people, and taken in the right way, cared for and properly governed, there is no reason why you should not be the happiest of Her Majesty's subjects. All you have to do in return for this care is to remain innocent, work hard, cultivate your lands and become wealthy.'[2] Innocent of some vices the Cook Islanders certainly are, but not innocent in the sense of being uncomplex or readily able to appreciate the virtues of becoming wealthy. Thus administrative

---

[1] Moss, 'The Maori Polity', *op. cit.* p. 23.
[2] See *Rt. Hon. R. J. Seddon's Visit to Tonga etc., op. cit.,* for a speech to the people of Rarotonga reported on p. 301.

policy needs measuring against the rule of reality, not of fantasy, and a knowledge of character structure provides one of the best rulers that the social scientist is at present able to suggest.

63
Rorschach Records

Rorschach records were collected from eighty-eight children, forty-five females and forty-three males, ranging in age from 7 years to 15 years 6 months, with a median age of 12 years. The purpose in using this test was not to study Aitutaki children as unique individuals, but to collect information about the kind of personality structure that appeared to be common to all the children, so that in this respect, information would be available about the way in which Aitutaki culture orders the experience of children growing up in this culture and thus gives them a common frame of reference for interpreting themselves and the world to themselves. The Aitutaki records have been analysed in considerable detail by Betty M. Spinley (Dr. Martha Anderson) and compared with a group of records collected from New Zealand children of about the same age. The results of the full analysis have been recorded elsewhere.[1] In the present context all that is necessary is to summarize the findings on the Aitutaki children and thus to show the way in which these records make it possible to analyse Aitutaki character structure at a deeper level than is possible from the previous summary of the more overt characteristics of behaviour.

The records of the Aitutaki children appear to show a well-defined character structure which may be defined in the following way:

1. The intellectual level of the children is low.

2. The children appear to be emotionally constricted, not broad and expansive in their approach to the world, but flat and withdrawing. Emotional states when they do occur are likely to be of a violent, eruptive kind.

3. Imagination is almost completely lacking. The children are matter-of-fact in their response to the world and their imagination, when used, is reproductive rather than creative.

[1] Betty M. Spinley, *A Study of Two Cultural Groups by the Rorschach Technique* (typescript, Jacob Joseph thesis), on file Library, Victoria University College, Wellington, New Zealand.

4. Anxiety is present, together with basic insecurity, and these two facets of the emotional life largely represent the response to a failure to control emotional-impulsive responses.

5. There is little apparent desire to see the world whole, but rather a directing of tendencies and interests onto the small details of the world together with a high degree of formalization about life which suggests that the culture provides all the major answers to life and the individual need concern himself in his decisions only about minor details.

6. Individuality is not stressed and there is no social approval for the person who thinks up novel ways of doing things. Novelties may be borrowed as fashions, but the culture itself is not interested in the development of new social, aesthetic, economic or other patterns of behaviour or institutional organization.

7. The personality structure seems to be fixed and rigid rather than plastic and modifiable. The records suggest that there will be no ready assimilation of new patterns of behaviour and change to new ways will be resisted rather than welcomed.

In sum Aitutaki children have sufficient similarities in their personality make-up which imply that the common form is one of low intellectual capacity; a flat constricted emotional life, given to occasional emotional outbursts; little use for imagination; basic anxiety and insecurity; interest only in minor details of the world; a particular interest in immediate sensory forms and in fixed, culturally determined status; little interest in individuality; a satisfaction with the present situation and little desire to change the patterns of social life.

It is important to remember in considering the congruence between the personality structure of these Aitutaki children and the previous discussion of character structure that the Rorschach interpretations were 'blind' interpretations. The interpreter knew the age, sex and 'race' of the children, but nothing more. Hence she was limited in her characterizations to what could be validly interpreted from the records themselves. The congruence between interpretation and observations thus becomes rather striking. Both methods of analysis remark upon easy-going acceptance of the status quo, upon emotional outbursts, upon the acceptance of group standards, and upon the existence of basic anxieties leading (as observation stresses) to occasional aggression and violence. The interpretations suggest in addition such variables in the pattern as low intellectual capacity, lack of imagination, and personality rigidity, and also indicate the characteristic way in which all the variables are put together into a rather special and characteristic Aitutaki configuration. That there is a special configuration is also suggested by the comparison between Aitutaki and New Zealand children, a comparison that is tangential to the present context, and, for this reason, not included here.

Finally, comparison between the Aitutaki Rorschach records and the only other Rorschach records readily available for a Pacific island people (excluding Maori and Micronesian records), those collected by Cook for a group of fifty males with a median age of 20·6 years,[1] indicates that in both groups of Polynesian people there are evidences for personality rigidity and valuation of the socially acceptable, a certain amount of emotional fluidity or lability together with a relative openness towards the world and finally a lack of individuality and an acceptance of conservatism. Cook is of the opinion that the relatively simple organization of Samoan culture has led to the development of a rather simple Samoan personality structure. If it were possible, he suggests, to re-structure Samoan culture so that it presented a series of challenges rather than of *faits accomplis* to the people then the most likely result would be a corresponding development in the intellectual achievements and personality structure of the people.[2] The argument is plausible certainly, and may apply equally to the Cook Islands, with this reservation, however, that what will be said later about the phenomenon of personality lag implies a far from simple relationship between psychocultural field and personality structure. If the relationship is not one of simple concomitant variation, then no amount of change in one variable (the cultural field) will necessarily result in a simple change in the same direction in the other variable (complexity of personality). In fact, one lesson from the study of culture contact situations is that people living in 'rigid' cultures tend definitely to resist increases in the complexity of their culture. They may borrow but they tend to absorb the new into a pre-set cultural mould. They do not often re-cast their mould to take care of possible new complexities. They simply reject that which cannot be fitted into the mould.

[1] P. H. Cook, 'The Application of the Rorschach Test to a Samoan Group', *Rorschach Research Exchange* (1942), 6: issue 2, April.
[2] P. H. Cook, 'Mental Structure and the Psychological Field: Some Samoan Observations', *Character and Personality* (1942), 10: 296-308.

64
Development of Character Structure

There is little detailed information that can be given about the development of character structure in the Aitutaki child. It has already been noted that infant care and child raising practices are mild and permissive. Toilet training is easy, food is generally plentiful and the sex interests of the child are treated casually. Discipline is of such a type as generally to lead to the building up of a shame rather than a guilt conscience, though it is probable that in many today the conscience structure tends to be an amalgam of both types. The expectable result of this childhood training would be a person with adequate impulse gratification, a rather tenuous and not very complex ego structure, and a group-bound super-ego. Impulse gratification would not necessarily carry the implication of a basic inner security so long as the ego-structure were not well integrated and the super-ego operated as a controlling factor only when the group became aware or was likely to become aware of deviant behaviour. This expectation is roughly born out by the analysis of character structure, but further field study is required before it would be possible to trace the developmental steps leading to the finished result.

65
Character Structure and Social Change

The analysis that has been presented of the Aitutaki character structure suggests no reason why simple borrowing of clothing, new house types, new foods, skills at reading, writing and spelling should not have occurred, nor any reason why techniques for using these one-time novelties should not have been absorbed into the technical knowledge of the culture. Hence simple changes of this sort occurred quickly. Similarly, if the weight of warfare created, as one suspects, unbearable amounts of fear and anxiety for the majority, there is no reason why this institution should not have snapped quickly, as it in fact did. There does not appear to be any doctrine or dogma of a Christian evangelical faith which would be repugnant to a Cook

Islander, with the exception of pre-marital chastity and post-marital monogamy. Thus in rather quick time Christianity, supported by 'lucky' hurricanes, famines, death-dealing diseases as well as by the personal efforts of the white missionary, was quickly absorbed. In fact, in some respects, Christianity is less repugnant to the value system of the Cook Islander than it is to many of the non-religious institutions of western European culture itself. Hence it is no paradox to say that the Cook Islands quickly became more Christian in outlook than the Christian culture from which Christianity was borrowed. Sex practices being based on approved impulse gratification did not yield readily to new ideological controls, even when these controls were reinforced by secular and material punishments. Christian standards of sexual morality are today observed by many, particularly the ageing and the old, but they are not practically observed, regularly and conscientiously, by many of the young.

Such nineteenth-century valuations as those of thrift, personal responsibility, the virtue of economic gain, the value of progress 'as the law of life' and change for the sake of change, did not secure any footing in the culture, even though they must have been part of the cultural background of missionaries, whalers, traders and other Europeans. The value-systems associated with these and other 'Middle-town' virtues would run counter to 'easy-goingness', personality rigidity, group-binding moral values. Thus there would be no dynamic motivation within the Cook Islander that would lead him to change more completely. Those islanders who, because of their more complete absorption of Christian and western European values, might have become agents for more far-reaching changes were withdrawn from the culture into an Institution for the Training of Native Teachers—twenty students and their wives each for four years of study and training; in the period 1839 to 1893, 490 men and women were so trained—and thereafter distributed far and wide over the western Pacific to evangelize in turn as they had been evangelized, and often to die in the unhealthy climates, the malarial and cannibal swamps of New Guinea and the Solomons.[1] The attempt to Christianize the people of New Guinea was thus made at the implicit cost of slowing down change in the Cook Islands; perhaps the Cook Islanders should be grateful that they were not temporarily forced or led to accept values basically at variance with

[1] R. Lovett, *op. cit.* pp. 352-353. Of the 52 couples that went to New Guinea between 1872 and 1891, 17 men and 23 women died of fever, 4 men and 3 women were killed, 3 men and 3 women returned to the Cook Islands.

their own culture by the continuing presence among them of those who by their choice of vocation were already on the way to becoming misfits in their own culture.

66
Social Change

Looking back at a century and more of culture contact in Rarotonga and Aitutaki one's abiding impression must remain an impression of cultural tenacity and stubborn conservatism rather than one of pronounced and lasting change. Certainly there have been changes on the periphery of life: changes in clothing, in tools, in communication, changes in religious ideology and practice; the disappearance of infanticide, cannibalism, institutional warfare, slow changes in polygamy and chiefly power. But despite these changes the people have remained tenaciously Polynesian, with their own characteristic social life, their own values and emotional attitudes, their own motivations and interests. Not the facts of change, but the resistances to change become emphatic when focus is switched from the externals of life to the psychological bonds that really hold a society together.

This judgment about Cook Islands society might perhaps be disputed by some authorities. Thus Linton, for instance, writes: 'The Polynesians were unique among historically minded peoples in that they never looked back to a Golden Age. The clan was likened to an upward reaching, outward stretching tree, always alive and growing. . . . This forward looking attitude made the Polynesians one of the least conservative of native peoples. They lived in anticipation that new things would be better than the old and were always eager for novelties.'[1] It may be true that the Polynesians never nostalgically dreamt of a Golden Age in the past—certainly not under conditions of aboriginal life, though some Polynesian groups have in modern times definitely lived in the past in order to provide themselves with a secure anchor against the vicissitudes of an urgent present—but on the other hand their supposed interest in novelty does not in fact seem to have led them further than an adaptation of western technology to island life and a rather complete borrowing of a set of religious beliefs which in many respects were similar to their own aboriginal ideology. If one thinks primarily of Tahiti, the Marquesas

[1] R. Linton and P. S. Wingert, *Arts of the South Seas* (New York, Museum of Modern Art, 1946), pp. 13-14.

and Hawaii one may be forced to think of social change as characteristic of Polynesia. If, on the contrary, one thinks of the Cook Islands, Tonga, Samoa and even New Zealand it is resistance to change and a strain of conservatism that strikes one most forcibly.

The key to this conflict of judgment may lie partly in semantic difficulties, partly in the effects of contact on a group's control of its land and on population numbers. Semantically, difficulty may arise from the use of metaphor. The Polynesian may have thought of his clan as an upward-reaching, outward-stretching tree, but equally and perhaps more often in the South and West Pacific, he thought of his clan as a sheltering tree with roots that stretched far back and deep into the past. Thus his clan was a direct linkage with heroic forebears and contemporary practices were valued because they kept tradition alive, not because they adapted tradition to a growing, changing present. Where therefore the Polynesian thought of the past as merely a continuation of the present backwards to the beginning of traditional time, it was conservatism, resistance to change that forced itself upon him. Apart from semantics, a group's continuing secure relationship to its land must play a role in determining the degree to which it remains an integrated unit. In New Zealand to a significant degree, in the Cook Islands and in western Polynesia the native peoples remained in control of their land or in control of enough of it to permit a continuing social life. Elsewhere in Polynesia atomization and alienation of titles have in some groups given rise to a landless people whose only method of survival has been found in urbanization or in a wage-earning plantation economy, neither of which is conducive to a continuing social integration. Finally, population changes may vitally affect social integration. Alcohol, disease and firearms reduced the New Zealand Maori population to a low level, but not low enough to force a disintegration of tribal life, whereas in the Marquesas depopulation was almost complete. Similarly the population of Rarotonga and Aitutaki declined substantially during the nineteenth century but since 1906 Aitutaki and Rarotonga have more than doubled their respective populations. Since then, a population of a minimum size is necessary for a continuation of traditional patterns of social life, some Polynesian groups have been fortunate enough to be able over the years to perpetuate themselves as functioning social groups, whereas others have simply lost this power through depopulation.

Depopulation may occur through the effects of alcohol, disease and firearms or it may result from temporary or permanent shifts in some groups of the population through the drawing-off of men in certain age groups for work in mines, plantations, public works or for army conscription. Some parts of the Pacific have in the past suffered severely through the operations of blackbirder and slaver, but in Polynesia such population changes have by now resulted in a more stable equilibrium. Until 1955 labour was recruited under supervision and on a yearly basis from the Cook Islands for work on the phosphate deposits at Makatea in the Society Islands. In 1949 no men from Aitutaki were thus employed, but from five other islands of the group about 7·4 per cent. of the men were absent from their homes at Makatea, a proportion of absentees, however, that would be too small to have any permanent changing effects on social organization. In the Pacific, as elsewhere, it is probably true to say that disintegration of society is most likely to occur only when change is so forced on the social structure of a society through disorganization of land control, patterns of leadership and the population basis of society that the society is no longer able to function as an integrated culture because the basic physical and social conditions of any society have disappeared.

When one has made allowance, however, for such factors as land control, population changes and attitudes to tradition the problem still poses itself in the study of culture contact and social change as to how and why certain peoples show a tenacious hold over their own social and dynamic integrations and why other peoples yield up these rather more readily in exchange for other motivations and integrations.[1] Conservatism and novelty are not characteristics of Polynesian society only. Differential cultural responses have been noted recently for Zuni and Navaho and a characteristic personality conservatism has been documented for a Wisconsin Ojibwa Indian group.[2] Herskovits expresses the general situation in the following

[1] Keesing, it will be remembered, has suggested that cultures may be thought of as either adaptive or rigid in their responses to new situations. See the previous discussion of the factors he lists as influencing acculturation on pp. 82-83, 123-125 above.

[2] Recent work is summarized in J. Adair and E. Vogt, 'Navaho and Zuni Veterans: A Study of Contrasting Modes of Culture Change', *American Anthropologist* (1949), 51: 547-561, and W. Caudell, 'Psychological Characteristics of Acculturated Wisconsin Ojibwa Children', *American Anthropologist* (1949), 51: 409-427. Of the increasing number of contributions that have been made to this topic over the past few years, perhaps the most important are those of A. Irving Hallowell now included in his volume entitled *Culture and Experience* (Philadelphia, University of Pennsylvania Press, 1955).

words: indigenous people 'have responded to the innovation in terms of their prior experience, accepting what has promised to be rewarding, and rejecting what seemed unworkable or disadvantageous. Where changes have been imposed on them, they have again responded in terms of their experience, with seeming complacence and inner rejection, or with open intransigence, or with a reconciliation of new form to traditional meaning.'[1]

In order to explain such differential changes in the culture contact situation, or even to explain the process of change itself, various theories have been suggested. A sociological explanation would be that of the Wilsons[2] who argue that from time to time oppositions and contradictions between different scales in a given society result in social maladjustments that force people to behave illegally (oppositions in the field of legal institutions), think illogically (oppositions in belief), and act unconventionally (oppositions of convention). The oppositions in all these sets of social relations result in behaviour that is inefficient and immoral, inaccurate and heretical, unskilful and ugly. Thus the oppositions become intolerable and compel change by giving rise to tendencies designed to equalize or even-up scale, reduce disharmonies and promote a new equilibrium in society. Social change that breaks up a primitive society and draws the primitive into the ambit of a more complex civilization involves an increase of scale so that the one-time primitive is now part of a social structure which has such characteristics as a wider range of material relations, a wider religious inclusiveness, a greater occupational specialization and a greater control of environment, greater religious variety, greater mobility. It is possible that the Wilsons' analysis represents a valid sociological statement of what happens when change takes place. However, for its understanding of the dynamic of change, the analysis relies heavily upon an expectation that people will change because of their appreciation of illegal, unconventional or illogical behaviour in themselves. But people often have difficulty in judging their own behaviour, and their insight into themselves is rarely equal to their interest in, and capacity to analyse, others' behaviour. With powers of rationalization far in excess of those of reason, people are often able to see black as white and the illegal as justified by the situation. Hence, if the sociological explanation of change is to be found in disharmonies of scale, the

[1] M. J. Herskovits, *Man and His Works* (New York, 1948), p. 482.
[2] G. and M. Wilson, *The Analysis of Social Change* (Cambridge, 1945).

SOCIAL CHANGE

psycho-dynamics of change are to be found in an understanding of how people are able, or not able, as the case may be, to appreciate the fact that disharmonies exist.

Two sets of psychological principles must be invoked to explain validly how social change takes place. The first set will be the principles of learning. The importance of drive, cue, response and reward in a theory of change has been analysed by Hallowell[1] and the first part of the present monograph has attempted to show, among other things, how learning theory can throw light upon the changes occurring in Rarotongan society after first white contacts and the introduction of Christianity. The second set of principles has to show how a given people recognize rewards, respond to certain situations as rewards and react to other situations as punishments. Simple principles that have often been invoked are principles of utility and prestige-imitation. It is clear that utility can often offer a simple explanation of change, particularly in the field of technology. Thus for the Cook Islander, iron is more useful than shell or stone for adz or fish hook, cotton goods more durable and useful than bark cloth, galvanized iron roofing more useful than coconut leaf thatch, sewing machines more useful than coconut slivers. At other times, however, people adopt changes not from utility, but rather from a tendency to imitate what has prestige for them. Thus the Cook Islander changes the pattern of his living to accommodate an elaborately-dressed double bedstead in his house—but he does not sleep in it, preferring a mattress on the floor, thus following the old-time sleeping habit. Or having adopted clothing, he wears particular styles of clothing, not particularly appropriate for his climate, in order to secure prestige for himself. But he has changed his culture in other ways too. He has become a nominal Christian, not entirely, one suspects, because the rewards for so changing were either utilitarian or increased prestige (though all human motives are complex, and rewards too) but because becoming a Christian fitted in with preferred persistent tendencies and thus brought pleasure, satisfaction and a freedom from anxiety. The Cook Islander has never responded passively to a culture contact situation, he has always been an active participator in the process of social change. Nor has social change merely added one more personal habit or cultural pattern to his life and culture. The situation has changed by changing the integration of his culture,

[1] A. I. Hallowell, 'Sociopsychological Aspects of Acculturation' in R. Linton (ed.), *The Science of Man in the World Crisis* (New York, 1945), pp. 171-200.

though the resultant total patterning has never been one to do violence to the persistent personality structure.

One further explanation of social change needs mentioning in this context and this explanation is Herskovits's theory of focus and reinterpretation. According to the theory, each culture has different dominant concerns. These dominant concerns are the focus of a people's culture, 'the area of activity or belief where the greatest awareness of form exists, the most discussion of values is heard, the widest difference in structure is to be discerned'.[1] Thus the focus of a culture will exhibit the most variable patterns, because a people will readily discuss it and alternative possibilities will receive a welcome hearing and be readily experimented with or frequently reinterpreted to fit them into the dominant focus of the people's lives. The concepts of focus, selectivity and reinterpretation therefore give a major psychocultural clue to the nature of social change.

On two grounds, however, it may be doubted how far these three concepts give the clue to social change. The first ground is that it is possible to account for the focus of a given society in terms of the character structure or group personality that the members of a given society share and thus conceptually to reduce focus to the perceptual anchorages derived from character structure. The second ground is that it is open to doubt whether a people is really prepared to discuss its dominant concerns or its most significant values because it is these concerns and values that it most takes for granted as the 'givens' of life. A people will be prepared to discuss certain values that are in focus, but these values are more likely to be peripheral or tangential values, or behaviour patterns temporarily in focus because a people's attention has been drawn to them. They may be prepared to select alternatives to these peripheral values and reinterpret them to fit in with the major values they live by and thus to introduce elements of change into their lives, but of the dominant concerns themselves they are more likely to refuse discussion than they are freely to change them. To the Cook Islander, for instance, as for all Polynesians, the two values of the sacred and the common are basic values and certainly dominant concerns, but they remain outside the focus of reinterpretation because any interpretation would strike directly to the heart of their culture. Thus change does not occur here, nor does it occur with the Polynesian in many other attitudes

[1] M. J. Herskovits, 'The Processes of Cultural Change' in R. Linton (ed.), *The Science of Man in the World Crisis* (New York, 1945), pp. 164-165, cf. also M. J. Herskovits, *Man and His Works, op. cit.* pp. 542-544.

and values equally saturated with deep feeling tone. The conclusion is reached, therefore, that selection and reinterpretation always occur over periods of time because social change, in the long run, is reintegrative, never a passive process of adding one element to another. But social change tends to affect the dominant concerns of a culture only when a people is so psychoculturally disorganized that it no longer values significantly its once-valued concerns. Ego-involvement has given place to ego-withdrawal or a temporary disintegration of an historically validated ego and change is then welcome because it may permit the re-establishment of a new ego structure.

The key to social change therefore is to be found in that which determines the swing of the ego backwards and forwards from outward-going participation to inward withdrawal. This swing seems to be basically fixed for a social group by its character-structure or group personality, just as for an individual, as a unique person, ego-involvement will be fixed by his own unique personality. The character structure of a group (basic personality type, status personality, social personality, preferred persistent tendencies and ethos appear to be terms with somewhat similar meanings) may be defined as that organization of needs, sentiments and attitudes within personality structure that determines the values of a self-view and a world-view which are common to the adult members of a distinct social group.[1] Character structure is accessible to study by depth psychology, social-anthropological techniques and personality tests. It is therefore of a different order as a concept from that of a group mind. In simple, relatively stable societies character structure will be much the same for all members of the group. In complex societies and in simpler societies undergoing rapid change there may develop subcultural variations on the basic character structure theme of the society as a whole or else members of the group may develop a primary character structure which is the group response to basic cultural values, fairly uniformly encapsulated through common infant-care and child-raising techniques, and in addition a secondary

[1] Summaries of various views about the nature of the concept of character structure or national character are to be found in J. J. Honigmann, *Culture and Personality* (New York, Harpers, 1954). Margaret Mead has also surveyed the field in her article 'National Character' in A. L. Kroeber (ed.), *Anthropology Today* (University of Chicago Press, 1953). Some of the methodological problems involved in the use of the concept are discussed in a paper by Inkeles and Levinson, 'National Character: The Study of Modal Personality and Sociocultural Systems' in G. Lindzey (ed.), *Handbook of Social Psychology* (Cambridge, Mass., Addison-Wesley, 1954), 2: 977-1020.

character structure which is a group response to sudden social change, imposed from without, and forcing upon each person a traumatic change of values.

Again in complex societies with subcultural divisions due to social caste, class, occupational and other types of division, the character structure of the group may be the resultant of a process that is analogous to the process of complementary schizmogenesis analysed by Bateson. Just as a society may compensate for warlike behaviour with complementary passive or feminine behaviour (as among the New Guinea Iatmul) or may compensate for dull routine by swinging to the opposition of a wild license (as in Polynesian Pukapuka),[1] so the character structure of a large national group may be due to the dovetailing of, say, complementary class-determined character structures. So long as the members of a group believe and feel themselves to be members of that group they must share values and attitudes in common, therefore there must be a common substratum of organized needs, sentiments and attitudes. This substratum will constitute the foundation upon which complementary structures can be built. If then, one observes from a distance one focuses on common behaviour and values (national character); if one observes more closely one focuses on class, caste or regional differences and so may overlook the complementary nature of the character structures thus observed.

It is further most probable that the character structure of a group penetrates or saturates in a varying degree different areas of culture. To continue the metaphor one might say that where the saturation is heavy (for example, in the field of moral values) change will be slight, but where the saturation is weak (as in the field of technology—but not in work organization or work motivation) then change will occur with ease. One may also rephrase the matter by saying that character structure provides the mould for a cultural

[1] Drunken bush orgies round the orange beer barrel, mentioned below, are probably also examples of a cultural compensation for the strict external enforcement of a severe evangelical morality. It is interesting to note that in medieval monastic culture a period of four days was set aside three times each year for the bleeding of the religious and subsequent relaxation of monastic rule so that what would otherwise be hours of work could be enjoyed in reading, repose and talking. Contemporary monastic culture has discarded bleeding but continues to use the principle of compensation in the institution of 'Lot' days when the religious may relax and enjoy pleasant relief from the severity of monastic discipline. See F. A. Gasquet, *English Monastic Life* (London, 1924), pp. 85-90; E. Power, *Medieval English Nunneries* (Cambridge, 1922), pp. 258-259; M. Baldwin, *I Leap Over The Wall* (London, 1949), pp. 178-179.

content. The content may be changed—warfare give place to organized competitive sports, informal education to school learning, aboriginal work to routine factory employment—but this change can go on without vitally affecting the mould of character structure.[1] In terms of ego structure, the conscious content of the ego changes, but not its unconscious roots. Along with cultural lag there can also be personality lag, so that a person faces one culture or a changed aboriginal culture with the character structure that fits him for another culture. Personality lag may result in personal maladjustment, but sometimes only when the person finds himself in a marginal position. So long as he spends most of his time with his own people he receives support for his own personality tendencies without suffering undue anxiety because he does not fit readily in a larger and more inclusive social group.

The relation of culture to personality is therefore rarely a matter of a simple and easy fit. So far from the two being little more than conceptually distinguishable aspects of the same social or organic matrix, in certain situations where social change is pronounced it is the lack of congruence between culture and personality that is marked—personality changes lag behind social changes. In other culture contact situations, however, it is character structure that determines the rate of social change. Persons sharing a given character structure will more or less all respond with indifference or ego-withdrawal to ideas and practices from another culture that are not congruent with their own character structure. Thus whether social change occurs or not will depend upon the feelings of a person. He will learn new ways of thinking and behaving if the results of his responding bring pleasure, but what will bring him pleasure cannot be determined on an *a priori* basis and without analysis of character structure. Conversely he will not learn if his response produces in him guilt, shame, a feeling of being made to appear ridiculous, or produce a flat lack of interest. As Murphy has remarked of the Arapesh man: in his rage he may sometimes hire a valley magician to

[1] Indeed, one may say more positively that the mould of character structure definitely determines the nature of the content, for instance, what kinds of work will appeal and what employment will be definitely rejected. Compare the case of the New Zealand Maori in Beaglehole, Ernest and Pearl, *Some Modern Maoris*, New Zealand Council for Educational Research, 1946, or that of the Iroquois in A. F. C. Wallace, 'Some Psychological Determinants of Culture Change in an Iroquoian Community', in W. N. Fenton (ed.), *Symposium on Local Diversity in Iroquois Culture*, Smithsonian Institution, Bureau of American Ethnology, Bulletin 149, 1951.

wreck vengeance on an enemy, but among the Arapesh the ethos of friendliness is 'too well defined to permit hostile ideas to enter often or remain long'.[1]

The measure of congruence between new pattern and old character structure is then the presence of ego-involvement or ego-withdrawal. There will either be a blindness to the cue for action or the model for imitation; or where the model is noticed (for character structure will determine many of what Murphy has called the 'perceptual anchorages' of the group), it may be noticed either as a 'thing in itself'—as, for instance, in the appreciation of the useful qualities of a knife—or else the model may be reinterpreted or restructured. In their first use of soap Rarotongans boiled it, then tried to eat it, finally threw it away. The model was not plainly observed and was restructured on an as-if food basis. Again after their first introduction to hymn-singing, the Cook Islanders have so reinterpreted the model that their singing of hymns is no longer recognizable as an English sound-pattern. Similarly they have accepted the game of cricket because it fits in with the strongly competitive drives in their character structure, but the rules and conventions of the game have been largely remoulded to render them acceptable in the types of rivalry which the game symbolizes.

The fact that the controlling governor of culture contact, other things being equal, is the character structure of the group and that the results of culture contact may be non-recognition, remoulding or rejection does not preclude an occasional fourth type of response which may be called 'institutional snapping'. In this connection it is plausible to think of different cultures as possessing different anxiety or tension levels, moreover the tension level may also be thought of as unequal in a given society. Thus the personal and social equilibrium may be disturbed in a variety of ways as the result of culture contact. In societies where anxiety-tension is low (for example, the Hopi), equilibrium is not easily disturbed; where tension is high (for example, the Dakota) equilibrium is easily disturbed, and once disturbed culture and personality have difficulty in finding a new equilibrium. Where tension is unequally distributed through the culture system institutional snapping may occur in those aspects of culture where the anxiety level is so high as to cause discomfort and distress among the people of the group, even though, with an absence of other examples or models prior to the culture contact situation being

[1] G. Murphy, *Personality* (New York, Harpers, 1947), p. 810.

SOCIAL CHANGE

initiated, the people concerned presumably went through the routine dictated by the customary patterns of the anxiety-causing institution.

If in the Cook Islands a comparison is made between the effects of the culture contact situation on tribal warfare, cannibalism, infanticide, polygamy and premarital sex customs, it is clear that the first three institutions collapsed almost immediately strong missionary pressure was brought against them. Thereafter the 'pagans' resorted to desultory semi-institutional violence in order to express their annoyance against the Christians, but even at this distance in time one can almost hear the sigh of relief that came from the majority of the population when the order went out: No more war or cannibalism: if you want to hate, be fanatic in the ways of the Lord; if you want to fight, fight sin under His banner. In a small island and with a small population warfare had doubtless created such extreme fear and discomfort that the institutional patterns broke at the first opportunity. With polygamy and sex morals on the other hand there was no sudden breaking of the old pattern. Polygamy in open or concealed form lasted for many years after the first missionary prohibitions (even today the Cook Islands probably practise monogamy 'with a difference') and premarital sex standards have probably changed very little over the past century. It would seem safe to assume that the institutions governing sex caused little anxiety or discomfort, the tension level was low, there was little community support for their change, whereas with warfare, cannibalism and infanticide there was wide community support.

Institutional snapping was partly due to the small population involved and to the fact that, although on Rarotonga, for instance, there were three tribal groups, these groups were living pretty well side by side and it was correspondingly hard to build up an in-group, out-group psychology, so that all who were not of one group could be considered natural or hereditary enemies. Strong in-group feelings together with a much larger population resulted in no institutional snapping for warfare among the New Zealand Maori, where the early traders' supplying of firearms and gunpowder resulted for some years in a crescendo of warfare, as old half-forgotten insults were paid off in bloodbaths rather than the former milder types of bloodletting. Economic factors do not seem to be important determining influences in the one case of Cook Islands institutional snapping or the other case of New Zealand institutional efflorescence. Both peoples could afford the luxury of institutional rigidity, therefore it was not a different relationship to an economic subsistence margin which caused the difference between rigidity and fluidity of institutional form.[1]

Anxiety may show a difference of level in a society relatively unaffected by culture contact. On the other hand, long-continued culture contact may result in building up anxiety levels in certain nstitutional forms which in turn results in personal behaviour which is either restless, leading to unbalanced compensatory behaviour, or to pronounced ego-withdrawal of an apathetic, lack-of-interest ii he world type. Unbalanced behaviour may also result in messianic revivals of behaviour appropriate to an earlier situation, but no longer realistic in a contemporary situation. The culture contact situation here fades into a typical minority-problem situation in which the 'space of free movement', to use Lewin's terminology, becomes restricted and persons respond to the restriction with an anxiety tension related in amount to the amount of restriction nvolved.[2] However, what constitutes a restriction of the space of free movement for any particular culture must depend upon the character structure of the culture. Hopi space of free movement has been restricted by culture contact with different cultural groups over several centuries without producing a lack of personal and group development perhaps because Hopi character structure shows marked inner resources of self-sufficiency. The Cook Islander has not the inner resources of the Hopi, but his culture now provides him with a number of compensatory outlets for floating anxiety and otherwise unchannelled aggression (alcohol and competitive sports) so that only sporadically has he felt a diminution of his space of free movement. He has been able to absorb the resulting restlessness and tension without resort to more than an occasional flare-up of aggression directed against the rather vaguely conceived agents of equally vaguely thought-of constructive institutions. External pres-

[1] In a previous article it was suggested that a 'rigidity of balanced tensions' leads to institutional snapping, but it is more probable that it is the unequal distribution of anxiety level which leads to breaks in those institutions where anxiety has banked up beyond the comfort level. See E. Beaglehole, 'Social and Political Changes in the Cook Islands', *Pacific Affairs* (1948), 21: 386-388. In *Culture and Personality* (New York, Viking Fund, 1949), pp. 123-126, Linton gives examples from Comanche and Tanala of abrupt breaks in institutional patterns and Kroeber suggests that economic explanation does account for certain south-west Indian tribes' position on a scale of relative institutional rigidity.

[2] K. Lewin, 'Psycho-sociological problems of a minority Group' in his *Resolving Social Conflicts* (New York, 1948), pp. 145-158.

sure would have to be great and long continued before the easygoing Cook Islander could ever think of himself as an unjustly treated member of a minority group.

Whether a people takes over the pattern of drinking alcohol appears to depend to a large degree on the amount of anxiety set free by the character structure of the people concerned. Horton has been able to show[1] from anthropological evidence that the drinking of alcohol tends to be accompanied by release of sexual and aggressive impulses; the strength of the drinking response in any society tends to vary directly with the level of anxiety in any society, and to vary inversely with the strength of the counter-anxiety elicited by painful experience during and after drinking—the sources of such painful experiences being the actualization of real danger or social punishments of various sorts. The main variables that Horton studied in connection with levels of anxiety were the hazards of subsistence economy (the more primitive the subsistence economy the greater the degree of insobriety) and those of culture contact (where culture contact involves damage to the subsistence economy strong insobriety will be present). The Cook Islanders' attitudes to drinking seem to be unrelated to any anxieties directly associated with subsistence economy hazards or indirectly to culture-contact hazards affecting subsistence. They thus contrast interestingly from a psychological viewpoint with the Hopi attitudes which are based upon a pattern of fear and restraint.

In the aboriginal culture, the drinking of fermented liquor was unknown in Polynesia. A drink made from *kava* root, a mild narcotic, was known almost everywhere (the two exceptions being New Zealand and Easter Island where the root would not grow in the cold climate), and readily drunk, often with elaborate ceremonial, sometimes as an excuse for pleasant sociability. But *kava* was not fermented nor had the Polynesians invented any technique for boiling and fermenting coconut sap, a highly intoxicating 'toddy' known in the Gilbert and Ellice Islands and in Pelew. Although Horton could not verify any relationship between insobriety and warfare, it is not improbable that in some parts of Polynesia warfare was enough of an emotional cathartic that the people had no need for alcohol as an aggression-release. The pattern of drinking alcohol was avidly adopted after culture contact resulted in the loss or

[1] D. Horton, 'The Functions of Alcohol in Primitive Societies: a Cross-Cultural Study', in C. Kluckhohn and H. A. Murray, *Personality in Nature, Society and Culture* (New York, 1948), pp. 540-550.

pronounced weakening of institutional warfare and therefore in the banking up of anxiety to a tension level that welcomed alcohol release. The inference can be safely drawn, at least, that Cook Islands character structure built into Cook Islanders (and still does) minor amounts of anxiety and lightly controlled aggression which could be readily released by alcohol. This anxiety is of a free floating type, due to the hazards of socialization, with its inevitable frustrations, but not specifically related to subsistence anxieties or to vague generalized culture contact hazards. The social controls and inhibitions of anxiety are rather slight. They dissolve readily under small amounts of alcohol. Contrariwise, the punishments for drinking alcohol are few and slight. At worst police prosecution and a fine or jail sentence, at best very mild social disapproval for pronounced insobriety, are the likely punishments. They are not severe in proportion to the rewards that come from the sociability of drinking parties and the feeling of comfort after tension and aggression have been released in a relatively harmless fashion.

Missionary records indicate the effects which came with the introduction of drinking to the Polynesian. Thus John Williams returned in May 1832 to Rai'atea (Society Islands) after an extended visit to Rarotonga. 'I was perfectly astounded', he writes, 'at beholding the scenes of drunkenness which prevailed in my formerly flourishing station. There were scarcely a hundred people who had not disgraced themselves; and persons who had made a consistent profession of religion for years had been drawn into the vortex.' The high chief had sanctioned the introduction of 'ardent spirits'. A trading captain sold the natives a small cask. 'This revived their dormant appetites, and like pent-up waters, the disposition burst forth, and, with the impetuosity of a restless torrent, carried the people before it, so that they appeared maddened with infatuation. As the small cask which had been imported was sufficient only to awaken the desire for more, they had actually prepared nearly twenty stills, which were in active operation when I arrived.'[1] Allowing for a pardonable exaggeration on Williams's part to make the black blacker, it is clear that alcohol appealed greatly to the Society Islander, specially when its consumption was approved by an important chief. From Rai'atea, alcohol was introduced into Rarotonga about 1850 and Buzacott reports: 'Drunkenness, a new vice in Rarotonga, made its appearance, in almost every part of the island

[1] J. Williams, *Narrative of Missionary Enterprise, op. cit.* pp. 405-406.

SOCIAL CHANGE

simultaneously, and required the strong arm of the law to quell it', particularly since inebriated young men were prone to injure 'each other in their drunken bouts.'[1]

With traders and even natives themselves taking part in an illegal trade to supply what alcohol they could import to a desiring populace, it was never possible in the nineteenth century to prevent the consumption of alcohol. Under the New Zealand administration, spirits, wines and beers are available to certain of the population on the production of a 'prescription' from a medical officer of health. Liquor for 'medicinal' or 'restorative' purposes is thus not available to the majority of the population, so that most brew fermented drinks from oranges. Such brewing, however, is illegal and the police make attempts to stop it by taking offenders to Court. But since most of the adult population are involved at one time or another in bush brewing, there is little popular support for police effort. It is significant that during the year 1948–49, 57·7 per cent. of the convictions in Rarotonga were secured for liquor offences as compared with 4·7 per cent. for theft and burglary, 13 per cent. for animal trespassing, 5·6 per cent. for 'loitering or remaining in a public place after 10 p.m. without reasonable excuse', the remaining 20 per cent. of the convictions ranging from 'adultery' (by married persons) to 'failure to register dogs'. The records held at Rarotonga 'may be taken as typical of the group' and indicate the 'petty nature of most of the cases'.[2]

Cook Islands culture thus seems to represent a deviant case when compared with Horton's summary of the variables involved in the consumption of alcohol in primitive societies. Not external hazards, but internal aggressive and anxiety pressures, seemingly unrelated to subsistence or acculturation pressures, appear to be the main determinants in Cook Islands alcohol consumption. But whereas among the Alorese, for instance, there is a constant fear that aggression, tenuously controlled, will break out in violence and hence a fear of intoxicants and comatose conditions,[3] among the Cook Islanders there is little fear of aggressiveness, even though it is also tenuously controlled, and so drinking is a pleasurable activity, indulged in even

[1] Sunderland and Buzacott, *Mission Life, op. cit.* p. 204. See also Gill's *Gems, op. cit.* p. 105.
[2] Cook Islands Report, 1949. The Annual Reports for both 1955 and 1956 note that liquor offences account for practically half the trials on criminal charges during each of these years.
[3] A. Kardiner, *The Psychological Frontiers of Society* (New York, 1945), pp. 117, 166 and 170.

though it is illegal. The character structure of the Cook Islander has not made him afraid of his own aggressiveness even though with him as with the New Zealand Maori, aggressiveness released through alcohol is likely to find an outlet in disorderly behaviour, personal assaults and destruction of property (but not, incidentally, in sexual assaults—a New Zealand white characteristic as a learned judge of New Zealand's Supreme Court remarked when comparing Maori with Whites). For this very reason, however, it is most probable that it will be prudent for some years to come to help the Cook Islander control his aggressiveness by making it difficult for him to procure spirits, wines and beers, other than the fermented drinks he will inevitably make and consume in semi-privacy of bush hideout or dwelling house.

A further good reason is to be found in the fact that many Cook Islanders find it almost impossible to use alcohol in moderation. This point was noticed fifty years ago by the first doctor in charge of the hospital on Rarotonga: 'I cannot recall a single one who has been able to restrain himself to drink habitually in moderation. Even the best of those who drink at all have been known to drink to intoxication.... Among the rank and file, those who live in the bush, there seems to be no restraint whatever, so long as the intoxicant can be found.'[1] The physician may have been making rather an extreme statement at the time, but the general tenor of his observation fits in so well with the all-or-none behaviour pattern of the islander as to make it substantially true.

One of the keys, therefore, to understanding the use made by people when they are free to borrow a pattern of alcohol consumption is an understanding of their character-structure, particularly of the role of aggressiveness and its control. Subsistence hazards may be a key variable in many cases, but there are other cases where a specific character structure, reflecting in some aspects economic factors, though not determined by them, will permit a people to drink easily, to drink with restraint and occasionally, or not to drink at all.

The discussion of character structure in this section may be summarized in the following propositions, some of which stem directly from, others being implicit in, the preceding argument:

1. Every cultural group is characterized by a basic personality or character structure which may be defined as that organization of

[1] Report from Dr. Caldwell to the British Resident, July 15, 1897, in New Zealand House of Representatives, *Appendices to the Journals* (1898), vol. 1, A-4, p. 11.

SOCIAL CHANGE

needs, sentiments and attitudes, developed in interpersonal relations, which determines the self-view and the world-view as these are common to all or most of the members of the group. Unique personalities are the result of constitutional influences inter-operating with character structure factors, idiosyncratic influences and status determinants.

2. Culture contact situations produce opposition, lack of conflict, fusion or imitation. Minor changes occur initially among a few of the population of the economically, politically or socially dependent group. Opposition to changes will result from anxiety induced by pressures thought of as threatening the economic, personal or social bases of group life. Acceptance of initial changes will come when leaders of the dependent people see advantages to themselves in new ways of behaving or in a new technology. Further changes will be accepted or rejected on the basis of the cultural and personal rigidity or adaptability of the dependent people. Strong external pressure may produce the appearance of change but, without alteration to character structure, such change will be superficial.

3. For people to change, they must learn new ways of behaving and believing, they must be able to appreciate rewards and punishments.

4. Rewards and punishments are often evaluated in terms of principles of utility or prestige or congruence with the dominant concerns of a culture.

5. Rewards and punishments are also evaluated in terms of their congruence with the specific organization of needs, sentiments and attitudes of a people. If new models are in congruence with a specific self-view or world-view they will be responded to with ego-involvement; if new models are not in congruence, they will be responded to with ego-withdrawal and anxiety, or will be reinterpreted before ego-involvement is possible.

6. Cultural change may be sudden (as in institutional snapping), or slow and segmental depending upon the level of internal anxiety in different aspects of the culture, the clearness of the models, the degree of re-interpretation necessary, and the intensity of the pressure to change.

7. A people which has been allowed to retain control of its customary land, sea and other economic resources, will normally choose among the possible elements offered for borrowing in such fashion as to

retain or quickly to regain their cultural equilibrium and customary character structure.

8. Normally environmental, historical and psychological factors operate over a period of time to determine the process of cultural change. At a particular moment or period, however, the character structure of a people, as this has been determined by the interoperation of environmental and historical influences with basic psychological needs will be the dominating factor in influencing a people's appreciation of models, therefore of what it can and does learn and therefore of cultural change.

9. No culture is totally rigid nor totally adaptable, but some cultures appear to be dominantly rigid or adaptable, when faced with pressures or opportunities to borrow from Western European cultures. This rigidity or adaptability is a function of the relative congruence between the character structure of the native society and that of the specific variant of Western European culture involved in the culture contact situation. But rigidity or adaptability will not necessarily characterize the same primitive cultures when meeting non-Western cultures.

10. In relatively stable societies personality and culture are part of the same organism-environment matrix. In changing cultures there may be personality lag as well as cultural lag. Whereas cultural lag is the outcome of a differential rate of institutional change, personality lag is due to the retention of a character structure from an earlier culture when a people is in fact trying to adjust or being forced to adjust to a new culture, with new values and attitudes not congruent with their old or surviving, character structure.

11. Personality structure is more rigid than cultural patterning. Because the older generations control the upbringing of the young members of a social group, older people will tend to develop in the young a personality structure congruent with traditional models. Young and old may, however, participate in a culture that is already strongly hybridized as the result of borrowing from the dominant alien group.

12. Cultural change may therefore proceed rapidly but the result will be a culture out of step with personality structure. When culture is not supported by a congruent personality, there will be an unintegrated culture with consequent signs of social disorganization. Culture and personality can be 're-aligned' by pressure on parents

or parent surrogates which will help them to develop a congruent personality through appropriate child-raising procedures for the youngest member of the group.

13. In sum, much social change may be explained by concepts derived from the facts of social structure (by the flexibility, the rigidity or the conflict of social patterns, for instance, or by the tendency for a social system to take up a new equilibrium after its balance has been disturbed). In critical instances, however, people have to change their patterned behaviour. They have to make new choices between apparently incompatible ways of acting. These choices are determined for the person by his enduring attitudes, themselves the product of the character structure he shares with other members of his own socio-cultural group and of his own unique personality. Unless what is chosen is congruent with character structure and personality the resulting disharmony will tend to force the person to reject the new or to modify it so that it becomes compatible with the already established, deeply-formed patterns of behaviour.

Conclusion

In concluding this case study of social change it is well to ask of the material the question that the psychologist might very well ask of his case history materials on the development of a person whom he has been intensively studying: how far is this case unique, how far has it more general features that can be applied to the study of human behaviour in a particular society. In social terms, how far is the story of social change in Rarotonga and Aitutaki unique, how far has it characteristics that link the Cook Islands' process of social change with social change elsewhere in Polynesia; and secondly, what is the relevance of the study of social change in the South Pacific for the general theory of social change and social stability?

Threading through the process of social change as it has occurred in the past five generations or so in the South and Central Pacific there are clearly some influences or factors which have made for uniqueness, others which have made for similarity. Considering for a moment the numerical factor at one particular date, it must have made for a unique situation in each island group that the percentage proportion of Europeans to natives in 1906 was about 95 in New

Zealand, 1·2 in Samoa, about 2 in Tonga and 4 in Rarotonga. In New Zealand the Maoris were very much of a minority group hanging on grimly to remaining lands and cultural integrity, whereas in Rarotonga the islanders were a large majority, living a free-and-easy life, unaffected by anxiety over European encroachment (with the exception of a tiny minority of chiefs who feared for their own status if changes were sudden or acute). Thus the numerical factor affected in unique ways these two communities and so the sequence and speed of social change were different in the two groups. Again, although the New Zealand Maori were only about 6 per cent. of the total population of New Zealand in 1906, the total Maori population at this date numbered a few over 50,000, in all at least twenty-five times as numerous as the natives of Rarotonga. In addition, the Maori lived on several millions of acres of land, whereas the Rarotongans had a mere 16,000 acres of domain to survey. Changes of a surface or static type are more likely in a population of 2,000 than in one of 50,000, particularly if the latter population is suspicious of change and of European pressure. Finally, intermarriage between Maoris and Europeans had probably been more frequent by 1906 in New Zealand than in Rarotonga. Because intermarriage is often a means whereby knowledge of a new culture is passed on to an indigenous people, this cultural transmission line functioned more effectively in New Zealand or again in Hawaii than it did in the Cook Islands.

Social change is likely to result not only from intermarriage with people of another homogeneous 'racial' stock but also from intermarriage and cultural contacts with a variety of racial groups in the one single melting pot. Thus one among several reasons why the native Hawaiian has probably changed most as compared with other Polynesian peoples has been intermarriage and cultural mingling with Europeans, Chinese, Japanese, Filipinos, Puerto Ricans and others. Only in Tahiti and Samoa have there been sizeable Chinese groups in contact with native peoples. In Samoa, however, the Chinese only made up about 6 per cent. of the total population in 1906 and today constitute barely 0·2 per cent. of this population.

This brief survey, therefore, suggests that taking the numerical factor alone there is every reason to expect a course of social change that will be unique for the island groups that have been mentioned. If one tries now to add the influences exerted by greater whaling and sealing concentration in New Zealand, the early individualization of

CONCLUSION

land titles and consequent alienations of land in Hawaii, missionizing from an early stage by Church of England, Evangelical and Roman Catholic missions in New Zealand as compared with single-mission conversions, continuation of native land tenure and subordination of whaling and trading contacts to mission control—to mention but three among many differences—in many Polynesian island groups, then there is good reason to judge that change in each group has occurred in its own unique way. Finally taking the factor of the prestige of native culture, one finds wide differences in Polynesia at different times in the social change process: on the one hand the fairly constant confidence and self-centred outlook of the Samoan who always has tended to think of himself as a superior sort of person and his culture as the flower of Polynesia; in the middle of the range the Cook Islander who does not think very much about his culture except to find it reasonably satisfactory; at the other end of the scale the Hawaiian or the New Zealand Maori whose history has been an alternation between the depressions and the exaltations of despair leading both at times to try and allay anxiety in messianic and nativistic movements.

A closer analysis of the Polynesian culture area which employed all of the factors that have been used earlier in this book would probably end up with many unique social processes, but also with a number of changes that appear to be fairly general, at least among the central and south Polynesian groups (excluding, that is, Hawaii and New Zealand). In most of these groups there has been a fairly uniform series of pressures operating over the years: single-mission evangelical Christianity; very low proportion of Europeans to natives; little exploitable land and few natural resources; rarely existent racial prejudice; subordination of economic and commercial exploitation to more powerful philanthropic influences; uniformity in the cultural equipment of the alien groups; much intermarriage; few and not extreme nativistic movements; gradual adjustment to introduced diseases and rapid recovery in population after initial decline—these, and probably many other factors, have tended to influence, in very roughly the same fashion, many island groups. Furthermore since such influences operated, not in a vacuum, but upon a people whose basic personality type has been formed along roughly identical lines by cultures which have cherished the same values, attitudes and outlook on life, the basic response to such externally operating factors has again been approximately the same.

SOCIAL CHANGE IN THE SOUTH PACIFIC

The island groups, in other words, have found some measure of compatibility between their own values and some of the values and emphases of evangelical lower middle-class western European civilization; they have proved adaptable when 'static' or overt behavioural change has been insisted upon (changes in clothing, use of firearms, new technical skills, church-going and the like), singularly resistant, even rigidly unadaptable, when dynamic or inner personality changes have been called for. Thus there has gone on side by side a process of fairly far-reaching outward or social change, and at the same time a stable personality configuration has resisted change by lagging far behind the social institutions and cultural forms with which a different personality configuration has been meshed in western European culture. No simple theory of a one-to-one relationship between culture and personality is adequate to account for situations where either personality or social lag are characteristic phenomena. Either several cultures may roughly fit the one and same personality configuration (in which case there may be no personality lag in culture contact situations) or else social change may operate only in certain parts or aspects of an indigenous culture, leaving the inner citadel of cultural values still intact and still relatively well adjusted to the basic personality structure of a people.

Assuming that pressures of the kind and intensity characteristic of Cook Islands history have been operating in a number of island groups to produce fairly similar overt social changes with a similar type of inner personality lag then one should expect to find in the Central and South Pacific the development of a contemporary native culture which is roughly similar on all the atolls and smaller high islands, and may be similar, after allowance is made for the inertia of larger populations, on the large high islands. This is in fact what one does seem to find. There are more similarities than differences in overt culture and personality dynamics between Rarotonga and Aitutaki on the one hand and the culture of Pangai in Tonga on the other. Extending the net still further it is interesting to note that Spoehr, on the basis of his studies of the contemporary culture of Majuro in the Marshall Islands concludes that present-day Majuro culture has sufficient affinities with Tongan village culture to make these two widely separated groups examples of a neo-island culture that appears to be stabilizing itself in the Pacific area.[1] It is

[1] A. Spoehr, *Majuro, A Village in the Marshall Islands*, Chicago Natural History Museum, Fieldiana: Anthropology (1949), 39: 253-256.

CONCLUSION

probable that the aboriginal cultures, including the value systems, of this Micronesian atoll people in the west and the Polynesian people of Tonga in the east were not sufficiently dissimilar but that they both tended to respond in the same way to pressures that were again essentially similar. The end result therefore of the culture contact process has been the development of similar variations on a similar cultural theme. The same cultural theme can now be elaborated in Rarotonga and Aitutaki, probably also in most of its essentials in the other islands of the Cook group. Hence from Majuro to Rarotonga uniformities have developed from the uniqueness of the social change process. This process in Rarotonga and Aitutaki has been, in sum, both unique and general.

This conclusion is at the present stage of contemporary Polynesian research only tentative and can very well form the core of a workable hypothesis for the ordering of further necessary research on contemporary island cultures. If the hypothesis is substantiated then it will have significant practical implications. Among others, this: assuming that administrators and social scientists in Pacific territories are likely to join hands more frequently and play God to island peoples, initiating and determining by policy a course of social change that has previously been left to empirical rule-of-thumb or accident, then policy will probably be itself partly based on the results of small-scale pilot experimentation. Such pilot studies, carried out in one of the contemporary island communities, Majuro for instance, should have results applicable to Rarotonga, without the need for reproducing the pilot experiment. Thus by working in well selected areas, results should be obtained that will be applicable to other areas in the Pacific. Time and money will be saved and policy grounded on fact, not theory.[1] Similarly, in the study of measures for improving Pacific island animal husbandry, fishery resources, land utilization, food crops, food production and marketing, all of which need study if island standards of living are to be noticeably raised,

---

[1] The South Pacific Commission has recently completed a pilot project on community development in Fiji, the results of which may be applicable to other Pacific island groups. See H. Hayden, *Moturiki. A Pilot Project in Community Development* (London, Oxford University Press, 1954). But note that such applications can only be made if a careful evaluation is available of the reason why some aspects of the project have failed, others have succeeded. This evaluation is conspicuously absent from many contemporary projects. Some comments on evaluation have been made in Ernest Beaglehole, 'Evaluation Techniques for Induced Technological Change', *International Social Science Bulletin* (1955), 7: 376-386.

what may be learnt by intensive study in carefully selected Pacific groups should be applicable to all others in the same stage of contemporary cultural development.

One further conclusion of the previous pages requires final emphasis in this context. Ultimately, it has been suggested, one of the important factors influencing change, the rate and sequence of change, even the probability itself of change, is the specific character structure of an island people. The dynamic aspects of personality configuration need to be kept in mind when planning changes, otherwise the administrator may meet puzzling resistances in what are, to him, obviously advantageous changes for the people concerned. For some desirable social changes, knowledge of character structure may not seem important, mosquito control, for instance. But it would have been possible to predict that the people of Aitutaki, because of their easy-going, all-or-none attitude to life, would be either indifferent to the necessity for mosquito control or else take to it with enthusiasm as a novelty, then quickly drop it as emotion cooled. No amount of demonstration would make the people efficient at this task. This seems to have, in fact, happened. Hence, if it is desirable to control mosquitos in the interest of filaria prevention, many energetic measures will be required: constantly changing and vivid appeals to competitive enthusiasms; constant supervision and control; legal penalties at the stage when at least 90 per cent. of the people seem to be actively interested in control measures. If therefore the knowledge of the psychology of a people must be kept in mind when planning mosquito campaigns, so much the more in programmes which demand new or changing work incentives, changing methods of land cultivation and the like. Social psychological factors may not be the sole key to understanding social change, but no attempt to direct social change is likely to be effective for very long which neglects a consideration of the role of dynamic personal influences in change and stability.

The second question that was raised at the beginning of this section referred to the relevance of the Cook Islands case study to change in contemporary western communities. It must be admitted that in the present state of our knowledge of social dynamics, the relevance is only slight. However it is true to say that a person who has soaked himself in the complexities of social change in a particular area of the non-literate world is likely to be increasingly embarrassed by the efforts of some of his colleagues in some of the

CONCLUSION

social sciences to explain social change in the western world. The specialist in Oceania or Africa or elsewhere is often unable to see the explanatory significance of challenge and response theories of social change, or of over-simple economic theories. He is likely to feel that Bloch's discussion of France's 'strange defeat' or Meinecke's explanation of Germany's 'catastrophe' are far too ambitious attempts to explain complicated processes, very largely perhaps because, although change is never merely additive but is always change in a configuration, none the less France and Germany are far too imprecise entities with which to work. Once the huge conglomeration of stratified cultures and sub-cultures, associations, communities and occupational groups that as a configuration make up contemporary France or New Zealand is broken down into its component parts then the social scientist may be in a position to trace resistances and change in each part and weigh the influence on each part of its integral relationship with all the others. Laborious and time-consuming as this process undoubtedly would be, it still remains true that it is more likely to be rewarding in the long run than the more immediately attractive molar explanations that inevitably lose in precision because they apply to such hugely complicated verbal entities.

Again, just as this Cook Islands study suggests the importance of psychological factors in social change, the importance, if one wishes so to phrase the matter, of national character, so the study of social change in larger modern social groups must also strive to formulate dynamic statements about the national character of the modern state. In this respect the small isolated primitive or folk community makes possible the application of hypotheses, the sharpening of conceptual tool, the testing of auxiliary instruments for collecting data. Thus what appears valuable for understanding folk society should also be valuable for analysing the dynamic group personality structure of the various sub-cultures that mesh one with another to form a modern civilization.

Thus a research wheel turns full circle. From the simple to the complex and back again, from the particular to the general and back to a fuller understanding and use of the particular, research in the social sciences follows the circle of scientific method that alone brings incontrovertible facts and makes possible firmly grounded policy.

Index

Abortion, 180
Abraham, M., 146 n.
Acceptance, phase of, 40
Adair, J., 239 n.
Adolescents, 49; church membership of, 195
Administration, 206-212
Adoption, 163; 164-166
Adultery, 28, 32, 44, 48, 49, 59, 61, 67, 72, 97, 197
Age composition of population, 134
Age grades, 184-185
Aggression, outlet in drinking, 98; in warfare, 171; of children, 186, 187; sickness and, 193; and character structure, 228-230, 248, 250-252
Aikman, C. C., 209 n.
Alcohol, introduction of, 44, 70, 71, 75-76, 250, 96-98; laws controlling use of, 107, 109, 112, 123; and aggression, 193; and social change, 238, 249-252
Allport, G. W., 208 n.
Amuri village, census of, 163
Andrews, Surgeon O. W., report on health, 117 n.; on population, 135 n., 141 n., 152, 193
Annexation, 102, 103; Resolution of, 113; debate on, 121
Anxiety, reduction of, 43, 44, 47, 233; and tension, 246, 248
Area, of Cook Islands, 3; of Aitutaki, 3, 6; of Rarotonga, 3, 6
Armitage, Elijah, 68
Arorangi, 30
Arrowroot, 39, 50, 69; crop value, 142; as food, 143, 145; in gift exchange, 155
Au local body, 152-153
Avarua, 51, 57

Baker, Shirley, 116
Bananas, 69, 76, 145
Banishment, 38

Baptism, 3, 48, 67
Bateson, G., 228 n.
Belcher, E., 56, 173 n.
Belshaw, H., 215 n.
Bible, The, 48, 77; sale of, 72, 88, 94
Birth rate, 135-136
Bligh, Captain, 7, 11, 14
Booth, merchant, 77
Bounty, The, 7, 12, 14
Bourke, Captain, 101, 102, 104-108
Bourne, 22, 31, 67
Breadfruit, 143
British Protectorate, 101-118; over Tonga, 116-117
Buchanan, J. C. R., 144 n.
Buck, Sir Peter, 7 n., 11, 57, 168 n., 224
Burial practices, 181, 193-194
Buzacott, Aaron, writings on social life, 11; biographical note, 25; arrival at Rarotonga, 30; retirement, 79; 31-130 *passim*.
Byron, Commodore, 7

Caldwell, Dr., 107 n.; 252 n.
Cannibalism, 43, 228, 247
Cassirer, E., 223 n.
Catholic church, missionaries of, 38, 39, 72-73; membership, 195
Caudill, W., 239 n.
Chalmers, James, biographical note, 26-27; 96
Chalmers, Mrs., 97
Character Structure, 5, 56, 123-124; importance of, 126; and work habits, 156, 157, 159; and children, 187; and social change, 224-237, 243-255, 260
Chare, James, 58
Chiefs, power of, 31-32; status of, 33, 197-198; warfare among, 33-34, 47; and land tenure, 106, 111, 112; lack of effective leadership, 114; rivalries among, 115-116; hierarchy of, 168-169; 175-176

Childhood, 183-191, 235
Chincha Islands, 96
Chinese, immigration of, 113, 119
Christian, F. W., 103 n.
Churches, building of, 15, 22, 39, 124; membership in, 37, 39, 45-46, 51, 53, 61, 88-89, 195-199
Circumcision, 188
Citizenship, New Zealand, 203-206
Clothing, 46, 56, 67-68, 77, 87, 161, 241
Coconut, 143, 144, 145; see Copra
Coffee, 69, 92, 93, 108; exports of, 120; production of, 215 n.
Commoners, 117
Congregational Church, 23, 195
Constitution Act, 110
Contraceptives, 180
Conversions, 47
Cook, Captain, 7
Cook, P. H., 234
Cook Islands, area of, 3; discovery of, 7; population, 3; annexation, 102
Cook Islands Amendment Act, 208
Co-operatives, producers, 208, 216; loan and savings, 216 n.
Copra, exports, 121; crop, 142, 215 n.
Cotton, 68, 88, 92, 108; exports, 120
Council, executive, 110; federal, 113; governing, 110; island, 114, 175, 207; legislative, 114, 208; municipal, 152-153
Courts of law, 58
Cowan, Tau, 144
Cults, 81, 82, 97
Cumberland, The, 13
Cumberland, K., 215 n.
Cunningham, 59, 68
Curacoa, H.M.S., 104
Curfew, 162
Currency, Chilean, 107-108

Dancing, 154, 155; circuit, 172-173; 226
Death customs, 191-194
Death rate, 41, 44-45, 135-136; for infants and children, 42, 45, 216
Descent, 177; groups, 169

Development Committee, Cook Islands, 215, 216
Diet, 143-146
Disease, 34, 45, 72, 117 n., 130, 136, 141; 191-194
Division of labour, 151-152
Divorce, 39, 177, 179
Drunkenness, 76, 98; see Alcohol
Dunbabin, T., 95 n.

East, Rev. Timothy, 24
Eating habits, 146
Economic development, 207, 209 n., 212-217
Economic organization, 142-143
Education, 134, 195-196; development of, 211, 217-218
Edwards, Captain, 14
Ellis, Rev. William, 50
Emigration, 71, 74, 82, 91; to Society Islands, 137; to New Zealand, 137-138; advisability of, 141; and depopulation, 238-239
Endeavour, The, 63
English, teaching of, 217
Epidemics, 34-35, 45
European settlers, 121; number of, 132, 255-266; tenure of land by, 146-147
Exham, R., 101, 103-104; report of, 108-109; 119

Family grouping, 164
Famine, 36
Fatalism, 46
Feeding of infants, 182, 183
Fines, legal, 57, 58
Firth, Raymond, 150 n., 168 n.
Fish, 143, 145
Fishing, 140
Flag of Protectorate, 104-105
Fletcher, Irene M., 25 n.
Flour, use of, 144
Food, 88, 143-146; cravings, 180; for marriage feast, 177; for nursing mother, 182
French visitors, 69-75, 80

INDEX

Fruit, 43; exports, 121, 215-216
Furnas, J. C., 141 n., 148 n.
Furniture, 87-88, 160-161
Furnivall, J. S., 144 n., 218

George, The, 75
Gerlach, J. C., 214 n.
German settlement, fear of, 102; in Samoa, 109
Gift exchange, 153, 154; in adoption, 166; dancing, 173; marriage, 177, 178; birth feast, 182; funeral, 194; motivation of, 226-227
Gill, George, biographical note, 26; 39, 46, 48, 72, 74, 76, 78
Gill, William, biographical note, 26; 39, 46, 49; retirement, 79 and *passim*
Gill, William Wyatt, biographical note, 27; 94, 96
Gilson, R. P., 101 n., 149 n.
Goals, 41
Goats, 15, 143
Gods, burning of, 15, 16, 17, 21, 40
Goodenough, 7, 13, 19, 63
Gosset, R. W. G., 12, 69
Gossner, 26
Grey, Sir George, 93, 96
Gudgeon, W. E., 57, 111 n., 117, 118, 148, 168, 174 n.
Guilt cultures, 228

Hailey, Lord, 204 n., 210
Hallowell, A. I., 239 n., 241
Hayden, H., 259 n.
Herskovits, M. J., 239, 242
Hertslet, Foreign Office Correspondence, 101 n., 104 n.
Hohman, 69 n., 91
Holmes, Susan, 139 n.
Homosexuality, 191
Honigmann, J. J., 243 n.
Horses, 77
Horton, D., 249
Households, income of, 142, 178; census of, 163
Houses, 82, 159-161
Hurricane, 36, 39

Immigration, 74, 80, 91, 93, 113, 118, 138
Impulse gratification, 56-57
Incest, 180
Income, 142, 178
Independence, 100-101, 116, 205
Infanticide, 129, 130 n., 228, 247
Infantile mortality, 135
Inkeles, 243 n.
Institutional snapping, 246-247, 253
Intellectual capacity, 219-223, 232
Intermarriage, 81-82, 91, 108, 256; laws forbidding, 101, 119; with traders, 122
Intervention, of French, 73, 101
Iro, native teacher, 48, 66, 73
Iron, 14
Irvine, Captain, 92-93

Jahoda, G., 220 n.
Jealousy, 186

Kainuku, 73
Kaitara, 66
Kardiner, A., 251 n.
Kava, 144, 249
Keesing, F. M., 40 n., 239 n.
Kerr, M., 220
Kinship, 166-167
Knutsford, Lord, 103
Krause, E. R. W., biographical note, 26; 92, 93, 94, 95
Kroeber, A., 248 n.

Lambert, S. M., 152, 191
Lamont, 58
Land, disputes over, 65; laws concerning, 103, 105, 119; tenure of, 106, 146-149, 169, 216, 238; control over, 165, 167; clearing of, 151
Large, J. T., 167 n.
Laws, code of, 28-30, 33, 38, 40, 44, 57, 76, 88; application to foreigners, 105, 108-109, 110, 112-113; offences against, 251
Leadership, 89, 114

Learning, 40, 41, 44, 79; in social change, 126, 241, 245
Lee, Ida, 11 n., 14 n.
Lemartine, The, 61, 70
Leprosy, 137, 191
Levinson, 243 n.
Lewin, K., 208 n., 248
Lewis and Hardwick, 77, 78
Lineages, 167
Linton, R., 237, 248 n.
London Missionary Society, 23, 39, 46, 50, 58; membership in, 195; library, 30 n.
Lopdell, Anne, 220
Lovett, R., 21 n., 24, 96, 236
Low, D., 11 n., 182, 184, 188
Luke, H., 27 n.

McArthur, Dr. Norma, 130 n.
McClare, Captain, 75
Macmillan, W. H., 149 n.
Makea, Chief, 19, 30, 34, 38; obituary of, 50, 110
Maladjustment, 81, 82
Mangaia, 57, 58
Maori, 93, 122, 123; population increase, 132, 134; birth and death rates, 135, 153; and social change, 238; character structure of, 245 n., 247, 256
Maraes, burning of, 15, 21 and *passim*, 184 n., 192
Marriage, 28, 32, 40, 44, 52 164-165, 176-180, 189, 190
Martin, K. L. P., 73 n., 82 n.
Mataiapo, 107, 167, 169, 170
Maude, H. E., 216 n.
Mead, Margaret, 212 n., 243 n.
Migration, planned, 216-217; *see* Emigration
Mills, C. H., 205
Missionaries, arrival of, 12, 14; Tahitian, 15; native, 15-18, 20, 31, 39, 41, 42, 95; L.M.S., 4, 125 and *passim*; Catholic, 38, 72-73; training of, 236
Money, attitudes toward, 157; collections of, 155, 177

Moss, F. J., 11, 34, 57, 58; resident agent of Rarotonga, 104-111, 113, 115, 118, 135 n., 148, 165, 170, 230-231
Motives, work, 149
Muller, Max, 26
Murder, 38
Murphy, G., 245-246

Nadel, S. F., 222, 223 n.
Naming, of adopted child, 166; of first-born, 184-185
Nativistic movements, 81, 98, 257
Newcomb, T. M., 208 n.
Newspaper, 99
New Zealand, trade with, 92, 93, 108; control by, 109, 113, 121; administration by, 203-218
Ngatangiia, 30, 75
Nutt, 61

Offences, legal, 57, 251
Omai, 27 n.
Oranges, 13; fermented, 57, 69, 76, 144, 251; trade in, 92; value of, 142
Orphans, 46
Orpheus, The, 96

Pa, Chief, 73, 108
Pakoti, J., 11 n.
Pandora, The, 14
Papeiha, 15, 23 and *passim*, 51, 230
Parliament, Cook Islands Federal, 110-111
Payment, 39, 48; gift, 49-50; to missionaries, 60; for work, 150-151
Pearl, R., 134 n.
Pembroke and Kingsley, 97 n., 124 n.
Peren, G. S., 214 n.
Personality, *see* Character Structure
Peruvian slavers, 95-96
Phosphate mines, 239
Physical characteristics, 11, 40, 42
Pigs, 16, 69, 143
Pineapples, trade in, 69, 92; fermenting of, 76

INDEX

Pitman, Charles, biographical note, 25-26; 28; arrival at Rarotonga, 30; retirement, 77 and *passim*, 100, 197
Pitman, Mrs. Charles, 31, 77, 78
Police, 31, 57-58; in mission theocracy, 106, 109; social status of, 197
Political development, 206-212
Polygamy, 29, 164, 247
Pomare, Queen, 73
Population, of Cook Islands, 3; of Rarotonga, 3, 41; of Aitutaki, 3, 6, 41, 61; European, 3, 38, 41, 44, 105, 120; of other races, 119; other islanders, 109, 138-139; density of, 139-141; changes in, 41, 45, 80, 93, 118, 216; and social change, 238; ratio of sexes in, 44-45, 57, 130, 135
Portuguese residents, 119
Poultry, 69, 143
Power, 47, 60, 100, 105
Pregnancy, 180-182, 189
Prendergast, Sir James, 112
Prestige factors, 82, 123, 230-231, 241
Primogeniture, 184-185
Pritchard, ex-Consul, 73
Progressive Association, Cook Islands, 175
Property, attitudes toward, 157
Protectorate, 101
Prout, E., 24
Public Health, 136-137, 213, 216
Punishment, 38, 43, 47, 52, 54, 57, 59-61; by fines, 109; for theft, 158; of children, 186-187; and disease, 192; and shame, 227; and social change, 241, 253

"Queens" of Rarotonga, 103

Racial mixtures, 133
Ranfurly, Governor, 103 n.
Raui, 152
Reading, 40
Reed, S. K., 141 n.
Religious groups, membership in, 195
Representation, 203-205
Revenues, 207

Rewards, 40-41, 44, 241, 253
Rice, 69
Rigidity, 123, 247-248, 254
Rivers, W. H. R., 46
Rorschach records, 232-234
Royle, Henry, biographical note, 27, 38-99 *passim*, 229

Sabbath observance, 57, 66
Samoa, Western, 132, 142
Schools, 37, 49, 217
Secondary industries, 216
Seddon, Richard, 109 n., 111, 113 n., 121, 304, 215-216, 231
Seniority, 167, 170, 184, 196
Seringapatam, The, 13
Seventh Day Adventist church, 195
Sex education, 188-189
Sexual relations, 98, 178-180, 189-191, 236
Shame cultures, 226-228
Shapiro, H. L., 11 n.
Sheep breeding, 88
Shipping, 215-216
Simey, T. S., 210 n., 215 n.
Singing, 154, 155, 172, 193-194, 225
Social-class structure, 167, 170
Social services, 142-143, 159, 213
Sorcery, 192, 228
Spinley, Betty M., 232
Spoehr, A., 258
Sports, 153, 154, 174, 226
Stace, V. D., 215 n.
Status, 196-199, 230-231
Stereotypes, 75
Sugar, 59
Suicide, 36, 48
Sunderland, J. P., 11 n; *see* Buzacott
Sweet potato, 68, 143, 145

Tacitus, The, 71
Tamatoa, Chief, 15
Tapairu, Chieftainess, 19, 20
Tapioca, 69
Taro, 143, 145
Tattooing, 168
Taxation, 142-143, 212

267

Technology, 11, 19, 40, 68, 241
Tensions, 174
Tere parties, 153-156
Theft, 77, 97, 157, 158, 182
Tiberio, 20, 22, 32
Tidman, A., 26
Time sequences, 40
Tinomana, Chief, 20-21, 30, 73
Tobacco, 75, 144
Tomatoes, 142 n.
Tonga, comparison with, 116-117; land tenure in, 148
Tonkin, Mrs., 24
Trade, export, 120-121
Traders, 12, 44, 69-75, 106, 122, 251
Trading, 68, 69, 75 n.; by missionaries, 77-78, 94; with New Zealand, 92, 99; in alcohol, 107-108, 111, 119
Traditional history, 168
Tribal grouping, 164, 167-170, 171
Tuberculosis, 136
Tubou, George, 116
Tupe, 63-67
Turner, Thomas, 58
Tyerman, Rev. A., 22 n.

Utility, principle of, 241

Vanilla, 92
Villages, 6-7, 30, 159; census of, 163; activities of, 172-176, 197, 225
Violence, anti-Christian, 33-34, 38, 40, 49, 58, 65, 247
Visiting, 153-156
Vogt, E., 239 n.

Walker, W. C., 122
Wallace, A. F. C., 245 n.
Warfare, 20, 33-34, 40, 115, 129; causes of, 171; 224, 228, 247, 249
Water supply, 144, 162
Weaning, 183
Whalers, 41, 90 and *passim*
Whiting, John, 228 n.
Wilkes, C., 69-70 n., 71, 90
Williams, John, 7, 11, 12; arrival at Aitutaki, 14-18; at Rarotonga, 19-23; biographical note, 24; on code of laws, 28-29; 31, 68 and *passim*, 198, 222, 250 and *passim*
John Williams, The, 96
Wilson, G. and M., 240
Work, habits of, 156-159, 162; organization of, 149-153
Wragge, 124 n.

For Product Safety Concerns and Information please contact our EU
representative GPSR@taylorandfrancis.com
Taylor & Francis Verlag GmbH, Kaufingerstraße 24, 80331 München, Germany

www.ingramcontent.com/pod-product-compliance
Lightning Source LLC
Chambersburg PA
CBHW061436300426
44114CB00014B/1713